Handbook of
Individualized Strategies
for
Classroom Discipline

W. George Selig, Ed.D. and Alan A. Arroyo, Ed.D.

Published by

WPS®
Publishers   Distributors

Western Psychological Services, Los Angeles, CA 90025

Copyright © 1995 by Western Psychological Services

Fifth printing: June 2006

Printed in the United States of America

9 8 7 6 5 4 3

ISBN: 0-87424-315-7

www.wpspublish.com

TABLE OF CONTENTS

Part 1
The Individualized Strategies System

Part 2
Problem Behaviors and Specific Intervention Strategies

LIST OF TABLES

LIST OF FIGURES

PREFACE

The Handbook of Individualized Strategies for Classroom Discipline is designed to help teachers, administrators, and other school personnel understand themselves, their students, and others. This Handbook provides specific strategies to positively impact student behavior and create a more effective and satisfying learning environment.

Part 1
The Individualized Strategies System

1
INTRODUCTION

Discipline problems in America's schools have reached crisis proportions. Over the last 15 years, survey after survey has pinpointed lack of discipline as one of the major problems in education (Gallup, 1984; Harris & Associates, 1993; National Education Association, 1982; "Problems of Discipline," 1978; U.S. Department of Health, Education, and Welfare, 1978). Meanwhile, researchers continue to stress the relationship between a safe, orderly school environment and learning (Brophy, 1986; Wang, 1992; Wang & Walberg, 1986). Because of this link between discipline and learning, as well as the need for improved classroom management, discipline is one of the nation's major education goals.

Discipline Alternatives for Teachers

In the past 20 years, numerous approaches to classroom discipline have vied for attention. Naturally, most experts claim their approach is best. Unfortunately, when teachers relied on one of these approaches and it did not work, they were left with few options.

Teachers need to be able to choose from a variety of intervention strategies (Charles, 1981; Curwin & Mendler, 1988; Jones & Jones, 1986). Wolfgang and Glickman (1986) state:

> It is the teacher who knows his or her own goals better than any outside "expert" and is the one who is most competent to decide and select those strategies most suitable for specific children ... Teachers possess the capacity to make decisions from alternatives. (p. 7)

Authorities recommend a variety of approaches, from simple counseling to behavior modification. Some approaches require a stronger personal relationship with students, whereas others require a more logical, problem-solving orientation. Still other approaches involve rules, rewards, and punishments. Given the diversity of student behavior in the classroom, teachers need to apply a wide repertoire of discipline and communication approaches; however, few have been prepared to do so (Charles, 1981; Harris & Associates, 1993).

The Individualized Strategies System

In response to the need for a continuum of discipline approaches, we developed the Individualized Strategies System. Along with over 40 general intervention strategies, two major variables were included in this system: behavior styles and levels of motivation. By assessing a student's behavior style and level of motivation, school personnel can choose the most appropriate intervention strategies from an array of options. Thus, school personnel are provided with the opportunity to broaden their repertoire of effective strategies while increasing classroom discipline and improving the learning environment.

Identifying a student's individual characteristics—such as level of motivation and behavior style—can provide school personnel with a better understanding of that student's strengths and needs. Such information can be generalized to affect teaching styles and academic decisions. It can also provide a road map for encouraging the growth and development of individual students; it is particularly valuable for developing effective inclusion approaches for students with disabilities.

Lastly, individualized strategies can help create safer schools by minimizing dangerous and explosive behavior. Some intervention strategies can eliminate a minor problem before it escalates; others can be used to handle more serious problems—such as fighting and anger.

Target Populations

This Handbook is designed to be used by school personnel with the following populations:
- Students who need extra support or strategies for dealing with challenging situations
- Students considered to be at risk for academic failure, dropping out of school, or expulsion
- Students with Attention Deficit Disorder (ADD) or Attention-Deficit Hyperactive Disorder (ADHD)

First-year teachers and school personnel not trained in dealing with students who have special needs may find the Handbook especially useful; however, people other than school personnel can also use the strategies with little modification. Parents, social service workers, probation officers, and juvenile corrections personnel should find the Individualized Strategies System helpful in dealing with aberrant behavior.

The System can be used with students from kindergarten through high school. Of course, some strategies are likely to be most effective with certain age groups. Teachers have been able to adapt specific strategies as necessary to suit a particular age group, however. In addition, due to the individualized focus of assessing each student's behavior style and level of motivation, teachers have implemented strategies that worked across gender, cultural, and ethnic differences.

Using This Handbook

The Handbook of Individualized Strategies for Classroom Discipline can be used in a very straightforward manner or as a tool for delving into a deeper understanding of a student's motivation and behavior. The Individualized Strategies System is like an automobile—you do not need to understand its complexities and inner workings in order to use it. Some people may want to use it to minimize specific undesirable behavior or encourage a more healthy, construc-

tive reaction to a situation. Others may also want to understand the basic constructs of the System. The Handbook is organized to accommodate both purposes.

Part 1 of the Handbook thoroughly examines the Individualized Strategies System. This first chapter summarizes the purposes, basic features, and potential target populations of the System. Chapter 2 is an overview of two assessment tools—Levels of Motivation and Behavior Styles—that make the intervention strategies more effective. Chapter 3 describes the four basic intervention strategy categories and the types of strategies within each category. It provides the basic concepts behind each strategy and answers the question "How does the System work?" which is analogous to understanding how the automobile operates. Chapter 4 explains how to use the System—with or without understanding why it works. Therefore, after reviewing chapter 1, you can proceed directly to chapter 4 if you so desire. Later, you can read chapters 2 and 3 for a more in-depth understanding of the construct of the System. Chapter 5 consists of three actual case studies that show how the System was effectively used to change students' behavior.

In Part 2 of the Handbook, intervention strategies are presented for the recurrent discipline problems that are encountered most frequently in the classroom. These discipline problems are organized alphabetically so that their listings in the Table of Contents can be used as an index.

2
ASSESSING A STUDENT'S NEEDS

Levels of Motivation

Levels of motivation are the stages students pass through on the road to maturity (Keefe, 1987). Sometimes a student may be motivated by the need for self-gratification. At other times, the need for approval takes priority.

There are four levels of motivation: Self-Absorbed, Approval Oriented, Interpersonal Loyalty, and Others Oriented (see Table 1). At each level, a student makes decisions based on certain needs, goals, and desires. Sometimes he or she reaches a new level only to slip backward when new circumstances arise (Hersey & Blanchard, 1982).

Level 1: Self-Absorbed

Individuals functioning at Level 1 are motivated by self-gratification, by the need to "get." In school, they are learning how, when, and where to do things. Teachers are responsible for directing and confronting them to stimulate growth. However, because this is a low level of motivation, confrontation may result in obstinate, rebellious, or apathetic behavior, depending on the student and the reason why he or she is on this level.

Level 2: Approval Oriented

Although still motivated by self-gratification, individuals at Level 2 can tolerate delayed gratification, if necessary, to gain the approval of someone significant. Students at this level are learning the reasons for doing things in certain ways, and they are learning how to be part of a productive group and how to work with others.

Level 3: Interpersonal Loyalty

Students at Level 3 are better able to delay personal gratification in order to meet their need for satisfying personal relationships and their need to be seen as competent. They tend to consider the thoughts of others and the needs of the group. Students at this level want to be responsible and they want to participate in making decisions. They will make an effort to exercise initiative and learn independent skills.

Level 4: Others Oriented

The thoughts and feelings of students at Level 4 are directed toward helping others—with no thought of personal reward or reciprocity. Students at this level are full and contributing members of society. They need opportunities to exercise their academic and interpersonal skills and the freedom to pace themselves, including setting their own goals and objectives. This type of student learns for the sheer love of learning.

Student's Current Level of Motivation

Understanding the characteristics of the four levels of motivation enables you to recognize and meet students' current needs while encouraging their progress to the next motivation level. By addressing the needs of individuals at their current level, you can help them gain the confidence to continue to grow. If a student's basic needs at a given level are not met, there is little chance that he or she will develop the tools necessary for further growth.

For example, you may want your students to act more independently in a science class. To accomplish this, you have decided to allow the students more opportunity to make decisions and set goals for themselves. Students operating at Levels 3 and 4 will thrive in this environment and will probably accomplish the objectives you have in mind. It is likely, however, that students at Levels 1 and 2 will have a very difficult time, particularly if they do not feel competent or if their interests are elsewhere. They will feel insecure, and their insecurity may be demonstrated through poor work or poor behavior. Give the students at lower motivation levels more direction and structure to enable them to participate productively.

A given student may demonstrate different levels of motivation depending on the difficulty of a task, his or her emotional stability, environmental factors, and the pressure around a particular situation. Although a general motivation level is usually evident, a student may fluctuate depending on the stressors that are active in his or her life during the course of the day. The key is to identify those stressors, determine the student's current motivation level, and provide the type of teaching and supervision necessary to encourage academic or behavioral improvement.

Behavior Styles

Researchers have identified 1,600 behavior patterns and divided them into four basic behavior styles. All four styles are generally blended within any given individual, with one or two styles exerting the most influence on how that person behaves (Gregorc, 1979; Marston, 1979).

Teachers should guard against the tendency to classify a student as manifesting one behavior style. People are not locked into a specific style of behavior, and they will not always respond in the same way. They tend to manifest different characteristics depending on the setting. For example, some people behave quite differently at work than they do at home. Successful relationships with students depend on how well the teacher is able to communicate with different behavior styles.

A behavior style is a set of observable behaviors. It is not a reflection of a person's innermost personality, values, or beliefs. It is merely a way to categorize a person's general behavioral style, which can be useful for predicting how that person will tend to communicate, learn, and respond in certain social situations.

We have identified two dimensions of behavior—responsive and directive—that help clarify the nuances of different personalities. Generally, people who want to control their environment are more directive; those who adapt readily to their environment are more responsive. These dimensions are independent of each other and remain more or less constant throughout life. When the four basic behavior styles are placed in quadrants relative to these dimensions (see Figure 1), it becomes relatively easy to predict how people will behave in most situations.

In general, the population is equally divided into the four quadrants, and no gender or racial group dominates any quadrant (Wilson Learning Corporation, 1990). Each quadrant has both positive and negative characteristics; no one style or dimension is better than another. There are, however, situations where one style is more effective than another. As people become more self-confident, they learn to adapt their behavior style to the situation and use the style that is most efficacious.

Characteristics of the four behavior styles are detailed in Table 2, which provides further insight into the dimensions of directiveness and responsiveness.

Once you have identified a student's level of motivation and prevalent behavior style, his or her personality profile will begin to emerge (see Table 3). With that information, you will be uniquely equipped to identify the most effective methods of communication, select appropriate motivational strategies, avoid creating stress and behavioral problems, and utilize the most effective teaching style.

Problem Behaviors

Teachers have always wrestled with discipline problems, but in recent years these problems have grown worse. Thirty years ago, gum chewing and cutting in line were considered major discipline problems. Today, problems such as drug abuse and teacher assaults have created a discipline crisis in schools. Based on extensive interaction with teachers during the development of the Individualized Strategies System, and consistent with numerous surveys conducted over the past decade, we have identified the following 46 behaviors as the most recurrent and troublesome classroom discipline problems:

Absenteeism

Anger

Anxiety

Arguing

Attention Span Problems

Baby Talk

Bossiness

Calling Out Answers

Cheating

Cutting in Line

Defiance

Dependence on Others

Disorganization

Distracting Others

Excuse Making

Fighting

Gum Chewing

Hallway Problems

Hygiene Problems

Hyperactivity

Inability to Settle Down

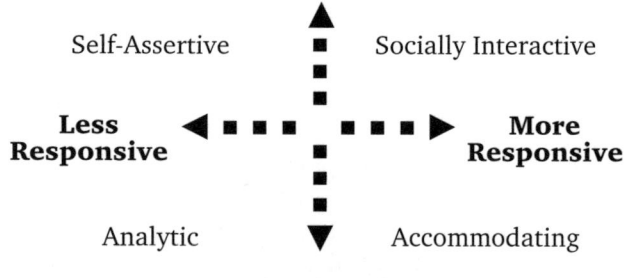

More Directive

Self-Assertive   Socially Interactive

Less Responsive   **More Responsive**

Analytic   Accommodating

Less Directive

Figure 1
Responsive Versus Directive
Dimensions of Behavior

Lack of Motivation

Late Assignments

Leaving Seat Without Permission

Losing or Mistreating Materials

Lying

Name Calling

Obscene Gestures

Oversensitivity

Physical Aggression

Profanity

Property Destruction

Shyness

Spitting

Stealing

Suspected Drug Use

Talking

Talking Back

Tantrums

Tardiness

Tattling

Teasing

Threats of Violence

Tilting Backward in Chair

Tripping Others

Whining

Part 2 of this Handbook presents a range of specific intervention strategies for each of these problem behaviors. The strategies are categorized by their degree of intrusiveness and by their applicability to given personality profiles.

Table 1
Levels of Motivation

	1. Self-Absorbed	2. Approval Oriented	3. Interpersonal Loyalty	4. Others Oriented
Motivating Forces	Self-gratification Fulfillment of basic survival needs Security Autonomy	Approval Recognition Prestige Acceptance	Affiliation and relationship Competence Respect Responsibility	Meeting the needs of others Justice Peace Truth
Characteristics	Is self-centered; wants his or her own way Becomes upset or aggressive when opposed or frustrated Does not trust others Has trouble respecting authority Is motivated by fear of punishment; may lie to avoid it Seeks tangible rewards for good behavior Has a short attention span; changes activities frequently Resists serving others Is unsympathetic Becomes jealous easily Complains about many things Uses other people's possessions without asking permission; fears request will be denied Attempts to gain advantages for himself or herself Weighs effort against tangible benefit Functions best when expectations are clear with few alternatives Has difficulty accepting the opinions of others, and often considers differing opinions as personal attacks	Continues to please self, but does so by gaining the approval of others Seeks approval from authority figures, peers, or others responsible for meeting his or her basic survival needs Is open to learning and growing Shows signs of self-discipline Plays the martyr and acts resentful if disciplined Accepts limited responsibility Learns from mistakes if given guidance Responds to verbal praise Loses interest in activities or subjects as social rewards decrease May be disruptive when trying to gain approval Envies others Is beginning to develop a sense of pride Seeks opportunities to be in the spotlight May fake interest to gain acceptance Enjoys competition that leads to recognition Directs conversation toward himself or herself to gain approval	Accepts rules and responsibility Wishes to contribute Trusts others and tries to earn their respect Judges others according to what is right Seeks approval by earning respect for accomplishments and good behavior Makes decisions based on reality Strives for competence Is able to concentrate Seeks affiliation with adults Compliments and praises others Expects a high level of performance from others Is occasionally critical, judgmental, legalistic, even merciless Is fairly secure in role and identity Is mostly a self-starter, with a fair amount of initiative Rethinks a position when new information is received Stands up for family and friends	Encourages, serves, and shows concern for others Does the proper thing, even when criticized Has little concern for self Achieves the highest possible potential Is very responsible Exhibits positive characteristics such as self-control, purposefulness, patience, initiative, and decisiveness Is a peacemaker Has internalized values Is less dependent on assurance from others Is confident Is at peace Is optimistic even when confronting difficulties Praises others in their absence Generally has healthy relationships Pursues knowledge, wisdom, and truth Feels an obligation to society

Table 1 (continued)
Levels of Motivation

	1. Self-Absorbed	2. Approval Oriented	3. Interpersonal Loyalty	4. Others Oriented
Prerequisites for Transition	Fulfillment of basic survival needs Increased interaction with others; need for self-gratification decreases as pleasure from the approval of others increases	Sense of personal responsibility Genuine concern for others Internalization of values	*Transition no longer a priority*	*Transition no longer a priority*
Appropriate Teaching Styles	Supervise closely and provide continual guidance Define expectations clearly and precisely; limit alternatives Establish concise, easily understood rules Clarify and explain goals frequently Provide tangible rewards for achievement Reassure and encourage the student frequently Intervene immediately when problems arise Teach the skills needed to master new material in small steps or units with specific deadlines Display the student's work as a reinforcement technique when he or she has done a good job Utilize strong eye contact when giving instruction	Provide moderate supervision Praise and encourage achievement frequently Emphasize personal accomplishment Encourage responsible, independent behavior Provide opportunities for recognition Communicate need for improvement, not perfection Establish precise expectations Allow limited involvement in decision making Focus student on living up to teacher expectations rather than on tangible rewards Prepare student for group discussion by assuring his or her mastery of factual information	Emphasize student's goals and aspirations Allow input about rules and expectations Maintain firmness, but acknowledge student as responsible and competent Encourage cooperative problem solving and group activities Provide less direct oversight Assure student that his or her goals are on target Communicate personal respect; validate student's ideas and thoughts Provide less correction and more information Invite participation in your goals Help student to accept your help	Supervise minimally Make decisions by consensus Engage in discussions regarding validity of values and standards Present problems and elicit solutions Set goals cooperatively Take a supportive role; allow maximum amount of freedom Provide ample opportunities for demonstration of desirable character traits Provide weekly assignments and allow student to establish timetable to meet deadlines Direct student toward opportunities to help others in class, school, or community When correction is necessary, allow student to devise a solution and a means of remedying the situation

Table 2
Behavior Styles

	Self-Assertive	Socially Interactive	Analytic	Accommodating
Emotional Needs	Admiration Recognition Authority Autonomy	Appreciation Recognition Attention Sociability	Being understood Affirmation Close personal relationships Order	Stable relationships Stable environment Structure Caring atmosphere
Characteristics	Extroverted Highly directive Controls to obtain results	Extroverted Moderately responsive Strives for personal impact on others	Introverted Moderately directive Attempts to control self and immediate environment	Introverted Highly responsive Needs to belong
Strengths	Gets immediate results Takes authority and guides projects through sheer determination Motivates others through his or her visionary abilities Completes tasks even amid criticism Instigates action once his or her vision is shared Enjoys change and accepts new challenges Makes quick decisions Enjoys solving problems Likes to take risks Enjoys competition Is innovative Prefers short projects	Is warm and outgoing Verbalizes well and is articulate Is the life of the party—witty and exuberant Approaches tasks intuitively and emotionally Has an energetic enthusiasm that can excite others Is optimistic Makes a favorable impression Is compassionate Enjoys contact with others Sells ideas Team planner Enjoys giving demonstrations	Excels at analytic projects Enjoys working under familiar circumstances; is cautious Excels in low-risk environment Is diplomatic Is devoted Is creative Pays attention to details, directives, and standards Is persistent and not easily exasperated Checks for accuracy and consistency Is orderly and organized Maintains a very pleasing work environment Adheres to rules	Works according to a pattern Is able to sit or stand in one place Never gets too excited Is patient and rarely gets angry Tends to be very stable Has a dry sense of humor Avoids getting involved in activities Listens and concentrates well—is responsive Calm; is able to calm others Diplomatic, practical, and objective Encourages loyalty among those he or she controls Accepts change very slowly; is cautious
Weaknesses	Ignores the needs of others when moving ahead on projects Is too forceful, even domineering May be prone to angry outbursts, but usually has self-control Deals harshly with others when they don't reach the goals he or she has set for them Retains grudges Wants his or her own way immediately Confronts others by beginning with a personal attack	Fluctuates emotionally May be impulsive and make snap decisions May be egocentric May not follow through with projects Oversells himself or herself Lacks attention to detail May waste time talking	Fluctuates emotionally—highs and lows can be significant Is a perfectionist Is indecisive Is overly sensitive to criticism Lacks humor and is unsociable May ask too many questions Overchecks information	Is insecure Conforms too easily; can be manipulated Lacks self-confidence Rates the opinions of others too highly Worries; can be unsettling Procrastinates and misses opportunities Lacks sense of urgency

Table 2 (continued)
Behavior Styles

	Self-Assertive	Socially Interactive	Analytic	Accommodating
Communication Styles	Communicates forcefully; gets right to the point Converses efficiently; tends to interrupt Discusses results and is action-oriented Uses physical presence to exert control Maintains direct eye contact Is impatient with delays	Is excitable Is persuasive Is talkative Discusses dreams and intuitions Is physically expressive Uses eye contact to enhance rapport	Speaks slowly and methodically Speaks seriously Is detail-oriented and thorough Discusses concepts, thoughts, and ideas Shows little emotion Avoids eye contact	Uses an easy, relaxed tone of voice Is patient Discusses feelings and relationships Avoids confrontational conversations Has a relaxed posture Avoids eye contact if relationship is strained
Preferred Learning Styles	Seeks utility Needs to know how things work Processes information abstractly[a] and actively[b] Focuses on one thing at a time Enjoys solving problems Prefers to work with unambiguous ideas Likes discovery-oriented inquiry Enjoys working on independent projects Likes to initiate discussion	Needs to know the purpose of things Processes information concretely[c] and actively[b] Enjoys variety Thrives on spontaneity; is adaptable Enjoys learning, particularly in groups and in open-ended projects Likes teaching others	Listens to and forms theories, concepts, and principles Seeks facts and continuity of ideas Values expert opinions Needs detail Thinks sequentially and analytically Processes information abstractly[a] and reflectively[d] Is interested in ideas rather than people Enjoys the traditional classroom setting	Seeks clarity and meaning Becomes personally and emotionally involved Listens and shares ideas Is interested in people and cultures Processes information concretely[c] and reflectively[d] Enjoys group projects but individual responsibility Prefers orderly presentations Likes "hands on" learning

[a]Learns best from principles, theories, and models.
[b]Learns best when processing information through physically moving or performing.
[c]Learns best from things that can be perceived through the senses of sight, sound, and touch.
[d]Learns best when processing information through thinking and feeling.

9

Table 3

Profiles by Level of Motivation and Behavior Style

Level of Motivation	Behavior Style			
	Self-Assertive	Socially Interactive	Analytic	Accommodating
1. Self-Absorbed	Does not generally seek help Attempts tasks or projects without understanding them Needs direction and ongoing evaluation Tends not to pay attention to details, but simply finishes the task Responds quickly—either negatively or positively—in a very assertive way Maintains his or her own position even when there is strong evidence against it Becomes very oppositional if challenged Expends purposeful effort only when convinced of benefit Attempts to direct or lead Desires proof to back up questionable statements from others	Avoids detail work Tends to be unaware of time Tries to socialize too much Asks "what if" questions May let desire for popularity get in the way of doing a task Is enthusiastic Is talkative Is overly confident Is outgoing Needs goals and objectives	Needs low-risk situations Needs a lot of explanation Needs organization Likes rules and standards Needs encouragement Likes step-by-step procedures Likes low-stress work Tends to ask many questions May check and recheck finished work Needs to feel safe	Needs time to adjust to a new task Is cautiously willing Is likely to procrastinate Is loyal Needs personal attention Needs understanding from the teacher Is productive if expectations are moderate Is a good listener Lacks a sense of urgency Does not require purpose in order to engage in a project or activity
2. Approval Oriented	Focuses on the task at the expense of other people or other responsibilities Wants to direct others even when not in a leadership role Tends to be overzealous when competing Likes to know exactly what is to be accomplished Takes risks—even inappropriately Wants to be perceived as powerful in class Tends to be very determined Is very observant May be reluctant to begin a new task for fear that it might draw negative attention	Gets along well with others Helps others look on the positive side Tries to gain popularity Is a good spokesperson for his or her group Is persuasive Likes to talk Likes to be neighborly Engages in attention-getting behavior Likes to be with people at the expense of finishing a task Is trusting	Avoids unpleasantness with others Likes to follow rules Likes regimentation Spends a lot of time on details May overdo planning before making a decision Tends to be serious Is very respectful May have difficulty in groups where tasks are delegated May be too cautious about joining in with others	Is amiable Becomes stubborn if pushed May not communicate vital information to others May not like to share credit Prefers working alone rather than with others Avoids leadership roles Likes to be part of a social group Does not like change Is low-key when working with others Likes being appreciated

Table 3 (continued)
Profiles by Level of Motivation and Behavior Style

Level of Motivation	Behavior Style			
	Self-Assertive	Socially Interactive	Analytic	Accommodating
3. Interpersonal Loyalty	Likes to delegate	Likes to look successful	Likes research projects	Is sincere
	Is very straightforward	Likes recognition	Is cooperative	Is willing
	Accepts challenges readily	Likes acceptance	Needs reasons for activity	Is dedicated
	Likes short, clear presentations	May be overly optimistic	Tends to have a narrow focus	Prefers to work alone when new tasks are being learned
	Likes and needs to be involved in decision making	Needs goals and objectives	Needs thinking time	Enjoys stable, routine tasks in cooperative groups
	May be overly directive when working with groups	May be persuasive without sound reasoning	Needs standard operating procedures	May procrastinate if expectations are too high
	May be abrupt when ready to move on to another task	May want more group discussion than is needed	May be tense at times if under stress	Is prone to listen while others make decisions
	Likes authority	May talk too much	May be overly cautious when making joint decisions	Is very patient with others
	Prefers short-term projects	Loves exciting projects	Tries to reduce risk in decisions	Is empathetic
4. Others Oriented	Likes independence	Benefits from assistance in managing time	Sensitive to others' feelings when offering suggestions	Tentative about making decisions that involve change
	Likes to set own pace	Desires others' support in setting goals and objectives	Avoids risky decisions	May put off unpleasant decisions
	May overlook details	Likes to spend time with others	Checks with teacher for confirmation regarding difficult decisions	Is very diplomatic
	Prefers activity over lengthy class discussions	Very careful about making unpleasant decisions	Desires more information than most other students	Is exceptionally patient
	Is very productive	Prefers working with others	Strives for perfection in form, procedure, and detail	Tends to be very well organized
	Presents his or her point of view with strong conviction	Motivates people	Is very idealistic	Needs more time to respond to pressure situations
	Accepts responsibility and leadership gladly	Needs to plan and concentrate on projects	Is extremely loyal	Is very dependable
	Tends to be an opinion leader	Invests himself or herself in meaningful tasks	Plans and executes projects well	Is most effective when handling one project at a time
	Organizes others effectively	Needs to be more realistic about time to complete tasks or projects	Is very dependable	Tends to be comfortable with the status quo

3

THE INTERVENTION STRATEGIES: DESCRIPTIONS AND GUIDELINES

Background and Development

For the past 50 years, theorists have articulated intervention strategies that they believed would either prevent or alter misbehavior. Most of these theorists were from the field of counseling psychology. Many were educators who were very specific about the design and proposed methodology of their intervention systems. As the interventions were used, however, it became apparent that none of them was successful with all students all of the time. Yet for every student there was at least one strategy that tended to be successful most of the time.

Although most teachers are familiar with some intervention strategies, few seem able to implement a wide variety of strategies—either because they are unaware of them or because they lack training in the appropriate use of additional strategies. Nevertheless, research clearly indicates that the more strategies teachers have at their disposal, the more successful they will be in maintaining appropriate classroom discipline.

With that in mind, we conducted an extensive study of the various intervention strategies available to teachers. We wanted to develop a system for determining which strategies would be most effective under various circumstances. We divided the strategies into four categories—Prevention, Limit Setting, Reinforcement of Limits, and Control—and put them in order by degree of intrusiveness (see Table 4), from the least intrusive in terms of classroom disruption (Prevention) to the most intrusive (Control). We also included strategies that involved outside agencies. We did not include Out of School Suspension and Expulsion as strategies, largely due to the ever-changing legalities concerning those decisions.

Because teaching styles vary, some teachers may find that a particular category would be more or less intrusive than what we have suggested. Generally, however, most teachers we consulted felt that the ratings were very accurate.

The strategies presented here are by no means exhaustive. For example, strategies for teaching new behaviors in a systematic fashion (e.g., social skills training or conflict resolution) are very effective, but are beyond the scope of this Handbook. The reader may refer to the Suggested Reading section of the Bibliography for sources of several other possible strategies. We have also found that teachers often use the strategies presented here as stimuli or springboards for creative solutions. We encourage you to combine, adapt, modify, and create strategies to arrive at the most effective method of intervention for you and the student.

Table 4
Intervention Strategies by Degree of Intrusiveness

Prevention	Limit Setting	Reinforcement of Limits	Control
Using a Businesslike Teaching Style	Announcing/Rehearsing the Rules	Stopping and Redirecting	Relocation Within the Classroom
Checking for Understanding	Using Affirmative Statements	Establishing Logical Consequences	Isolation Within the Classroom
Ignoring Misbehavior	Disguising Directives	Asking "What" Questions	Removing Stimuli
Increasing Physical Proximity	Describing Misbehavior as It Occurs	Setting Achievable Goals	Exclusion From Fun Activities
Nonverbal Communication	Direct Commands	Positive Peer-Group Reinforcement	Coordinating Outside Intervention
Using Humor to Relieve Stress	Modeling Expected Behavior	Token Rewards	Time Out
Asking Adult Questions	Appealing to Values	Tangible Reinforcement	Time Out for a Specified Period or Activity
Introducing Role Models	Reflecting Verbal Responses	Charting Progress	Requiring a Plan for Improvement
Identifying Idealized Characters	Probing for Motives	Using Written Contracts	Deducting Points for Misbehavior
Probing for Values	Student Self-Monitoring	Suggesting Parental Intervention Strategies	Detention
Sharing Authority and Decision Making	Exchanging Information With Parents		Having a Parent in the Classroom
Alerting Parents to Concerns			

Least Intrusive ▲ … ▼ Most Intrusive

PREVENTION

The low-key intervention strategies in the *Prevention* category are standard operating procedures in most well-managed classrooms; however, some of them may be either missing from a teacher's repertoire or used inconsistently. They generally require little extra teaching time and minimal intrusion into potentially disruptive behavior. These strategies are appropriate for students who have enough internal control to correct their misbehavior with a minimum amount of teacher assistance.

Using a Businesslike Teaching Style

Some students learn only in a serious, controlled environment. Businesslike teaching requires a highly organized lesson plan so that students know what they should be doing at all times. When using this strategy, you should continue to be caring, supportive, and approachable, especially during lunch and recess.

▶ **Implementation Guidelines**
1. Design lesson plans that include good opening statements, transitions, and closing statements.
2. Structure the entire school day—including group activities.
3. Dress in a conservative, mature manner.
4. Structure behavior in the classroom with logical, easily understood rules and procedures.
5. Allow very little open discussion time.

▶ **Positive Student Responses**
1. Rapid transition from a playful attitude during nonwork time to a serious attitude during work time.
2. Longer attention span during teaching sessions.
3. Increased respect for the teacher.

▶ **Negative Student Responses**
1. Perceived lack of love and caring from the teacher.
2. More reserved relationship with the teacher—even in off-task time.
3. Frustration with the level of concentration demanded. Frequent breaks may be necessary initially.

Checking for Understanding

Make sure that the student understands the assignment. Frustration caused by confusion or misunderstanding can lead to talking, laughing, or heightened activity. Simply ask the student to repeat the directions or presentation to prevent such problems.

▶ **Implementation Guidelines**
1. Explain directions or present information in a number of ways (e.g., orally, in writing, or using diagrams, outlines, or flow charts).
2. Give instructions that approximate the actual task as closely as possible.
3. Ask students to repeat or demonstrate your instructions.
4. Rephrase directions or present information differently if there is confusion.
5. Demonstrate solutions for one or two items, or answer one or two questions.

▶ **Positive Student Responses**
1. Attention to task without further misbehavior.
2. Improved understanding, although further clarification may be necessary.

▶ **Negative Student Responses**
1. Increased frustration after several unsuccessful attempts.
2. Reluctance to attempt to understand explanations.

Ignoring Misbehavior

Often students will repeat misbehavior if they receive reinforcement of any kind. A student may misbehave to temporarily steal the teacher's attention. Ignoring such behavior can be very effective. Remove the reinforcement, and the student's behavior is useless and will most likely cease. Of course, this method can only be used for less disruptive behavior.

▶ **Implementation Guidelines**
1. Note repeated misbehavior that consistently receives attention.
2. Decide whether the behavior could be allowed to continue for a short period of time, even at an increased level, without significantly disturbing the rest of the class.
3. Ignore the misbehavior the next time it occurs.
4. Expect a temporary increase in the misbehavior until the student realizes that he or she is no longer achieving the desired response.

▶ **Positive Student Responses**
1. Increased misbehavior that decreases once the student realizes that such behavior no longer receives attention.
2. Attempts to gain attention in more positive ways—by raising his or her hand, participating in discussions, or answering questions.

PREVENTION *(continued)*

▶ **Negative Student Responses**

1. Continued misbehavior, unaffected by teacher's lack of interest; attention may not be the student's motivation.
2. Behavior so disruptive to the rest of the class that another form of discipline is necessary. You may want to continue to use this strategy in conjunction with another approach, but you should set limits on how disruptive the student can be.

Increasing Physical Proximity

Many students feel comfortable misbehaving only when they think they are out of your reach or attention. Such disruptions may happen so frequently that almost constant correction is necessary, which wastes valuable teaching time and fragments the entire lesson. You can continue the lesson and reduce the student's misbehavior by exercising greater control of his or her proximity—that is, spending more time near the misbehaving student. If this method is used consistently, the student will eventually adapt to your presence and continue to behave while you are further away. If you approach the student only when he or she is acting up, your presence may prove more of a distraction than a correction.

▶ **Implementation Guidelines**

1. Circulate throughout the classroom, especially while teaching.
2. Walk up and down the aisles near the misbehaving student without interrupting the teaching process.
3. Sit on an empty desk or chair near the student.
4. Ask the student questions, or focus discussion near him or her.

▶ **Positive Student Responses**

1. Decreased misbehavior when you are near.
2. Eventually, increased attention even when you are not in the vicinity.

▶ **Negative Student Responses**

1. Obvious signs of increased anxiety when you are very near.
2. Decrease in answering questions or participating in discussions. Student may be more quiet, but he or she is not really listening when you are near.

Nonverbal Communication

Most teachers have a repertoire of nonverbal communication techniques; however, such physical communication is probably used inconsistently and without prior thought. This strategy requires consistent, premeditated nonverbal communication to achieve discipline. When used purposefully and consistently, certain looks, hand signals, or head movements can let a student know what is expected without time-consuming and potentially embarrassing words. Use nonverbal communication to acknowledge positive performance as well as negative behavior.

▶ **Implementation Guidelines**

1. Physically acknowledge positive behavior—smile, nod approval, or make a gesture of satisfaction (e.g., thumb held up in conjunction with a smile).
2. Physically acknowledge negative behavior—raise your eyebrows, scowl, frown, roll your eyes, shake your head, or stare menacingly.
3. Record your physical responses for a while to determine the ratio of positive expressions to negative expressions. If you are responding more to negative behavior, try to increase your use of physical expression to acknowledge positive behavior.

▶ **Positive Student Responses**

1. Increased attentiveness.
2. Misbehavior suppressed quickly, without distracting other classmates.

▶ **Negative Student Responses**

1. Sarcasm or mimicry.
2. Confusion—verbal communication may be necessary.

Using Humor to Relieve Stress

Students sometimes take certain situations very seriously—the simplest problems can be stressful, causing insecurity and illogical behavior. Using humor in the midst of stress can comfort students and communicate to them that everything will work out fine.

Humor can also be used with students who are about to misbehave. If, for example, you see that a student is crumpling up paper every time he or she makes a mistake, a humorous comment can indicate that you see the action, while allowing the student to do the right thing without feeling confronted. (For example: "Let's please use an eraser, so we don't wipe out the entire rain forest.") Humor is an effective way to say that, although misbehavior will not be tolerated, this situation is not viewed as serious because the student can be trusted to do the right thing.

▶ **Implementation Guidelines**

1. Do not use mean or sarcastic humor.
2. Use humor when a student seems insecure or about to panic, is becoming too serious or negative, is on the verge of misbehaving to create a diversion, or is trying very hard but becoming frustrated.
3. Use humor that the student will understand.

▶ **Positive Student Responses**

1. Laughter or smiling.
2. Renewed confidence and willingness to approach the situation from a different angle.
3. Friendly, yet respectful behavior.

▶ **Negative Student Responses**

1. Sarcasm or disrespect.
2. No response at all.
3. Crying or anger; accusations of insensitivity.
4. Use of humor at inappropriate times.

Asking Adult Questions

At any given time, an individual's behavior is an expression of one of three internal modes—child, parent, or adult. The child mode is a reflection of feelings and experiences recorded internally during childhood. The parent mode is also recorded during childhood—in response to the child's parents' actions and reactions. The adult mode is internalized when the student's rational abilities are being developed; it becomes more dominant as the years pass and continues throughout life. Try to maintain adult social transactions while affirming the creativity of the child, the restraint of the parent, and the rational thoughts of the adult.

▶ **Implementation Guidelines**

1. Assume that the student is operating in the adult mode.
2. Ask questions that would meet the needs of the adult mode. For example, if a student spills paint in the classroom, the parent-to-child question would be "Didn't I warn you about making a mess?" The child-to-parent question would be "Why do I always have to clean up the mess?" The adult-to-adult question would be "What can I get for you so that you can clean this up?" Focus on the specific problem, not on possible causes or blame.
3. Revert to the parent mode only if adult-to-adult communication is not working.
4. Never revert to the child mode when communicating with a student.

▶ **Positive Student Responses**

1. Increased acceptance of responsibility; improved behavior.
2. Increasingly adult reactions to situations.
3. Improved attitude and relationships.

▶ **Negative Student Responses**

1. Assumption of parent-mode or child-mode attitude.
2. Assumption of distorted adult role and loss of respect for authority.
3. Continued misbehavior.

Introducing Role Models

One of the most important ways students learn is by studying a role model. Teachers, peers, and idealized characters are the most common role models. The teacher, of course, should always try to be a good role model. In addition, because students notice peers who receive rewards, you can sometimes eliminate the need for endless demands for obedience by moving the focus to rewarding proper behavior.

▶ **Implementation Guidelines**

1. Use one of the following types of role models.
   - *Teacher.* Model the behavior you expect from your students. If you are consistently late, for example, the students will likely show less respect for time. If you are consistently well-mannered, the students may show more respect for manners.
   - *Peer.* Use students as examples of proper behavior—point out and affirm the behavior you would like other students to emulate.
   - *Idealized Character.* Identify a role model that the students respect, and encourage them to demonstrate the best qualities of that person. (See "Identifying Idealized Characters" in this chapter for more detail.)
2. Reward those who imitate the correct behavior.

▶ **Positive Student Responses**

1. Emulation of students who receive rewards for proper behavior.
2. Emulation of the positive qualities modeled or discussed.

▶ **Negative Student Responses**

1. Unnatural or undesirable imitation of attributes of another student's personality.

PREVENTION *(continued)*

2. Disillusionment as the result of unsuccessful attempts to change. Be patient and encouraging.
3. Lack of interest in rewards for modeling correct behavior. Find more attractive rewards.

Identifying Idealized Characters

Determine which role models or characters the student might want to be like. Look for traits in that character that the student should imitate, and encourage such behavior. The role model could be a current real-life figure or a character in literature, film, or television.

▶ **Implementation Guidelines**

1. Talk with students about which characters (potential role models) they consider to be most important.
2. Ask students to reveal the things they admire most about those characters.
3. Identify the qualities that students are expected to imitate.
4. Reward students who imitate the correct behavior, and point out behavior that is similar to that admired in an idealized character.
5. Point out significant examples of inappropriate behavior that are inconsistent with the traits of an idealized character.

▶ **Positive Student Responses**

1. Identification and emulation of positive role models.
2. Discovery of additional positive characteristics in existing role models.

▶ **Negative Student Responses**

1. Inability to distinguish good characteristics from bad characteristics.
2. Placement of blame for misbehavior on the idealized character's example.
3. Concentration on the idealized character's flaws as an excuse for misbehavior.
4. Unnatural imitation of attributes of the idealized character's personality. Concentrate on correct behavior, not overall personality.
5. Disillusionment at not being able to act well enough to receive rewards. Be patient and encouraging.
6. Lack of interest in rewards for modeling correct behavior. Find more attractive rewards.

Probing for Values

Under certain circumstances, students tend to express their attitudes, aspirations, purposes, interests, and activities. By looking for and encouraging such situations, the teacher can gain insight into why certain behaviors are present. That information can enhance understanding between the teacher and his or her students.

▶ **Implementation Guidelines**

1. Watch for situations in which students reveal their values. If convenient, encourage continued conversation at those times.
2. Identify subjects that interest the student. Then, in a one-on-one situation, bring up those subjects and probe for additional insights into the student's values.
3. Look for consistent, repetitive responses to make sure that the values expressed are not simply the student's mood of the moment.

▶ **Positive Student Responses**

1. Recognition of a contradiction between values and misbehavior.
2. Willingness to question values that are causing conflict and misconduct.
3. Reassessment of or renewed commitment to values.

▶ **Negative Student Responses**

1. Excuses for misbehavior, such as "That's just the way I am."
2. Unwillingness or inability to verbalize values.
3. Insecurity and confusion.

Sharing Authority and Decision Making

Encourage students to imitate the attributes of a democratic society. Students are not only affected by their peers; they can also be primary motivators. By allowing peers to express their opinion of a student's behavior, you utilize one of the most significant sources of behavior reinforcement. Although peers have a tendency to reinforce a student's bad behavior, the teacher can form a group that redirects peer attention. Within such a structure, peers are encouraged to help improve each other's behavior.

PREVENTION *(continued)*

▶ **Implementation Guidelines**

1. Design a group structure—either formal or informal—for use during class meetings (e.g., assign a class president, vice president, etc.).

2. Decide what behavior should be discussed by the class.

3. Decide what behavior should be punished by the class. Present a list of suggested consequences for misbehavior.

4. Schedule class meetings on a regular basis.

5. Avoid letting students vote on proposed punishment, but obtain consensus whenever possible.

6. Retain veto power, but use it only when absolutely necessary.

▶ **Positive Student Responses**

1. Agreement with peer decisions; improved behavior.

2. Participation—without vindictiveness—in the discussion of a peer's problem.

▶ **Negative Student Responses**

1. Use of group to pinpoint certain peers for retaliation.

2. Fear of retaliation for speaking up.

3. Unfairness in regard to another student's problem because of recent punishment by the group.

4. Resistance to consequences handed down by the group.

5. Complaints of unfair treatment.

Alerting Parents to Concerns

Alerting parents to your concerns about a student's behavior is the first strategy that involves parents in the classroom discipline process. Parents have primary responsibility for their child, and they should know if something unusual is happening. When discussing the student's behavior, be unemotional and direct. Do not alarm the parents unless the situation is critical. As objectively as possible, describe how the student's behavior has changed, so that the parents have detailed information to help them work on the problem. Be very careful not to place blame, suggest causes, or lead the parents to solutions. The goal is to gain additional insight and/or allow the parents to intervene once they have the necessary information.

▶ **Implementation Guidelines**

1. Determine the severity of the student's problem. If it is serious, be very frank with the parents; however, if it is not serious, avoid alarming them. They may be shocked to receive a call from their child's school.

2. To avoid misunderstandings, decide how to communicate your message before calling.

3. Avoid suggesting a cause or solution.

4. Write down any information the parents provide that might be helpful in solving the student's problem.

▶ **Positive Parental Responses**

1. Genuine concern for their child's needs.

2. Willingness to provide new information about the problem.

3. Expression of interest in other aspects of the student's performance and behavior in the classroom. Hopefully the parents will see you as a part of the solution.

4. Willingness to try a new approach with the student to try to decrease misbehavior.

▶ **Negative Parental Responses**

1. Punishment of the student because of your call.

   Note. The student might attempt to punish you for making the call. Such a response does not mean that it was wrong to make the call, but it does indicate that further work is necessary.

2. Making excuses for their child and blaming you for his or her problems. This is often a temporary response; the parents probably already suspect that something is wrong.

3. Ignoring the problem.

LIMIT SETTING

Limit Setting strategies are necessary when behavior problems occur despite the use of Prevention strategies. Many of the strategies in this category require some restructuring of the student's environment, which will involve a minimum to moderate amount of the teacher's time. These strategies are appropriate for students who have enough internal control—with support from the teacher—to correct their own behavior.

Announcing/Rehearsing the Rules

Students need to know their boundaries. When rules are vague, they do not know what is expected. The rules and procedures essential for a good classroom atmosphere should be logical and clear. Although the teacher should take the lead in rule development, student input and feedback to the rules will tend to encourage adherence. Once the rules are developed, be businesslike and repeat the rules frequently until they are fully understood. Establish reasonable consequences for breaking the rules, and be prepared to follow through.

One key to the successful implementation of rules is consistent rehearsal. By rehearsing the rules—and the consequences for breaking them—students become familiar with them and are more apt to follow them. Rehearsing is a good way to check the degree of understanding concerning the rules. It is also a time for students to practice the behaviors and procedures necessary to comply with the rules. Social skills training and conflict mediation skills may best be taught at this juncture. (See the Suggested Reading section of the Bibliography for resources.)

▶ **Implementation Guidelines**

1. Choose rules, with appropriate student input, that are necessary for a good classroom atmosphere and announce them (e.g., say, "There is to be quiet during work time. Raise your hand and stay in your seat when you want to speak. Stay in line when walking in and out of the classroom."). Introduce no more than five to seven rules—too many can diminish the effect of those that are most important.

2. Make the consequences for breaking the rules logical and clear.

3. Post the rules conspicuously.

4. Repeat the rules at the beginning of each day until the students can recite and follow them automatically. Repeat the consequences occasionally. Have the students paraphrase and explain the rules and consequences on a regular basis.

5. Add or change rules that are burdensome, unnecessary, or unworkable. Rehearse new rules and consequences.

6. Increase the frequency of rule rehearsal when a rule is not being followed, or before and after holidays.

7. Notify parents of the rules and consequences, as well as any subsequent changes.

8. Enforce the rules consistently. One infraction without consequences can damage the students' perception of your resolve.

▶ **Positive Student Responses**

1. Students voice a commitment to the rules.

2. Willingness to paraphrase and discuss the rules and consequences.

3. Fewer instances of rule breaking.

4. Demonstrated remorse for misbehavior.

5. Open discussion of a rule with someone who is on the verge of breaking it.

▶ **Negative Student Responses**

1. Student interpretation of the rules varies widely. This may be due to a lack of clarity in how the rules are stated.

2. The student may not understand a rule or the reason behind it.

3. Nonparticipation in rule rehearsal. This may indicate a need for student ownership and understanding of the rules.

4. Lack of remorse after breaking a rule. The consequences (positive or negative) may not be effective.

5. Open rebellion against a particular rule; if many students seem to have a problem with it, it may be inappropriately stated, explained, or understood.

Using Affirmative Statements

If a student is disruptive because of a need for attention, try to determine what behavior that student exhibits that actually deserves positive attention, and encourage that behavior. If you find it difficult to discern such behavior, it may be because the student is not doing activities that he or she is capable of doing well. Change the student's environment or responsibilities and then acknowledge positive behavior in the new role. Students can go from attention-getting behavior to helplessness very quickly. They need reassurance that they are capable of becoming important members of the class, and they need to actively develop

LIMIT SETTING *(continued)*

those capabilities. Look for a student's strengths, design areas where those strengths can be used, and encourage and acknowledge success.

► **Implementation Guidelines**

1. Find the student's areas of interest and ability.
2. Design activities that encourage involvement in those interests and abilities.
3. Emphasize the need for improvement, not perfection.
4. Match the student with others who are willing to help him or her.
5. Avoid placing students in competition with each other.

► **Positive Student Responses**

1. Renewed interest in schoolwork; sense of being a vital part of the class.
2. Acknowledgment and understanding of other students' roles.
3. Decreased need for attention.
4. Increased self-confidence.

► **Negative Student Responses**

1. Lack of interest in the activities chosen for them. The teacher may have chosen the wrong activity, or the student may have discovered that he or she is not interested after all.
2. Inability to succeed; frustration.
3. Distrust of praise because of empty praise for earlier, poor performance.

Disguising Directives

Some students will correct their misbehavior with just a glance from you or a verbal hint. Others need a disguised verbal directive; they would confront a direct command. Not all students confront direct demands, but for those who do, it can create a strained relationship. By disguising a demand in such a way that students perceive they have been asked to do something rather than commanded to, they may respond without confrontation. For example, "How are you doing with your reading?" is a question that allows the student to feel that he or she has a reasonable choice of responses. Use this strategy as a warning or last step before you are forced to make a direct demand.

► **Implementation Guidelines**

1. Give the class as a whole a hint that those who are misbehaving are sure to notice.
2. Give a disguised verbal directive to the target student if he or she does not respond to the hint.
3. Try to avoid unintentionally inviting a confrontation. Negative facial expressions may invite hostility even when the words being spoken are fairly calm.

► **Positive Student Responses**

1. Compliance with no sign of regret.
2. Response to the hint with no need for further directives.

► **Negative Student Responses**

1. Resentment, even if ultimately obedient.
2. Continued need for direct demands.
3. Confrontation.

Describing Misbehavior as It Occurs

Many students fail to recognize that their actions affect others, and they may therefore cause a disturbance without knowing they've done anything wrong. They may also act in a way that leads you to believe they are about to misbehave. For example, a student who taps his or her foot faster and faster as a math problem is being worked on may be on the verge of an outburst of some kind. Assume that the student will do the right thing once made aware of his or her actions. Then, instead of correcting the student, describe what he or she has just done, or is doing. Once this has been done, the student should correct the situation.

► **Implementation Guidelines**

1. Describe to the student exactly what you see happening (e.g., say, "I notice you are tapping your foot fast and loud"). Avoid suggesting a solution to the problem.
2. Wait for some sign that the student understands how his or her behavior could constitute a problem. Allow him or her to solve the problem or suggest a solution.
3. Describe the impact of the student's action on other students (e.g., say, "When you raise your voice, some of the other students can't concentrate and may stop working").

LIMIT SETTING *(continued)*

▶ **Positive Student Responses**

1. Cessation of misbehavior.
2. Signs of understanding the problem.
3. Suggested solutions.

▶ **Negative Student Responses**

1. Inability to understand the problem. You might have to give a more detailed description.
2. Little or no change in behavior even after learning the effect it has.

Direct Commands

Direct, assertive commands, spoken with authority, should be used to tell students specifically what to do or not to do when rhetorical questions or softer commands do not work. Direct commands should be positive and void of put-downs or absolute statements. If, for example, a student is not doing his or her seatwork, you could say, "Please, start your seatwork immediately." Avoid statements like, "You're doing it again—spacing out. You'd better change that lazy attitude. You sure are a disappointment to your parents." Finally, direct commands should not be punitive—for example, it would not be appropriate to say, "Stop acting like a baby, and keep your hands to yourself."

▶ **Implementation Guidelines**

1. Try some of the other strategies first, if possible.
2. Think of a positive way of stating the command.
3. Anticipate situations where commands must be given, and practice your tone and posture.
4. Analyze responses.

▶ **Positive Student Responses**

1. Immediate return to work or cessation of misbehavior.
2. Return to work or cessation of misbehavior after a minute or two.

▶ **Negative Student Responses**

1. Defiance.
2. Defensiveness or attempts to place blame on others.

Modeling Expected Behavior

Modeling the desired behavior is one of the best teaching methods available. Because students learn from the teacher's example or demonstration, wise teachers model the academic and social behavior they want to encourage. By modeling the appropriate student response, whether in word or in deed, you provide the student with instructions about how to act properly. The modeled behavior could range from ways to approach academic tasks to ways to comply with rules and behavioral expectations. Significant deviations from the model may then be treated as intentional misbehavior requiring stronger intervention. This strategy is a quick and effective response to the numerous disruptions that occur during the course of a school day.

▶ **Implementation Guidelines**

1. Analyze the student's misbehavior and determine whether he or she has learned the correct behavior. Remind the misbehaving student of the correct way to act.
2. Model the correct behavior.
3. Consistently behave as you would like to see the students behave.

▶ **Positive Student Responses**

1. Repetition of the modeled actions.
2. Self-correction without the need for a model.

▶ **Negative Student Responses**

1. Repetition of the same misbehavior with no sign of awareness that it is wrong.
2. Enjoyment of the one-on-one attention this strategy affords. Certain types of misbehavior may increase—especially with academic modeling.

Appealing to Values

By watching how a student reacts in various situations, you can discover what values he or she possesses (see "Probing for Values" earlier in this chapter). Most students have established values that allow them to behave properly. If a student exhibits behavior that is obviously contrary to his or her established values, point out how the student normally acts, and ask why his or her current behavior is different.

By forcing students to think about why they decide to behave improperly, you can encourage them to discover what makes them go against what they know is right. With that knowledge, they may be able to resist the temptation to misbehave in the future.

▶ **Implementation Guidelines**

1. Observe and record the student's values.
2. Upon misbehavior, contrast the student's typical, proper behavior with his or her misbehavior.

LIMIT SETTING *(continued)*

3. Ask the student to think carefully about the situation and consider why his or her good values were abandoned.

4. When privacy seems necessary, ask the student to write out his or her answers.

5. Make sure that the student understands the expected behavior and expresses the values necessary to demonstrate that behavior.

▶ **Positive Student Responses**

1. Ability to express frustration and talk with you.

2. Inclination to correct misbehavior before it is fully manifested.

▶ **Negative Student Responses**

1. Inability to evaluate misbehavior or to articulate why it occurs.

2. Continued behavior inconsistent with the student's spoken values.

Reflecting Verbal Responses

Students often say superficial things that have a deeper message; however, they may be quickly corrected for outward behavior before their more deep-seated problem can be revealed. You can encourage them to verbalize their real message by paraphrasing their words. Often, when students realize how their actual words sound, they try to express their feelings more accurately. Given time, they may then be better able to recognize and solve their own problems.

▶ **Implementation Guidelines**

1. Listen to the student, and try to determine his or her hidden message.

2. Paraphrase that message.

3. Continue to paraphrase such messages until no further clarification is forthcoming.

4. Do not try to guess what the underlying problem may be—just reflect what is actually said. For example, consider the following dialogue.

STUDENT: I hate math.

TEACHER: Math makes you unhappy?

STUDENT: Yes, I just want to drop it or fail.

TEACHER: You feel like giving up on it?

STUDENT: I try and try, but I keep getting D's in the dumb course.

TEACHER: No matter what you do, nothing works. Right?

STUDENT: Well, I haven't tried everything. There are those tutoring sessions after school.

TEACHER: Tutoring sessions may be an option.

▶ **Positive Student Responses**

1. Decreased anxiety and agitation.

2. Increased cooperation.

▶ **Negative Student Responses**

1. Accusations that you are parroting what the student is saying.

2. Continued misbehavior in spite of having a chance to vent and reflect.

Probing for Motives

this one applies to us.

Students are goal-oriented, and their actions can often be attributed to attempts to achieve one of the following inner goals: attention, power, revenge, or helplessness. The teacher must discover which of these inner goals is motivating the student's misbehavior and then learn how to redirect that energy constructively. When dealing with misbehavior, ask yourself whether that behavior reveals one of the student's inner goals. If you can determine which inner goal is motivating the student, you can intervene appropriately and avoid the possibility of reinforcing the misbehavior.

▶ **Implementation Guidelines**

1. Immediately after the student's misbehavior, consider the following four questions and corresponding motives:

   • Do I feel annoyed? Attention-getting may be or is likely the student's goal.

   • Do I feel beaten or intimidated? Power may be or is likely the goal.

   • Do I feel wronged or hurt? Revenge may be or is likely the goal.

   • Do I feel incapable of reaching this student in any way? Helplessness may be or is likely the goal.

2. Respond to the appropriate motive as follows:

   • If attention-getting is the student's goal, deprive him or her of attention by quickly directing others to another task without recognizing the misbehavior. If the misbehavior persists, isolate the student and exclude him or her from further participation in class activities. Later, you might want to reveal your suspicion that attention was the student's goal.

   • If power is the goal, do not allow open conflict. State any applicable rules and consequences, and then move on with the activity at hand. If necessary, let the student engage in another activity until he or she can be dealt with one-on-one. As much as possible, give the student positive positions of power (e.g., lunch monitor).

LIMIT SETTING *(continued)*

- If revenge is the goal, the student will need a lot of care, whether or not he or she seems receptive. Find out why the student feels hurt, teach forgiveness, and work out the conflict that caused the problem initially.
- If helplessness is the goal, the student has lost a lot of hope. Be patient and attempt to show the student where he or she is most capable. Occasionally switch from regular, difficult classroom activities to activities in which the student has interest or talent. Spend extra time later working on the areas of difficulty.

▶ **Positive Student Responses**

1. Cessation of earlier misbehavior.
2. Verbalization or realization of inner goals.
3. Anticipation of the need for correction by seeking help.

▶ **Negative Student Responses**

1. Continued misbehavior based on the same inner goal, which indicates that the strategy needs to be altered.
2. Slightly altered misbehavior—the problem was probably not diagnosed correctly.
3. Slow response to intervention.

Student Self-Monitoring

Only when students are made aware of their behavior and the effect it has on others can they take responsibility for maintaining proper behavior and gaining self-control; however, most students who are prone to misbehavior are unable to control their actions without some guidance. For such students, begin by pointing out unacceptable behavior and explaining proper behavior. Once the student understands what is expected, work together to set reasonable, specific goals and devise a way to monitor the student's progress.

For example, a student may be having difficulty getting through science experiments without disrupting the class. You and the student observe that about 15 minutes into an experiment, he or she begins to act up. You both agree that, after working for 10 minutes, the student will go to the front of the room to speak to the teacher and evaluate his or her behavior. The student should be responsible for remembering when to talk to the teacher. The teacher should encourage the student and send him or her back to work for another 10 minutes. This schedule continues until the student's

goal is reached. When the student is able to concentrate on the task for 10 minutes at a time, extend the intervals to 15-minute stretches. As the student continues to meet goals, grant more responsibility. Make sure the student monitors his or her own progress and knows when the goal is reached. Focus on accomplishments rather than failures. Having students record and graph their progress is often a helpful feedback system for teachers, parents, and administrators, as well as the students.

▶ **Implementation Guidelines**

1. Define the misbehavior to be addressed.
2. Without the student's notice, make a notation each time you observe the behavior.
3. Discuss your notations with the student to insure that the problem is understood.
4. Devise a step-by-step plan to eliminate the misbehavior.
5. Work with the student to set realistic goals for each step. For example, if the student speaks out before raising his or her hand or being called on, and this occurs 10 times per day, have the student reduce the number of incidents by 2 each day until the misbehavior is eliminated.
6. Have the student maintain a neat, handwritten chart to monitor his or her progress.
7. Establish a reward for the successful completion of each goal. Increase the reward if the student exceeds the goal.
8. Once a goal is consistently attained, set a new goal.

▶ **Positive Student Responses**

1. Interest in charting as a game; willingness to chart other misbehavior.
2. Increased awareness of personal actions and signs of increased self-control.
3. Improved relationship with the teacher.

▶ **Negative Student Responses**

1. Inability to meet goals; tendency to become discouraged. Set the goals lower if the student seems to be trying.
2. Lack of interest in the process; no effort to maintain chart or meet goals.
3. Overemphasis on charting at the expense of academic performance.
4. Resumption of prior misbehavior while working on new goals.

LIMIT SETTING *(continued)*

Exchanging Information With Parents

Up to this point, the student's parents have simply been told of his or her misbehavior in the classroom (see "Alerting Parents to Concerns" earlier in this chapter). You should try many strategies to curb the student's misbehavior, either directly or indirectly, before involving the parents further in the discipline process. If you feel that you need more information about the student, however, it may be helpful to ask the parents about what they think may be causing the problem. Do not ask the parents for solutions, but allow them to work through the problem. On the other hand, if they ask for guidance or help, it should not be refused. Remember that parents have primary authority over their child—do not diminish their feeling of responsibility.

▶ **Implementation Guidelines**

1. Determine the severity of the problem, and decide how to approach the parents.

2. Write down questions before calling.

3. Remind the parents of their child's earlier problems, and describe the other strategies you have used to try to correct the misbehavior. Defend your view of the situation with facts. If the problem is serious, be frank. If it is not very serious, avoid alarming the parents. They will probably be distressed to receive another call from you. Do not accuse or threaten. Avoid suggesting a solution.

4. Write down any information that might be helpful in understanding and solving the student's problem.

▶ **Positive Parental Responses**

1. Genuine concern for their child and his or her needs.

2. Willingness to provide new information that gives you more understanding about the situation.

3. Curiosity about other aspects of the student's performance and behavior in the classroom. Hopefully, the parents will see the teacher as part of the solution.

4. Improved relationship with the student that leads to a decrease in the misbehavior.

▶ **Negative Parental Responses**

1. Punishment of the student because of your call.

   Note. Student may be resentful and attempt to punish you for calling his or her parents. Such a response does not mean that it was wrong to make the call, but it does indicate that further work is necessary.

2. Making excuses for their child and blaming you for his or her problems. This is usually a temporary response; the parents probably know that something is truly wrong.

3. Ignoring the problem or not providing helpful information.

REINFORCEMENT OF LIMITS

Reinforcement of Limits strategies should be used when the student's behavior dictates the need for a moderate amount of extra teaching time and attention. The strategies in this category involve the use of direct commands, charts, and various other reinforcements of previously defined limits. These strategies are based on the assumption that, although the student does not have enough internal control to correct the problem on his or her own, with the teacher's intervention the situation can be appraised and corrected.

Stopping and Redirecting

To stop and redirect a student's inappropriate behavior, first let the student know that the misbehavior has been discovered by asking him or her to stop, then redirect the student's attention to the task at hand. For example, if a student begins to doodle instead of working on math problems, say, "Stop drawing on your paper. Begin your first math problem." This is a clear message without a lot of extra information. Hopefully, the student will accept the lack of fanfare and get to work.

▶ **Implementation Guidelines**
1. Determine what is preventing the student from paying attention, and ask him or her to stop that behavior.
2. Tell the student what he or she should be doing.
3. Shortly thereafter, check to see if the student has obeyed.

▶ **Positive Student Responses**
1. Quick return to schoolwork.
2. Realization that you are able to determine what the student is doing on a regular basis.

▶ **Negative Student Responses**
1. Instigation of commotion to show displeasure at being forced to do something.
2. Brief period of obedience followed by a return to misbehavior.

Establishing Logical Consequences

When presented in terms of obvious cause-and-effect relationships, one of the best ways to maintain classroom discipline is to establish logical consequences for certain behaviors. For example, students can readily understand that if they fool around in the hallway—running, pushing, or shoving—and fall on the floor, they will very likely be hurt. Similarly, it can be made clear that if students fail to turn their work in on time, they will be required to stay after school to complete it. Another approach is to direct students to leave a class in the same order as they arrived, in order to encourage on-time behavior.

▶ **Implementation Guidelines**
1. Make a list of common classroom rules.
2. Establish logical consequences for breaking the rules.
3. Rehearse the rules, and the consequences for breaking them, with the students until they fully understand.

▶ **Positive Student Responses**
1. Understanding and acceptance of the consequences for his or her actions.
2. Curiosity about the logical consequences of other actions.

▶ **Negative Student Responses**
1. Failure to see the correlation between his or her actions and their consequences.
2. Anger toward you for administering the consequences.

Asking "What" Questions

Asking a "what" question in response to misbehavior (e.g., "What are you doing?") forces a student to address the misbehavior rather than offer the myriad excuses that a "why" question elicits. Do not stop asking "what" until the student verbalizes a response that indicates that he or she realizes that the given action or reaction was inappropriate. Then form an agreement with the student to stop the misbehavior. Agree on a consequence for the misbehavior if it continues.

▶ **Implementation Guidelines**
1. Ask a "what" question that addresses the student's misbehavior.
2. Get the student to describe his or her misbehavior without making excuses for it.
3. Ask a "how" question (e.g., "How did this outburst help you get the answer to your math problem?").
4. Ask another "what" question (e.g., "What would be a better way to handle your math question next time?"). Make suggestions if the student runs out of solutions.
5. Establish a verbal plan for improvement that includes consequences for continued misbehavior.

REINFORCEMENT OF LIMITS *(continued)*

▶ **Positive Student Responses**

1. Enthusiastic acceptance of the agreement.
2. Compliance with the solution that was agreed upon.

▶ **Negative Student Responses**

1. Defiance and refusal to adhere to the agreement.
2. Excuse making.
3. Taking advantage of the time and effort involved in the process and causing frequent trouble.
4. Confusion, frustration, depression, or resentment. Work with the student to negotiate a more realistic agreement.

Setting Achievable Goals

Some students have so many problems that it seems impossible to correct them all without constant discipline. This can be frustrating for both you and the student. By establishing a goal, identifying the steps necessary to achieve that goal, and rewarding the successful completion of each step, you and the student can see improvement. Start with an achievable goal that must be attained before other problems can be resolved—even if it's not the desired end result. Additional training in social skills or conflict resolution may be necessary. (See the Suggested Reading section of the Bibliography for resources.)

▶ **Implementation Guidelines**

1. Decide which misbehavior is most troublesome and should be worked on first.
2. Set a major goal for ending that misbehavior and identify the steps necessary to achieve that goal. For example, if a student is causing disturbances during math, the ultimate goal may be for him or her to remain seated and on task throughout the class period. The first step could be for the student to simply stay awake the entire class period. Once that is accomplished, responding in class or taking notes 50% of the time may be the next step. Finally, staying on task the same amount of time as the other students in the class may be the desired end result.
3. Reward the successful completion of each step. Use praise or tangible reinforcement until the problem ceases.

4. Move to the next step only when the prior one has been successfully attained; work on one problem at a time. If a step seems unachievable, break it into smaller steps. For example, if a student is having trouble remaining seated throughout a class period, first have him or her stand next to the desk, then kneel on the chair, then, finally, sit down.

▶ **Positive Student Responses**

1. Improved ability to correct his or her own misbehavior.
2. Increased awareness of misbehavior.
3. Decreased trouble in other areas and improved self-control.

▶ **Negative Student Responses**

1. Loss of control in areas that are receiving less attention.
2. Failure to progress to the next step after various attempts.

Positive Peer-Group Reinforcement

Pressure from peers can be used to help motivate students to behave appropriately. One such method would be to reward the entire class for their combined effort toward a goal. For example, announce that there will be one hour of free time if the entire class solves 1,000 math problems correctly. The students will encourage one another to work toward that goal. Be very careful, however, not to allow one individual to be singled out as the cause of failure. Instead, teach students to depend on each other for help and encouragement.

▶ **Implementation Guidelines**

1. Determine the overall level of motivation of the class; it should be at least Level 2 (Approval Oriented) for peer-group reinforcement to be effective.
2. Set a realistic goal for the class.
3. Closely monitor progress toward the goal.
4. Teach and model the behavior needed to achieve the goal.
5. If the goal is not reached, show the class how they could have been successful.

REINFORCEMENT OF LIMITS *(continued)*

▶ **Positive Student Responses**

1. Positive response to pressure from peers.
2. Genuine remorse at letting down peers; desire to do better next time.
3. Enhanced sense of belonging in the class. The whole class may act more unified as a result of having to depend on one another.

▶ **Negative Student Responses**

1. Anger at the disappointment their peers are communicating and even retaliation against the more vocal students.
2. Inability to handle pressure from classmates—depression, rejection. You may need to restrain the class.
3. Inability to keep up his or her share of the group's responsibility.

Token Rewards

Rewards can be used to encourage correct behavior and discourage negative behavior; however, overuse of rewards can be time-consuming and ineffective. On the other hand, a program based on tokens (e.g., points on a chart, chips, or stickers) that can be redeemed for a significant reward may encourage students to demonstrate appropriate behavior over a period of time. Earning tokens is rewarding in itself—students learn the value of working toward a goal and persevering until that goal has been attained.

▶ **Implementation Guidelines**

1. Determine what prizes or privileges students will try to earn—(e.g., less homework, a magazine, leading a group game, or a positive note home to parents). Allowing the students to choose from a menu is often the best approach.
2. Decide how many tokens will be needed to redeem a prize and what behavior will be required to earn tokens.
3. Make a verbal or written contract that spells out the agreement.
4. Be sure that the contract is fair, clearly understood, honest, positive, and systematic.
5. Reward tokens intermittently.

▶ **Positive Student Responses**

1. Improved attitude about appropriate behavior.
2. Increased responsibility for appropriate behavior and work.

▶ **Negative Student Responses**

1. Objection to the length of time required to earn a prize. You may need to increase the chances of winning tokens and decrease the length of time it takes to earn a reward.
2. Lack of interest in the reward; try upgrading it.

Tangible Reinforcement

Some students need tangible rewards that provide immediate satisfaction before they can be induced to behave appropriately or demonstrate a new skill. Food is the most common tangible reinforcement—special privileges and permission to participate in games or activities are also effective rewards. In addition, awarding special time with the teacher can be an inducement to improve behavior.

▶ **Implementation Guidelines**

1. Select the most appropriate tangible reward. If you want to use food, choose nutritious, inexpensive food items (e.g., popcorn or peanuts).
2. Define the behavior to be rewarded.
3. Decide on the frequency of rewards.
4. Switch to token rewards once behavior is within appropriate limits.

▶ **Positive Student Responses**

1. Increased positive behavior.
2. Improved relationship with the teacher (if the reward is extra time with the teacher).

▶ **Negative Student Responses**

1. Failure to increase positive behavior. Try a different reward.
2. Improved behavior only when motivated by immediate, tangible rewards.

Charting Progress

Sometimes students don't realize what they are doing or how often they are doing it. Charts are an effective and easy way for you and the student to monitor misbehavior and check progress. Appropriate behavior is often achieved one step at a time, and charting is essential for setting and working toward goals. The teacher's chart also encourages students to monitor themselves. When their activity is written down, students are better able to focus on improving their behavior and increasing their understanding of what proper behavior is.

REINFORCEMENT OF LIMITS *(continued)*

▶ **Implementation Guidelines**

1. Identify the student's misbehavior, define the appropriate behavior, and discuss the problem with the student, making sure he or she understands.

2. Set a goal—or a series of steps toward a goal— to correct the misbehavior.

3. Write the goal on a chart so that it can be monitored (e.g., reduce talking without permission from 10 times per day to zero in the next week).

4. Establish a reward, if appropriate, for meeting the goal.

▶ **Positive Student Responses**

1. Immediate interest in meeting the goal; increased self-confidence.

2. Increased awareness of his or her actions; increased self-control.

3. Improved relationship with the teacher.

▶ **Negative Student Responses**

1. Frustration and discouragement. Lower the goals if the student seems to be trying.

2. Lack of involvement in the process, and lack of interest in the goals.

3. Overemphasis on behavioral goals at the expense of academic achievement.

4. Resumption of prior misbehaviors while working on new goals.

Using Written Contracts

Combine strategies such as Setting Achievable Goals, Token Rewards, and Charting Progress to create a systematic plan to deal with misbehavior. First, define the expected behavior, then establish some basic guidelines for achieving that goal. Have the student agree— in writing—to follow those guidelines. This strategy lets you spend less time dealing with misbehavior and more time encouraging correct behavior while maintaining a system that is fair and consistent.

▶ **Implementation Guidelines**

1. Define the behavior you want the student to demonstrate.

2. Discuss with the student the system to be used to achieve that behavior, and agree on the details.

3. Write down the agreement and have the student sign it along with you. Others (e.g., parents or the principal) can also sign if appropriate.

4. Reward the student only when all of the conditions of the contract have been met. Negative consequences for the student not fulfilling the contract should also be stated, and meted out if necessary.

▶ **Positive Student Responses**

1. Adherence to the plan and increased concentration on correct behavior.

2. Enthusiasm about the agreement and the rewards.

3. Improved attitude about good behavior.

4. Increased responsibility for his or her behavior and work.

▶ **Negative Student Responses**

1. Lack of desire to work for rewards; potential to return to poor behavior.

2. Overemphasis on the agreement and excessive amount of time discussing or arguing the rules or rewards.

Suggesting Parental Intervention Strategies

By this time, you have made the parents aware that there is a problem with the student's behavior, and you have collected more information (see "Alerting Parents to Concerns" and "Exchanging Information With Parents" earlier in this chapter). Because the student's misbehavior has continued, it is time to enlist the parents' help in deciding how the student should be handled. Before contacting the parents, determine how you think they could help solve the problem. They have probably been working on some method of correction, but because the problem persists, the teacher can assume that their efforts have not really helped. In fact, the parents may welcome suggestions, even if they don't express their appreciation.

▶ **Implementation Guidelines**

1. Think of ways that the parents could help (e.g., by drilling the student on an academic problem or rewarding their child each time a note is sent home reporting positive behavior). You cannot assume at this point that the parents know how to change the student's behavior.

2. Call the parents and remind them of the facts concerning the problem, but this time, suggest some solutions.

3. Come to an agreement as to what the parents will do and plan to monitor the progress on that agreement.

REINFORCEMENT OF LIMITS *(continued)*

▶ **Positive Responses**

1. Increased closeness between the student and his or her parents.

2. Parents show renewed interest in their child and express relief that there is hope for him or her. Parents may call to give you progress reports. You will probably see improvement in the student's classroom behavior.

▶ **Negative Responses**

1. Parents express resentment at your intrusion; they may tell you to stay out of their business.

2. Student displays increasing resentfulness that you are using his or her parents to correct the problem. This may be especially true if the parents become unnecessarily harsh.

3. Increase in student's misbehavior at home if the parents find it difficult to control him or her. Your suggestions may have merely drawn battle lines for the unruly child.

CONTROL

Control strategies are required when the student's behavior problems are frequent, intense, or highly disruptive. In such cases, a great deal of teacher intervention is needed; most of the strategies in this category require constant adult supervision. Use these strategies with students who have little or none of the internal control needed to stop their own misbehavior and correct themselves.

Relocation Within the Classroom

This is the first and least intrusive of a series of strategies that call for moving students to a less problematic location when misbehavior persists. For example, if a student is drawing pictures instead of concentrating on the assigned task, move him or her to the front of the classroom. Placing the student in a new environment underscores the need for better behavior. It also frees the student from the environment that contributed to his or her trouble.

Before using this strategy, be sure that the misbehavior in question does not merit more serious, possibly punitive, intervention (e.g., detention).

▶ **Implementation Guidelines**

1. Identify the object or person that is contributing to the student's misbehavior.
2. Move the student to another location in the classroom—closer to you and away from the distraction—without disrupting the lesson plan.
3. Leave the student in the new location for a specified time or until the desired behavior is demonstrated.

▶ **Positive Student Responses**

1. Decreased misbehavior in the new location; possible preference for the new location.
2. Decrease in other misbehavior potentially related to the original location.
3. Increased ability to concentrate.

▶ **Negative Student Responses**

1. Other misbehavior of a less obvious nature in order to avoid relocation.
2. Increased disruptive misbehavior as part of a deliberate attempt to be relocated and thereby avoid participation in class activities.

Isolation Within the Classroom

If you have tried several strategies unsuccessfully, and the student's behavior is disruptive, it may be necessary to move him or her to an isolated area within the classroom. Such an area should be out of the direct view of the other students and free of extraneous stimuli. The isolated student should be allowed to listen to the class but should not be allowed to participate. You may have the student work on an assignment independently, providing the work is commensurate with the student's skill. Allow the student to return when a new class activity begins or when his or her assignment is completed satisfactorily. This strategy allows the student to remain in the learning environment without being disruptive.

▶ **Implementation Guidelines**

1. Decide which misbehavior requires the use of this strategy.
2. Designate a readily available area for the student to relocate to—a hot seat from which other students cannot be bothered.
3. Discuss the purpose of relocation with the class and the requirements for being allowed to rejoin the class.
4. Follow through exactly as described to the class.

▶ **Positive Student Responses**

1. Improved behavior while in the hot seat.
2. Increased ability to curb misbehavior.

▶ **Negative Student Responses**

1. Disruptive behavior even while in the hot seat.
2. Preference for the hot seat.
3. Overuse of this strategy may result in too many students in the same situation, which may make it impossible to provide effective isolation.

Removing Stimuli

Remove objects that tempt students to create a disturbance. For example, if a student is tapping his or her pencil, walk over and take the pencil without interrupting the lesson. By removing the stimulus, you stop the distracting behavior and keep the lesson going so

CONTROL *(continued)*

that other students are not disturbed. Sometimes you may need to interrupt the class to intervene appropriately. Either way, remove the stimulus object to stop the student's behavior.

▶ **Implementation Guidelines**
1. Determine whether a particular stimulus is causing misbehavior.
2. Remove the stimulus without disrupting the class or lesson plan.
3. Later, explain to the student why the object was removed.
4. Replace the stimulus after a time to see if the student is able to handle the temptation it provides.

▶ **Positive Student Responses**
1. Improved behavior once the stimulus is returned.
2. Request for the stimulus to be returned, with assurances that the misbehavior will not continue.

▶ **Negative Student Responses**
1. Use of another stimulus to continue similar misbehavior.
2. Reaction to other stimuli that were previously not a problem.
3. Overreaction to the object being removed.

Exclusion From Fun Activities

Students participate in a variety of academic, and sometimes entertaining, activities during the school day. Some students cannot contain their excitement during fun activities and may become highly disruptive. Other students take advantage of the confusion that comes with fun activities by misbehaving. Excluding such students from activities they want to participate in can stop their misbehavior and motivate them to behave correctly. The embarrassment of being removed and missing the fun may be motivation enough for the student to stop misbehaving.

▶ **Implementation Guidelines**
1. Warn the students that anyone who disrupts an activity will be excluded from that activity.

2. Consistently exclude disruptive students, including the first student to be disruptive, so the other students will realize that you are serious.
3. Excluded students may observe the activity from a distance as long as they can remain in the vicinity without being a disturbance.

▶ **Positive Student Responses**
1. Immediate cessation of misbehavior.
2. Increased enthusiasm and productivity upon being allowed to rejoin the group.

▶ **Negative Student Responses**
1. Resentment and continued disruptive behavior even after exclusion from the activity. You may need to remove the student from the classroom.
2. No improvement; student wasn't particularly interested in the given activity.

Coordinating Outside Intervention

Because teachers spend a great deal of time with their students, they are often the first to notice when a student has a problem that requires outside intervention. If you think that a student needs extra help, first consult the school's policy concerning such action—especially if you suspect abuse or neglect. Then contact an outside agency or the parents to initiate action.

Sometimes parents initiate outside intervention. You may be asked to cooperate with an agency by observing the student or recalling various behavior patterns. For example, if the parents hire a psychologist to help their child, you may be a valuable source of information for that psychologist. The same is true for students on medication for hyperactivity or depression. Sharing information with the doctor is important for his or her understanding as well as yours. Of course, permission should be obtained from the parents for sharing information with agencies or doctors.

▶ **Implementation Guidelines**
1. Keep accurate records of the student's behavior patterns for use by school personnel, the student, his or her parents, or an outside agency.

CONTROL *(continued)*

2. Call the parents if there is a problem with the student that calls for action you are unable or unqualified to handle. Contact an agency or the principal if there is a problem that the parents are causing and it could be considered illegal (i.e., parental neglect or abuse). Check your local school system's policies in this regard.

3. Cooperate fully with programs to help the student.

▶ **Positive Agency Responses**

1. Work toward a common goal for the benefit of the student.
2. Serious consideration of your information.
3. Cooperation and willingness to share helpful information with you.

▶ **Negative Agency Responses**

1. Unwillingness of any of the participants in a coordinated effort to continue with the suggested treatment.
2. Disregard for your information.

Time Out

Although a student may have an outburst of uncontrollable anger, he or she generally has little desire or ability to maintain that anger for a long time. If you move the student to a nonstimulating atmosphere, he or she may cool off and regain the ability to think and act rationally. This area should be outside of the classroom. If the source of anger is another student, separate the students until they have cooled off rather than insisting that they immediately reconcile or apologize. If a project is causing anger, the student should be allowed to cool off and get beyond the frustrating point that triggered the rage before he or she tries again. If the student is angry at you, let him or her cool off before you confront the problem. Once the anger has subsided, he or she may be allowed to return to class. Later, instruct the student to behave respectfully toward adults, and discuss appropriate ways to handle frustration.

▶ **Implementation Guidelines**

1. Determine whether the student has lost the ability to act rationally.
2. Move the student to a designated area, away from stimulating objects or people.
3. Bring the student back into class only after he or she has cooled off.

4. Try to resolve the problem that caused the anger.
5. Increase the amount of time spent in isolation for each subsequent offense throughout the day.

▶ **Positive Student Responses**

1. Increased self-control while in time out.
2. Increased ability to find a solution to the problem once he or she has returned to the classroom.
3. Decreased reliance on anger and increased use of discussion to resolve problems.

▶ **Negative Student Responses**

1. Inability to cool off.
2. Continued tendency to become angry at little things.
3. Increased anger; violence.
4. Loss of valuable class time because of need for isolation.

Time Out for a Specified Period or Activity

Establish rules in advance for the use of time out as a penalty for disruptive outbursts. The idea is to give the student a calm environment in which to collect himself or herself. In addition, the student may better appreciate being with others after experiencing some isolation and may make an effort to avoid the situation as much as possible. Students can be temporarily relocated for a specified amount of time and/or given an activity to complete before being allowed to return.

▶ **Implementation Guidelines**

1. Identify the types of behavior that will cause this response and explain the purpose and use of time out to the students.
2. Designate a readily available relocation area away from any stimulating objects or people.
3. Increase the amount of time spent in isolation and/or the amount of work to be completed for each subsequent offense throughout the day.
4. Follow through consistently, as explained to the class.

▶ **Positive Student Responses**

1. Improved behavior.
2. Increased self-control.

CONTROL *(continued)*

▶ **Negative Student Responses**

1. Preference for isolation.
2. Overuse of this strategy may result in too many students in the same situation, which may make it impossible to provide effective isolation.

Requiring a Plan for Improvement

Sometimes students' misbehavior or anger is disruptive, and they must be separated from the rest of the class (see "Isolation Within the Classroom" and "Time Out" earlier in this chapter). To encourage such students to come to terms with their misbehavior and why it occurs, require them to submit a plan for improved behavior in the classroom before allowing them to return. Before you accept a student's plan, explain the reasons for certain behavior requirements.

▶ **Implementation Guidelines**

1. Identify the type of behavior that will get this response and communicate that to the class.
2. Designate a relocation area.
3. Have any student who breaks the rules submit a plan that addresses the following questions: What did I do? Why is it a problem? What rule did I break? How do I plan to avoid this problem?

   Note. It is important for the student to answer the question "What did I do?" by stating exactly what he or she did, without blaming others and thus disowning personal responsibility. The most critical question to answer is "How do I plan to avoid this problem?" A menu of possible strategies may be needed for the student to choose from. Additional training in social skills or conflict resolution may also be necessary. (See the Suggested Reading section of the Bibliography for resources.)
4. Discuss the plan and encourage the student to think of reasons why the plan will or won't work.
5. Enforce the student's adherence to the plan. If the misbehavior continues, have the student complete another plan to stop the same behavior. Be sure the second plan is different, as the first one didn't work.

▶ **Positive Student Responses**

1. Development of a workable plan or at least an increased interest in analyzing the situation.
2. Adherence to the plan.
3. Intelligent, valid defense of his or her plan.

▶ **Negative Student Responses**

1. Disruptive behavior while isolated.
2. Lack of interest in developing a plan or analyzing misbehavior.
3. Constant arguing about the plan and its intentions that disrupts the whole process.

Deducting Points for Misbehavior

Adults lose money when they pay a speeding ticket, which usually motivates them to check the speedometer more often. Similarly, it may be necessary to take away something a student has earned in order to get his or her attention. (Note that this strategy can only be used in combination with the Token Rewards or Tangible Reinforcement strategies discussed earlier.)

Teachers utilizing this strategy have generally found it to be either quite effective soon after implementation or not successful at all. If it does not appear to be bringing about the desired results, then before abandoning it in favor of another approach, you may want to consider increasing the frequency with which points are awarded, and/or increasing the desirability of the rewards for which points can be redeemed.

▶ **Implementation Guidelines**

1. When this strategy is employed to correct group misbehavior, post a list of violations and the number of points (or tokens) that will be deducted for each offense. Individual behavior problems, however, should be handled through private discussions with the student.
2. Give the student a warning before actually beginning to deduct points.
3. Deduct points exactly as warned, if the student continues to misbehave.
4. Increase the number of points deducted for each subsequent offense.

▶ **Positive Student Responses**

1. Immediate cessation of misbehavior.
2. Increased enthusiasm and productivity.

CONTROL *(continued)*

▶ **Negative Student Responses**

1. Resentment and disruptive behavior. You may have to remove the student from class.

2. No improvement; lack of interest in the reward process.

3. Misbehavior continues immediately after the warning. Without further warnings, begin to deduct points exactly as you have stipulated.

Detention

Most teachers keep students after school as punishment or as a chance to catch up on academic time lost because of misbehavior during the day. Although both of these reasons have merit, there is another, equally important, reason for using detention as a form of discipline—to establish a better relationship with the student and learn his or her academic weaknesses.

During the day, there is little time to focus on one student. If a student needs extra attention, it is better to provide it after school so that the other students can continue to receive quality instruction during school hours. Without the distractions typical during regular school hours, you may be able to find out what is bothering a student or what academic material he or she has not grasped. Detention should seldom consist of just having a student sit alone as punishment. The teacher or a tutor should use the time to strengthen the student's academic weaknesses, which may be causing frustration and contributing to misbehavior.

▶ **Implementation Guidelines**

1. Make it clear that detention will be used as a method of discipline. Also specify the type of behavior that will result in students being kept in detention, and the length of time for which they will be detained. Be sure to explain that students who are given detention will have to remain in the classroom after school so that they and the teacher will have each other's full attention.

2. Use detention to develop a relationship with the student. Ask questions that reveal who the student is and what his or her needs and frustrations are.

3. Identify problem areas that affect the student's performance and attitude about school.

4. If possible, supply remediation in those areas of weakness that may be contributing to the behavior problems (i.e., social skills training or study skill strategies).

5. Work with the student to help him or her see problem areas and how to work toward improvement.

6. End the detention on a positive note if at all possible.

▶ **Positive Student Responses**

1. Improved relationship with you during detention.

2. Ability to work on an area of frustration during detention.

3. Participation in creating a plan to correct behavior.

4. Improved attitude after detention.

▶ **Negative Student Responses**

1. No improvement in relationship with you; refusal to attempt to develop a relationship.

2. Refusal to concentrate on skill problems.

3. Continued frequent disruptions during class; enjoyment of detention.

Having a Parent in the Classroom

If the student continues to misbehave after the other parental involvement strategies have been tried (see "Alerting Parents to Concerns," "Exchanging Information With Parents," and "Suggesting Parental Intervention Strategies" earlier in this chapter), a parent should be brought into the classroom to observe the situation firsthand.

Often, the student will behave while his or her parent is in the classroom, in which case you can simply try to show the parent the classroom environment and the situations in which misbehavior typically occurs. If, however, the student continues to misbehave even with his or her parent in the classroom, it is an indication that the parents have little control over the student, even in the home environment. Your primary role at that point is to work with the parents to gain control over the student's behavior. Without support and help from home, many discipline approaches will fail. Perhaps the most important aspect of having a parent in the classroom is that it shows the student that you and his or her parents are working together to solve the problem.

▶ **Implementation Guidelines**

1. Make sure you have tried all of the preceding strategies for parental involvement. This is the last strategy that calls for voluntary parental involvement.

CONTROL *(continued)*

2. Ask one or both parents to attend a typical class period and to stay for at least one hour. This will give the student time to settle into his or her routine. Choose an hour when the student is normally prone to misbehave.

3. Let the student know that the parent will be coming to class to observe. It should not be a surprise to the student.

4. Have the parent sit in the back of the classroom. Ask him or her to observe without becoming involved in classroom activities.

5. Schedule some time afterward to discuss the student's behavior that day and the behavior normally experienced in the same setting on other days.

6. Work with the parents to develop a plan to bring the student back into line. The principal and outside agencies may also be involved.

▶ **Positive Responses**

1. Improved behavior that continues after the parent's visit.

2. Increased parental involvement with the student's education.

▶ **Negative Responses**

1. Changed behavior due to parental presence that returns to poor behavior once the parent leaves. The student may not be responding to strategies the parents are trying at home after consulting with the teacher.

2. Little change in the student's misbehavior during the parent's visit. Little parental enthusiasm for changing the approach to dealing with their child.

3. The parent may be a disruptive factor in class, or the student may not see the parent as having power. A cooperative, significant person other than the parent (i.e., an older sibling, a parole officer, or a grandparent) may be more helpful.

4
How to Use the Individualized Strategies System

Using the Problem-Solving Worksheet

The Individualized Strategies System matches intervention strategies for specific behavior problems with a student's personality profile to increase the probability of success. In order to select and implement the most effective intervention strategies for an individual student, you must complete the Problem-Solving Worksheet (WPS Product No. W-315B). A completed sample Problem-Solving Worksheet is presented in Figure 2.

After you have entered the student's identifying information at the top of the worksheet, follow the instructions on the worksheet to identify his or her problem behavior, level of motivation, and behavior style. This information enables you to select the intervention strategies that are most likely to be effective for that individual.

Identifying the Problem Behavior

Problem behaviors are troublesome habits or reactions that students may exhibit in the classroom or some other school setting. If the behavior is recurrent, it is likely to interrupt learning for the student or for others.

For descriptions of each of the problem behaviors addressed in this Handbook, see Table 5. After reviewing Table 5, decide which of the listed problem behaviors best matches the target student's most recurrent and troublesome behavior. Write the name of this problem behavior on the designated line of the Problem-Solving Worksheet.

Identifying the Level of Motivation

Level of motivation describes a student's development toward an internal locus of control. Knowing a student's level of motivation can help the teacher or other school professional determine what drives that individual's behavior. Such information can be used to determine the degree of structure and control—external or internal—that the student needs in order to perform successfully. See chapter 2 for a comprehensive description of the levels of motivation.

The Level of Motivation Checklist, which is found on the reverse side of the Problem-Solving Worksheet (see Figure 2), can help you to identify a student's level of motivation. Think of the student's behavior in a specific setting, such as the classroom or the hallway, then check each item that generally applies to that individual. Total the number of checks in each column. The level with the highest number of checks is the one that best describes the student. If two levels have the same number of checks, review Table 1 for information that will help you to decide which level is the most applicable for the individual in question.

Identifying the Behavior Style

An individual's behavior style is the pattern of action he or she exhibits when relating to people, projects, or events. As discussed in chapter 2, the following four behavior styles have been identified for use with the Individualized Strategies System: Self-Assertive, Socially Interactive, Analytic, and Accommodating.

The Behavior Style Checklist on the reverse side of the Problem-Solving Worksheet (see Figure 2) helps you to identify a student's behavior style. As with the Level of Motivation Checklist, think of the student in the context of a particular setting, then check the items that describe the behavior you observe most often. Total the number of checks in each column. The behavior style with the highest number of checks is the one that best describes the student. If two behavior styles have the same number of checks, review Table 2 for information that will help you to decide which style best characterizes that individual's behavior in the specific setting you have chosen.

Selecting the Appropriate Strategies

In the table located on the front of the Problem-Solving Worksheet, find the column for the behavior style that you have identified as best describing the target student. Go down that column to the row containing the level of motivation you have identified for the student. Place a check mark at the point where the column and the row intersect.

Next, refer to Part 2 of this Handbook's Table of Contents, and locate the problem behavior to be addressed. The page number listed for each problem behavior denotes the beginning of the section that outlines strategies designed to address that behavior. The strategies are grouped into the four categories discussed in chapter 3: Prevention, Limit Setting, Reinforcement of Limits, and Control. Like these categories, the individual strategies are presented in the order of their intrusiveness, starting with the least intrusive.

Throughout Part 2 of this Handbook, the strategies suggested for use in correcting the specified problem behaviors are preceded by coded tables like the one shown on the Problem-Solving Worksheet. Compare the location of the mark you have placed in the worksheet table with the same location on these other tables. A black square at the intersection of the student's behavior style and level of motivation indicates that the intervention strategies immediately following that table are the ones with the highest probability of success for this student.

Consider the first intervention strategy that would be appropriate for use in addressing the student's problem behavior, and determine how effective you think it would be, based on your knowledge of the student. Continue to read the appropriately coded intervention strategies for the selected problem behavior until you find the one that you believe will be most effective. The Problem-Solving Worksheet includes spaces for recording the name and page number of the strategy you select, as well as several lines on which you can note the results achieved by employing that strategy. This information is useful if you later wish to review the strategy you chose or to consider alternative strategies for dealing with the same problem behavior.

You may also want to review Table 6, which is an alphabetized list of all the basic intervention strategies used in the Individualized Strategies System, with brief descriptions of each strategy. (The strategies are discussed in greater detail in chapter 3.)

Implementing an Intervention Strategy

Once you have completed the Problem-Solving Worksheet, you are ready to implement the strategy you have selected. Use the strategy more than once,

preferably over a period of several days, to determine whether it is effective, and record the results on the Problem-Solving Worksheet. Based on those results you have four options:

1. Continue to use the strategy.
2. Modify the strategy or combine it with other strategies.
3. Select one of the other strategies suggested for use in addressing the same problem behavior. This new strategy should be chosen, like the previous one, in accordance with the student's behavior style and level of motivation.
4. If none of the preceding options seems appropriate, review all the general strategies listed in chapter 3. Select a strategy you think would work and adapt it to the problem behavior.

Figure 2 presents the completed Problem-Solving Worksheet for Patti, a high school student who continually talked in the classroom without permission and distracted the rest of the students. Patti's teacher, Mr. Hall, completed the worksheet based on his perception of her behavior in the classroom. After reviewing Table 5, he decided that Patti's most troublesome and recurrent problem behavior was talking.

Turning to the section of Part 2 devoted to the problem of talking, Mr. Hall looked at the coded tables preceding the intervention strategies, in order to find the strategies that were most likely to succeed, given Patti's behavior style (Socially Interactive) and level of motivation (Level 2). He read the first such strategy, Stopping and Redirecting, and thought it might work. He entered the name of that strategy and its page number on the Problem-Solving Worksheet.

Mr. Hall tried the strategy of Stopping and Redirecting for 3 days in a row, and he noted that Patti's talking decreased considerably. He decided to continue to use this strategy every time Patti's talking was a problem.

If Stopping and Redirecting had not been successful, Mr. Hall could have modified the strategy or tried the next appropriately coded strategy in the same section of Part 2: Asking "What" Questions. He also had the option of combining those strategies or reviewing the general strategies in chapter 3 to find an entirely new strategy. The use of modified and combined strategies is illustrated in the case studies presented in chapter 5.

Handbook of Individualized Strategies for Classroom Discipline
Problem-Solving Worksheet
by W. George Selig, Ed.D. and Alan A. Arroyo, Ed.D.

Published by

WPS WESTERN PSYCHOLOGICAL SERVICES
Publishers and Distributors
12031 Wilshire Boulevard
Los Angeles, California 90025-1251

Student's Name _Patti Masterson_

Age _15_ Gender: ☐M ☑F Grade _10_

Date _10/19/94_ Teacher's Name _Mr. Hall_

Instructions

Review the list of problem behaviors in Table 5 of the *Handbook of Individualized Strategies for Classroom Discipline* (WPS Product No. W-315A), and enter the problem behavior for this student on the designated line below. Complete the Level of Motivation Checklist and the Behavior Style Checklist on the reverse side of this worksheet. Then, in the table below, place a check mark at the intersection of this student's behavior style and level of motivation. In Part 2 of the Handbook, compare this table with the coded tables that precede the intervention strategies suggested for addressing this student's problem behavior. A black square at the same intersection of behavior style and level of motivation indicates that the strategies immediately following that table are the ones with the highest probability of success for this student.

Problem Behavior _Talking_

Level of Motivation	Behavior Style			
	Self-Assertive	Socially Interactive	Analytic	Accommodating
1. Self-Absorbed				
2. Approval Oriented		✓		
3. Interpersonal Loyalty				
4. Others Oriented				

Intervention Strategy _Stopping and Redirecting_

Page Number _217_

Results _Responded fairly well. Talking without permission has decreased considerably. Will continue using this strategy._

W-315B

Figure 2
Sample Problem-Solving Worksheet

Level of Motivation Checklist

Review the levels of motivation described in Table 1 of the Handbook. Then think about a specific setting (e.g., a classroom or the hallway), and check the items below that describe this student's typical behavior in that setting. Total the check marks for each level of motivation. The level with the highest number of check marks is the one that best describes this student.

Level 1 (Self-Absorbed)	Level 2 (Approval Oriented)	Level 3 (Interpersonal Loyalty)	Level 4 (Others Oriented)
☐ Usually wants his or her own way	☑ Pursues certain subjects, activities, or hobbies in order to win approval	☐ Wants to be respected for his or her ideas	☐ Seeks opportunities to help others
☑ Has a very short attention span, and changes activities often	☑ Demands attention	☑ Is loyal and will stand up for family or friends	☐ Often praises peers, even in their absence
☐ Is very possessive of his or her belongings	☑ Completes most tasks, but seeks verbal praise for his or her efforts	☐ Is even tempered and self-controlled	☐ Is self-motivated; enjoys feeling productive
☐ Uses other people's belongings without asking permission	☐ Is considered to be a show-off	☐ Enjoys organized group activities	☑ Volunteers for necessary tasks
☐ Becomes angry or resentful if opposed	☐ Demands admiration for his or her achievements	☐ Has a healthy appreciation of rules, and likes strong adult guidance	☐ Is able to make decisions objectively
☐ Gets unusually upset when contradicted	☑ Enjoys participating in competitive activities, but is upset if his or her efforts go unrecognized	☑ Strives for competence	☐ Can converse with adults on their level
☑ Often must be told specifically what behavior is expected before he or she will comply	☐ Is quick to judge peers	☑ Enjoys being part of a particular group	☑ Is generally optimistic
☐ Has a low trust level	☑ Behaves best when he or she is the center of attention	☑ Enjoys the company of adults, both family members and others	☐ Is able to stand up for his or her beliefs, even in the face of criticism
	☑ Loses interest in a task if not given constant attention and encouragement		
2 Total Checked	**6** Total Checked	**4** Total Checked	**2** Total Checked

Behavior Style Checklist

Review the behavior styles described in Table 2 of the Handbook. Then think about a specific setting (e.g., a classroom or the hallway), and check the items below that describe this student's typical behavior in that setting. Total the check marks for each behavior style. The style with the highest number of check marks is the one that best describes this student.

Self-Assertive	Socially Interactive	Analytic	Accommodating
☐ Is outspoken, opinionated, assertive	☑ Uses facial expressions and hand movements when talking	☐ Is systematic and well-ordered—prefers to have a plan or method	☑ Has an honest, sincere, low-key style—doesn't appear to mislead people
☑ Is active, restless—has difficulty staying in one place	☐ Expresses himself or herself well verbally	☐ Seems very organized	☐ Likes routine—is predictable and not quick to change
☐ Is persistent—keeps pushing until goal is reached	☑ Tends to be cheerful, sees the bright side of situations	☐ Seems prepared for most events or activities	☐ Seems mild tempered
☐ Is decisive—makes decisions easily and sticks with them	☑ Is persuasive—can present ideas convincingly	☐ Tries hard to avoid unwanted surprises	☐ Is humble and modest about accomplishments
☑ Usually wins arguments or debates	☐ Is open-minded—open to others' ideas	☐ Seeks details	☑ Is compassionate—tends to be one of the first to help someone who is sick or hurting
☐ Tells people what he or she thinks	☑ Is friendly and outgoing	☐ Keeps records	☐ Is reserved around new people or in new situations
☐ Gets right to the point	☐ Doesn't mind changing plans and is flexible	☐ Is restrained and usually very self-controlled, seldom loses temper	☐ Takes time to think things through and get in touch with his or her feelings
☑ Usually takes a leading role in a group	☑ Enjoys being around people most of the time	☐ Appears to be steady and calm	☑ Is tenderhearted—usually approaches people in a gentle, soft manner
☐ Is productive—works hard and gets a lot done	☑ Likes change and diversity	☐ Is often critical of self or others	☐ Is empathetic—considers other people's thoughts and feelings
☐ Does not change mind easily once he or she has formed an opinion	☑ Is usually talkative	☐ Prefers to thoroughly understand a new task or situation before trying it	☐ Prefers an organized environment that is free from unexpected change
☐ Likes to work independently and is able to do so effectively	☐ Expresses affection and appreciation for others	☐ Is analytic—approaches most problems in a logical fashion	☑ Appears ready to defend and protect others—especially those in a weaker position
☐ Is competitive—strives to be first in most things	☐ Is original—thinks of new and different ways to do things	☑ Is usually careful and tactful when communicating with others	☐ Is stable—acts sensibly and responsibly
☐ Tends to be result oriented	☑ Enjoys discussing goals and dreams	☐ Is thorough—often checks things two or three times	☑ Is usually calm, easygoing, and relaxed
3 Total Checked	**8** Total Checked	**1** Total Checked	**5** Total Checked

Figure 2 (continued)
Sample Problem-Solving Worksheet

Table 5
Problem Behaviors

Problem Behavior	Description
Absenteeism	Chronic, willful absence from school for a class period, a day, or any other length of time
Anger	Sudden, keen displeasure manifested by an outburst of wrath or hostility; a sense of resentment, unjust treatment, or injury
Anxiety	Worry or uneasiness about a situation
Arguing	Disputing, quarreling
Attention Span Problems	Not focusing on a task or activity for an appropriate length of time
Baby Talk	Use of verbal conversation that is significantly below age or maturity level
Bossiness	Inappropriate use of physical or verbal communication to manipulate or control others
Calling Out Answers	Responding to questions without waiting to be called on (especially troublesome in large group discussions)
Cheating	Copying other students' answers, taking credit for other students' work, or inappropriately accessing information
Cutting in Line	Stepping into a waiting line of students inappropriately
Defiance	Refusing to obey a person in authority
Dependence on Others	Reluctance to engage in an activity without an overdependence on help from the teacher or from peers
Disorganization	Inability or unwillingness to organize work habits, school materials, notes, supplies, and so on
Distracting Others	Diverting other students' attention from their assigned tasks
Excuse Making	Continual requests that allowances be made to avoid obligations, assignments, responsibility, or accountability
Fighting	Physical conflict intended to inflict harm on another
Gum Chewing	Chewing gum or eating without permission
Hallway Problems	Misbehavior in the hallway
Hygiene Problems	Lack of attention to personal cleanliness—for example, bad odor, dirty or messy hair, or dirty or messy clothes
Hyperactivity	Excessive activity, short attention span, or inability to concentrate or remain still
Inability to Settle Down	Inability or unwillingness to refrain from excessive and inappropriate activity at the beginning or end of activities or during transitions between activities
Lack of Motivation	Little or no interest in learning or completing assignments
Late Assignments	Inability or unwillingness to complete assignments within the allotted time frame
Leaving Seat Without Permission	Impulsively or inappropriately leaving seat without permission
Losing or Mistreating Materials	Losing assigned materials, treating them carelessly, or not maintaining them in good condition

table continued on next page...

Table 5 *(continued)*
Problem Behaviors

Problem Behavior	Description
Lying	Answering untruthfully, or creating untrue scenarios regarding behavior or activities
Name Calling	Intentionally insulting another person by calling him or her names or making derogatory references to his or her family, friends, or belongings
Obscene Gestures	Physical actions that communicate an offensive message
Oversensitivity	Taking unwarranted offense from harmless or meaningless remarks, glances, or the perceived attitudes of others
Physical Aggression	Aggressive physical behavior such as pushing, shoving, hitting, or tripping
Profanity	Foul, profane, or inappropriate language
Property Destruction	Any activity that results in damage to or destruction of property
Shyness	Fear or reluctance to communicate with or relate to others
Spitting	Forcefully ejecting saliva from the mouth
Stealing	Taking property without the owner's permission
Suspected Drug Use	Behavioral or physical indications that the student may be taking drugs—for example, sudden or steady decline in achievement on tests, classwork, or projects; missed classes; a decline in personal hygiene; or constantly bloodshot eyes
Talking	Verbal communication at a time when it is not permitted, or excessive communication that infringes on the rights of others
Talking Back	Verbally responding to a teacher in a manner that is a direct challenge to the teacher's authority or an inappropriate response to a direction or question
Tantrums	Acting out frustration or uncontrolled anger—for example, kicking, screaming, biting, verbal outbursts, or holding one's breath
Tardiness	Regularly arriving late for class, school, or school events
Tattling	Continuously bringing the teacher stories about other students' misbehavior
Teasing	Excessively taunting other students, making fun of the physical or behavioral peculiarities of others, humiliating another student in front of others, and so on
Threats of Violence	Overtly stating intent to physically harm another; physical stance, body language, or other form of intimidation that leads others to believe that physical harm is intended
Tilting Backward in Chair	Rocking backward in chair so that only two legs of the chair remain on the floor
Tripping Others	Deliberately causing another student to fall
Whining	Complaining, begging, or making requests in an irritating, childish manner

Table 6
Intervention Strategies

Strategy	Description
Alerting Parents to Concerns	Contact parents to express your concern about the student's attitude or behavior.
Announcing/Rehearsing the Rules	Establish specific rules for behavior in the classroom in order to define boundaries, expectations, and the consequences for misbehavior. Review these rules regularly.
Appealing to Values	Confront the student about his or her misbehavior, and compare it to the positive values he or she holds.
Asking Adult Questions	Use adult-oriented questions to appeal to the student's rational abilities.
Asking "What" Questions	Ask "what" questions until the student acknowledges his or her misbehavior; do not accept excuses.
Charting Progress	Use charts to monitor misbehavior and check the student's progress.
Checking for Understanding	To avoid misbehavior caused by frustration, have the student repeat instructions to make sure that he or she clearly understands what is expected.
Coordinating Outside Intervention	Coordinate help or support from an outside source (e.g., a mental health or family service agency, the legal system, etc.).
Deducting Points for Misbehavior	Deduct tokens or withhold privileges the student has earned.
Describing Misbehavior as It Occurs	Describe to the student what he or she has just done, is doing, or is about to do.
Detention	Keep the student after school for a specified period of time.
Direct Commands	Make specific demands, spoken with authority, concerning the student's behavior.
Disguising Directives	Disguise verbal directives to get the student to behave and to avoid confrontation.
Establishing Logical Consequences	Establish logical consequences for certain behaviors.
Exchanging Information With Parents	Work with the student's parents to gather information that might help resolve the problem.
Exclusion From Fun Activities	Exclude the student from an activity he or she enjoys.
Having a Parent in the Classroom	Bring one of the student's parents into the classroom to observe the student's behavior there.
Identifying Idealized Characters	Encourage the student to imitate the positive behavior of an idealized character.
Ignoring Misbehavior	Eliminate the student's payoff for inappropriate attention-getting behavior by refusing to acknowledge it.
Increasing Physical Proximity	Spend more time near the student throughout the class period.
Introducing Role Models	Acknowledge positive behavior that the student should model.
Isolation Within the Classroom	Temporarily move the student to an isolated area of the classroom where he or she can continue to work.
Modeling Expected Behavior	Demonstrate by example the behavior you want the student to exhibit.

table continued on next page...

Table 6 *(continued)*
Intervention Strategies

Strategy	Description
Nonverbal Communication	Use eye contact, body movements, or hand signals to gain the student's attention.
Positive Peer-Group Reinforcement	Provide incentives for peers to motivate students to behave appropriately.
Probing for Motives	Ask yourself questions to determine the goal behind the student's misbehavior.
Probing for Values	Listen for and encourage the student to express closely held values.
Reflecting Verbal Responses	Verbally reflect the essence of a student's argument in order to clarify his or her true feelings.
Relocation Within the Classroom	Move the misbehaving student to a less problematic location within the classroom.
Removing Stimuli	Remove any object that acts as a stimulus for misbehavior.
Requiring a Plan for Improvement	Separate the student from the rest of the class, and have him or her prepare a plan for improved behavior. Do not allow the student to return to the classroom until he or she presents an acceptable plan.
Setting Achievable Goals	Establish achievable goals to improve behavior step-by-step.
Sharing Authority and Decision Making	Give peers some authority to help stop a student's misbehavior.
Stopping and Redirecting	Stop the student's inappropriate behavior, and redirect his or her attention to the task at hand.
Student Self-Monitoring	Have the student monitor his or her own behavior using charts or other means to record progress.
Suggesting Parental Intervention Strategies	Enlist the parents' help in correcting the student's behavior.
Tangible Reinforcement	Give students tangible, immediately satisfying rewards for appropriate behavior.
Time Out	Move the student to a nonstimulating environment so that he or she can cool down and regain the ability to think rationally.
Time Out for a Specified Period or Activity	Establish rules in advance for the use of specified periods of time out in response to angry outbursts.
Token Rewards	Over a period of time, reward students who demonstrate appropriate behavior with tokens that can be redeemed for a prize.
Using a Businesslike Teaching Style	Maintain a serious, businesslike atmosphere in the classroom.
Using Affirmative Statements	Verbally acknowledge and emphasize the student's strengths and achievements.
Using Humor to Relieve Stress	Use humor to lighten a stressful situation.
Using Written Contracts	Have the student agree, in writing, to follow a plan for improved behavior.

5
CASE STUDIES

Although the Individualized Strategies System has proven most successful when used as described in chapter 4 of this Handbook, teachers have also successfully combined strategies or created new strategies tailored to specific situations. The following case studies illustrate how teachers and support personnel have used the system. These examples demonstrate just how effective school personnel can be when given a range of intervention strategies matched with a student's personality profile.

Case Study 1: Tony

Background

In any sixth-grade classroom, there is likely to be a wide range of physical types and sizes. Tony was at the large end of that size range. Everyone, including the teacher, Mrs. Beck, was aware of Tony's formidable frame; his intimidating posture and comments served as further reminders of his size.

Tony often confronted fellow students who had inadvertently offended him in some way. He was suspected of physically abusing other students, but he was never caught in the act, and students would not speak up against him.

When frustrated by academic work or angered by a comment he perceived to be negative, Tony demonstrated oppositional behavior toward the teacher. He often argued with her face-to-face and tried to get in the last word. His demeanor was threatening. After reviewing Table 5, Mrs. Beck concluded that Tony's major problem was defiance.

Use of the Individualized Strategies System

Mrs. Beck completed the Problem-Solving Worksheet for Tony (see Figure 3). According to the Behavior Style Checklist, Tony was self-assertive. He also had a significant tendency toward socially interactive behavior. According to the Level of Motivation Checklist, Tony was functioning at Level 1 (Self-Absorbed) in the classroom. In other settings, such as sports, he was functioning at Level 2 (Approval Oriented)—unless he felt he was being treated unfairly by his teammates or the coach.

Mrs. Beck referred to Part 2 of this Handbook to find the recommended intervention strategies for defiance. Under Defiance, she located the strategies that would be appropriate for self-assertive behavior styles at Level 1. She reviewed all of the recommended strategies and picked the one she thought would work best—Deducting Points for Misbehavior.

Mrs. Beck developed a plan whereby Tony would be given four tickets at the beginning of each class period (i.e., Math, Language Arts, etc.). If, throughout a period, he demonstrated respectful behavior toward his peers and the teacher, he could keep the four tickets. He would lose one ticket every time he was defiant.

If he kept 90 out of a possible 120 tickets during the week, he could select a reward from a list of two or three possibilities (e.g., 15 minutes at the computer, 10 minutes listening to music, or a "no homework" pass). He would also receive a note to take home, commending him for his achievement.

Initially, Mrs. Beck saw some improvement in Tony's behavior. On Monday and Tuesday, he kept 40 out of 48 tickets, but his behavior deteriorated on the following 3 days of the week. Rather than give up on the strategy she had chosen, Mrs. Beck decided to modify it by allowing Tony to select a reward every 2 days if he kept 36 of the 48 tickets earned during that time. The modification worked.

Within 3 weeks, the strategy had been further modified so that Tony's only reward was a note to take home, with an occasional "Nice job, Tony!" written on the blackboard. His behavior toward his peers and teacher improved noticeably, and very few incidents of intimidation occurred. Other students actually wanted Tony in their cooperative groups. His grades went up, and the frequency of his arguing and disrespectful behavior decreased to nearly zero. He still expressed anger and frustration at times, but a verbal or nonverbal reminder was all that was needed for him to maintain control. Eventually the intervention strategy of Deducting Points for Misbehavior was eliminated and replaced by a weekly note sent home if his behavior was generally appropriate (a variation on another intervention strategy—Using Affirmative Statements).

Summary

Tony's case demonstrates how the Individualized Strategies System can be utilized with minimal modifications. Because the teacher understood that students whose level of motivation is at Level 1 may need more immediate positive feedback, she was able to successfully adjust the intervention strategy.

Tony's case also illustrates how an intrusive strategy such as Deducting Points for Misbehavior can eventually be phased out and replaced with a less intrusive strategy. The main goal of any discipline plan should be to encourage self-control. Tony obviously rose to the occasion. Perhaps even more important, Tony's level of motivation increased as the intervention strategies were administered. Success is not always so comprehensive and readily apparent, but teachers have found that it happens more often than might be expected.

As in most disciplinary situations, Tony's problems may have had an academic root. Because many students who act out are underachievers, decreasing their negative behavior and increasing their motivation often improves academic achievement. In this case, Tony became more receptive to feedback from his peers and the teacher. His academic strengths became more apparent as he learned to participate in positive ways.

Handbook of Individualized Strategies for Classroom Discipline
Problem-Solving Worksheet

by W. George Selig, Ed.D. and Alan A. Arroyo, Ed.D.

Published by

WPS WESTERN PSYCHOLOGICAL SERVICES
Publishers and Distributors
12031 Wilshire Boulevard
Los Angeles, California 90025-1251

Student's Name _Tony Drew_

Age _12_   Gender: ☑M ☐F   Grade _6_

Date _11/8/94_   Teacher's Name _Mrs. Beck_

Instructions

Review the list of problem behaviors in Table 5 of the *Handbook of Individualized Strategies for Classroom Discipline* (WPS Product No. W-315A), and enter the problem behavior for this student on the designated line below. Complete the Level of Motivation Checklist and the Behavior Style Checklist on the reverse side of this worksheet. Then, in the table below, place a check mark at the intersection of this student's behavior style and level of motivation. In Part 2 of the Handbook, compare this table with the coded tables that precede the intervention strategies suggested for addressing this student's problem behavior. A black square at the same intersection of behavior style and level of motivation indicates that the strategies immediately following that table are the ones with the highest probability of success for this student.

Problem Behavior _Defiance_

Level of Motivation	Behavior Style			
	Self-Assertive	Socially Interactive	Analytic	Accommodating
1. Self-Absorbed	✔			
2. Approval Oriented				
3. Interpersonal Loyalty				
4. Others Oriented				

Intervention Strategy _Deducting Points for Misbehavior_

Page Number _106_

Results _Gave Tony four tickets at the beginning of each class period, and took one back each time he was defiant. He has gone from needing a reward every 2 days to needing only occasional verbal and written praise in order to maintain respectful behavior. Will continue the written and verbal encouragement, along with occasional one-on-one talks._

W-315B

Figure 3
Problem-Solving Worksheet for Case Study 1

Level of Motivation Checklist

Review the levels of motivation described in Table 1 of the Handbook. Then think about a specific setting (e.g., a classroom or the hallway), and check the items below that describe this student's typical behavior in that setting. Total the check marks for each level of motivation. The level with the highest number of check marks is the one that best describes this student.

Level 1 (Self-Absorbed)	Level 2 (Approval Oriented)	Level 3 (Interpersonal Loyalty)	Level 4 (Others Oriented)
☑ Usually wants his or her own way	☐ Pursues certain subjects, activities, or hobbies in order to win approval	☑ Wants to be respected for his or her ideas	☐ Seeks opportunities to help others
☐ Has a very short attention span, and changes activities often	☑ Demands attention	☐ Is loyal and will stand up for family or friends	☐ Often praises peers, even in their absence
☑ Is very possessive of his or her belongings	☐ Completes most tasks, but seeks verbal praise for his or her efforts	☐ Is even tempered and self-controlled	☐ Is self-motivated; enjoys feeling productive
☑ Uses other people's belongings without asking permission	☑ Is considered to be a show-off	☐ Enjoys organized group activities	☐ Volunteers for necessary tasks
☑ Becomes angry or resentful if opposed	☐ Demands admiration for his or her achievements	☐ Has a healthy appreciation of rules, and likes strong adult guidance	☐ Is able to make decisions objectively
☑ Gets unusually upset when contradicted	☑ Enjoys participating in competitive activities, but is upset if his or her efforts go unrecognized	☐ Strives for competence	☐ Can converse with adults on their level
☑ Often must be told specifically what behavior is expected before he or she will comply	☐ Is quick to judge peers	☐ Enjoys being part of a particular group	☐ Is generally optimistic
☐ Has a low trust level	☑ Behaves best when he or she is the center of attention	☐ Enjoys the company of adults, both family members and others	☐ Is able to stand up for his or her beliefs, even in the face of criticism
	☐ Loses interest in a task if not given constant attention and encouragement		
__6__ Total Checked	__4__ Total Checked	__1__ Total Checked	__0__ Total Checked

Behavior Style Checklist

Review the behavior styles described in Table 2 of the Handbook. Then think about a specific setting (e.g., a classroom or the hallway), and check the items below that describe this student's typical behavior in that setting. Total the check marks for each behavior style. The style with the highest number of check marks is the one that best describes this student.

Self-Assertive	Socially Interactive	Analytic	Accommodating
☑ Is outspoken, opinionated, assertive	☐ Uses facial expressions and hand movements when talking	☐ Is systematic and well-ordered—prefers to have a plan or method	☐ Has an honest, sincere, low-key style—doesn't appear to mislead people
☑ Is active, restless—has difficulty staying in one place	☑ Expresses himself or herself well verbally	☐ Seems very organized	☐ Likes routine—is predictable and not quick to change
☑ Is persistent—keeps pushing until goal is reached	☐ Tends to be cheerful, sees the bright side of situations	☐ Seems prepared for most events or activities	☐ Seems mild tempered
☐ Is decisive—makes decisions easily and sticks with them	☑ Is persuasive—can present ideas convincingly	☐ Tries hard to avoid unwanted surprises	☐ Is humble and modest about accomplishments
☐ Usually wins arguments or debates	☐ Is open-minded—open to others' ideas	☐ Seeks details	☐ Is compassionate—tends to be one of the first to help someone who is sick or hurting
☑ Tells people what he or she thinks	☐ Is friendly and outgoing	☐ Keeps records	☐ Is reserved around new people or in new situations
☑ Gets right to the point	☑ Doesn't mind changing plans and is flexible	☐ Is restrained and usually very self-controlled, seldom loses temper	☐ Takes time to think things through and get in touch with his or her feelings
☐ Usually takes a leading role in a group	☐ Enjoys being around people most of the time	☐ Appears to be steady and calm	☐ Is tenderhearted—usually approaches people in a gentle, soft manner
☐ Is productive—works hard and gets a lot done	☐ Likes change and diversity	☑ Is often critical of self or others	☐ Is empathetic—considers other people's thoughts and feelings
☑ Does not change mind easily once he or she has formed an opinion	☑ Is usually talkative	☑ Prefers to thoroughly understand a new task or situation before trying it	☐ Prefers an organized environment that is free from unexpected change
☑ Likes to work independently and is able to do so effectively	☐ Expresses affection and appreciation for others	☐ Is analytic—approaches most problems in a logical fashion	☐ Appears ready to defend and protect others—especially those in a weaker position
☑ Is competitive—strives to be first in most things	☑ Is original—thinks of new and different ways to do things	☐ Is usually careful and tactful when communicating with others	☐ Is stable—acts sensibly and responsibly
☑ Tends to be result oriented	☐ Enjoys discussing goals and dreams	☑ Is thorough—often checks things two or three times	☐ Is usually calm, easygoing, and relaxed
__9__ Total Checked	__5__ Total Checked	__3__ Total Checked	__0__ Total Checked

Figure 3 *(continued)*
Problem-Solving Worksheet for Case Study 1

47

Case Study 2: Jolene

Background

Mrs. Davis was concerned about Jolene's off-task behavior. The third grader was outgoing and friendly and never seemed to be intentionally disruptive, yet she always seemed to be either inattentive or attending to things other than her assigned task.

The Pupil Personnel Service (PPS) team recommended that one of its members observe Jolene in the classroom setting. Jolene was recorded as being off task 90% of the time during a creative writing period. The observer also noted that Jolene was out of her chair at least 10 times within that 30-minute period.

Jolene's parents informed Mrs. Davis that Jolene had been diagnosed as having Attention Deficit Disorder (ADD); however, they had decided not to continue to give her medication because of its ineffectiveness during previous experiences.

Use of the Individualized Strategies System

Mrs. Davis completed the Problem-Solving Worksheet to determine what could be done to help Jolene succeed (see Figure 4). According to the checklists, Jolene's behavior style was socially interactive, and as for her level of motivation, she was functioning at between Level 2 and Level 3 in the classroom.

Having identified Jolene's major problem as a short attention span, Mrs. Davis turned to Part 2 of this Handbook and located the section devoted to Attention Span Problems. There she read through the strategies recommended for use with students who shared Jolene's behavior style and level of motivation. After reviewing several of the suggested strategies, Mrs. Davis decided that Student Self-Monitoring would work. Jolene's parents were willing to cooperate, especially if it meant that medication would not be necessary.

Mrs. Davis met with Jolene and her parents to discuss Jolene's charting strategy and goals, which included:

- Working at a task until finished
- Staying in her chair
- Paying attention

A 30-minute creative writing period was held twice daily. For a week, Mrs. Davis kept a written record of Jolene's progress during that period. Every 15 minutes, she wrote *yes, no,* or *sometimes,* depending on Jolene's success in meeting her goals. At the end of each day, Jolene plotted the number of yeses she received that day on a graph as follows:

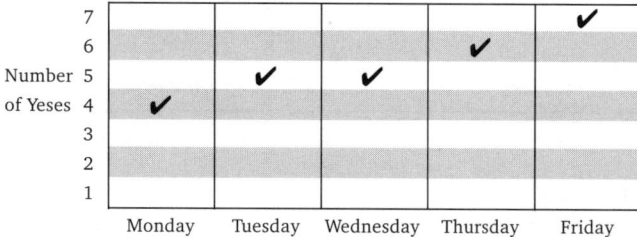

As the chart shows, Jolene made steady progress and was soon on task 80%–90% of the time. Mrs. Davis stopped monitoring every 15 minutes because she saw that Jolene was catching herself when she was off task.

Jolene's parents were pleased with her apparent progress. She was much happier, but she came home exhausted because she put so much effort into achieving the goals. The parents decided to resume counseling. They indicated that if the counselor felt it was necessary, they would try medication again. They thought that would make Jolene's improvement less stressful for her.

Jolene continued to use the self-monitoring strategy until the end of the year. During that time, she slipped occasionally, but her recovery was quick and self-motivated.

Summary

Mrs. Davis was in a situation thousands of teachers face daily. Their classrooms each contain at least one child who has been diagnosed as having ADD, and who is not being treated with medication. Instead of giving up in despair, however, Mrs. Davis attempted a strategy that has been found to work for many children with ADD—charting.

In this case, Mrs. Davis provided feedback and Jolene completed the chart. One successful modification of this strategy would be to cue the student periodically to check his or her own on-task behavior. The student is cued by a cassette tape in a portable player near his or her desk. Some teachers have the student use an earphone so that other students will not be disturbed. At preset intervals, the tape emits a bell or beep that the teacher previously recorded. The cue reminds the student to check the appropriate box on his or her goal sheet. Of course, the student has to be at a high enough level of motivation to have the internal control to self-monitor in this manner. Peer mentors have also been used successfully to monitor the on-task behavior of students with ADD.

When the efforts of school personnel are successful, both the student and his or her parents are encouraged. In fact, parents are often more willing to seek appropriate assistance outside the school after they observe successful school intervention. Experts report that successful treatment of ADD requires home, school, medical, and sometimes psychiatric intervention. Once the school takes the initiative, parents feel encouraged to implement other approaches as well.

Handbook of Individualized Strategies for Classroom Discipline
Problem-Solving Worksheet

by W. George Selig, Ed.D. and Alan A. Arroyo, Ed.D.

Published by

WPS WESTERN PSYCHOLOGICAL SERVICES
Publishers and Distributors
12031 Wilshire Boulevard
Los Angeles, California 90025-1251

Student's Name ___Jolene Rusnick___

Age ___8___   Gender: ☐M ☑F   Grade ___3___

Date ___1/16/95___   Teacher's Name ___Mrs. Davis___

Instructions

Review the list of problem behaviors in Table 5 of the *Handbook of Individualized Strategies for Classroom Discipline* (WPS Product No. W-315A), and enter the problem behavior for this student on the designated line below. Complete the Level of Motivation Checklist and the Behavior Style Checklist on the reverse side of this worksheet. Then, in the table below, place a check mark at the intersection of this student's behavior style and level of motivation. In Part 2 of the Handbook, compare this table with the coded tables that precede the intervention strategies suggested for addressing this student's problem behavior. A black square at the same intersection of behavior style and level of motivation indicates that the strategies immediately following that table are the ones with the highest probability of success for this student.

Problem Behavior ___Attention Span Problems___

Level of Motivation	Behavior Style			
	Self-Assertive	Socially Interactive	Analytic	Accommodating
1. Self-Absorbed				
2. Approval Oriented		✓		
3. Interpersonal Loyalty				
4. Others Oriented				

Intervention Strategy ___Student Self-Monitoring___

Page Number ___78___

Results ___Self-monitoring focused Jolene on her off-task behavior and served as a reminder to get back on task. She has learned to be attentive, stay in her seat, and focus on assigned tasks. Will continue this strategy, but with less teacher intervention. To help maintain her new behavior pattern, will implement a program of affirmative statements and weekly one-on-one discussions of her behavior.___

W-315B

Figure 4
Problem-Solving Worksheet for Case Study 2

Level of Motivation Checklist

Review the levels of motivation described in Table 1 of the Handbook. Then think about a specific setting (e.g., a classroom or the hallway), and check the items below that describe this student's typical behavior in that setting. Total the check marks for each level of motivation. The level with the highest number of check marks is the one that best describes this student.

Level 1 (Self-Absorbed)	Level 2 (Approval Oriented)	Level 3 (Interpersonal Loyalty)	Level 4 (Others Oriented)
☐ Usually wants his or her own way	☑ Pursues certain subjects, activities, or hobbies in order to win approval	☑ Wants to be respected for his or her ideas	☑ Seeks opportunities to help others
☑ Has a very short attention span, and changes activities often	☐ Demands attention	☑ Is loyal and will stand up for family or friends	☐ Often praises peers, even in their absence
☐ Is very possessive of his or her belongings	☑ Completes most tasks, but seeks verbal praise for his or her efforts	☐ Is even tempered and self-controlled	☐ Is self-motivated; enjoys feeling productive
☐ Uses other people's belongings without asking permission	☑ Is considered to be a show-off	☐ Enjoys organized group activities	☑ Volunteers for necessary tasks
☐ Becomes angry or resentful if opposed	☐ Demands admiration for his or her achievements	☐ Has a healthy appreciation of rules, and likes strong adult guidance	☐ Is able to make decisions objectively
☐ Gets unusually upset when contradicted	☑ Enjoys participating in competitive activities, but is upset if his or her efforts go unrecognized	☐ Strives for competence	☐ Can converse with adults on their level
☑ Often must be told specifically what behavior is expected before he or she will comply	☐ Is quick to judge peers	☑ Enjoys being part of a particular group	☐ Is generally optimistic
☐ Has a low trust level	☑ Behaves best when he or she is the center of attention	☑ Enjoys the company of adults, both family members and others	☐ Is able to stand up for his or her beliefs, even in the face of criticism
	☑ Loses interest in a task if not given constant attention and encouragement		
_2_ Total Checked	_6_ Total Checked	_4_ Total Checked	_2_ Total Checked

Behavior Style Checklist

Review the behavior styles described in Table 2 of the Handbook. Then think about a specific setting (e.g., a classroom or the hallway), and check the items below that describe this student's typical behavior in that setting. Total the check marks for each behavior style. The style with the highest number of check marks is the one that best describes this student.

Self-Assertive	Socially Interactive	Analytic	Accommodating
☐ Is outspoken, opinionated, assertive	☑ Uses facial expressions and hand movements when talking	☐ Is systematic and well-ordered—prefers to have a plan or method	☐ Has an honest, sincere, low-key style—doesn't appear to mislead people
☑ Is active, restless—has difficulty staying in one place	☐ Expresses himself or herself well verbally	☐ Seems very organized	☐ Likes routine—is predictable and not quick to change
☐ Is persistent—keeps pushing until goal is reached	☑ Tends to be cheerful, sees the bright side of situations	☐ Seems prepared for most events or activities	☑ Seems mild tempered
☐ Is decisive—makes decisions easily and sticks with them	☐ Is persuasive—can present ideas convincingly	☐ Tries hard to avoid unwanted surprises	☐ Is humble and modest about accomplishments
☐ Usually wins arguments or debates	☑ Is open-minded—open to others' ideas	☐ Seeks details	☑ Is compassionate—tends to be one of the first to help someone who is sick or hurting
☑ Tells people what he or she thinks	☑ Is friendly and outgoing	☐ Keeps records	☐ Is reserved around new people or in new situations
☐ Gets right to the point	☑ Doesn't mind changing plans and is flexible	☐ Is restrained and usually very self-controlled, seldom loses temper	☐ Takes time to think things through and get in touch with his or her feelings
☑ Usually takes a leading role in a group	☑ Enjoys being around people most of the time	☐ Appears to be steady and calm	☑ Is tenderhearted—usually approaches people in a gentle, soft manner
☐ Is productive—works hard and gets a lot done	☐ Likes change and diversity	☐ Is often critical of self or others	☑ Is empathetic—considers other people's thoughts and feelings
☐ Does not change mind easily once he or she has formed an opinion	☑ Is usually talkative	☐ Prefers to thoroughly understand a new task or situation before trying it	☐ Prefers an organized environment that is free from unexpected change
☐ Likes to work independently and is able to do so effectively	☐ Expresses affection and appreciation for others	☐ Is analytic—approaches most problems in a logical fashion	☐ Appears ready to defend and protect others—especially those in a weaker position
☐ Is competitive—strives to be first in most things	☑ Is original—thinks of new and different ways to do things	☐ Is usually careful and tactful when communicating with others	☐ Is stable—acts sensibly and responsibly
☐ Tends to be result oriented	☑ Enjoys discussing goals and dreams	☐ Is thorough—often checks things two or three times	☐ Is usually calm, easygoing, and relaxed
_3_ Total Checked	_9_ Total Checked	_0_ Total Checked	_4_ Total Checked

Figure 4 *(continued)*
Problem-Solving Worksheet for Case Study 2

Case Study 3: James

Background

Mr. Carson could usually rely on James to be quiet and diligent, and he needed someone with those qualities in his fourth-period algebra class. Although the other students in that group were capable, they were immature and unmotivated.

James, however, began to show a change in behavior. He would come to class before the bell and pace around the room. When class began he would take his seat, but would tap his foot or beat the desk with his pencil. In addition, James began to participate less in class. When he did speak, he would spurt out his answer quickly without looking up from his paper. Mr. Carson determined that the behavior James was demonstrating was anxiety—worry or uneasiness about some situation.

Use of the Individualized Strategies System

As shown in Figure 5, the Problem-Solving Worksheet completed by Mr. Carson identified James as having an analytic behavior style with strong accommodating tendencies. Mr. Carson shared this information with James. At first, James thought he was more socially interactive, but after reviewing the characteristics on the Behavior Style Checklist, Mr. Carson and James agreed that James had more of the reflective tendencies of an analytic and accommodating style than the extroverted behavior of a socially interactive individual. According to the Level of Motivation Checklist, James had been operating at Level 3 until recently.

In Part 2 of this Handbook, Mr. Carson found the section that presented intervention strategies for Anxiety. He decided to try the first two strategies recommended for students whose behavior style is analytic or accommodating and whose motivation is at Level 3—Checking for Understanding and Increasing Physical Proximity. During class, Mr. Carson made sure that James understood the questions being asked and the assignments given, and he also made a point of spending more time near where James was seated. Despite these efforts, James's anxious behavior continued.

Mr. Carson felt that James's current level of motivation had fallen to Level 2. Therefore, he decided to use strategies consistent with that level of motivation as well as James's analytic behavior style. Mr. Carson reviewed two strategies for analytic or accommodating behavior at Level 2—Using Affirmative Statements and Reflecting Verbal Responses.

First, Mr. Carson tried Using Affirmative Statements. In accordance with the instructions for this strategy, he commented positively whenever James volunteered anything in class. For example, if James gave a correct answer, Mr. Carson would be sure to say something like, "Correct as usual, James. You really studied this chapter." If James's answer was not correct, Mr. Carson would comment on any part of the answer that was correct and say, "Close. You gave a good effort on a tough problem." Normally, this strategy is successful with students at Levels 2 or 3, but it did not work for James. He seemed to be growing even more nervous.

Mr. Carson implemented the next strategy—Reflecting Verbal Responses—after class one day. He and James were alone in the classroom. Mr. Carson described some of the behavior he had observed and asked, "What's up?" It took a couple of modifications of that question before James opened up. As James spoke, Mr. Carson paraphrased what James said, as follows:

"Well, I don't like it when you always call on me," said James.

"Does it seem like I call on you a lot?" responded Mr. Carson.

"Well, not a lot. Maybe it's what you say after I answer. Even if I'm wrong, I feel like you're pointing me out, making me into someone special," explained James.

"My reinforcing or rewarding your efforts makes you feel different from the others," paraphrased Mr. Carson.

"Yeah, and I hear about it on the bus. 'James is suckin' up to Carson.' I want to do well in school, but I don't want everyone to think I'm a nerd."

"You're caught between a rock and a hard place. You don't know what to do."

"Yeah."

Then there was silence. Mr. Carson and James agreed to meet the next day and continue their discussion. After James left the room, Mr. Carson turned to the general strategies in chapter 3 of this Handbook. Because the specific strategies recommended in Part 2 had already been employed without success, he knew he now needed a different approach.

After reviewing the strategies, Mr. Carson decided to try Asking Adult Questions. When Mr. Carson met with James the next day, they reviewed what James had said about the problem. It became apparent that even before Mr. Carson had used the initial strategy (Checking for Understanding), James had felt singled out. Mr. Carson discovered that some immature members of the class were putting pressure on James not to apply himself.

Mr. Carson made the transition to a problem-solving mode by asking James an adult question: "How can we solve this problem so that you can participate in class without feeling that the others will joke about you on the bus?" James thought a minute. Mr. Carson reminded James that his basic tendencies were to be a good thinker and to ask questions (analytic traits) while being sensitive about how he and others feel (an accommodating trait).

Mr. Carson had James look at some of the strategies in Table 6 to see if that would spark an idea. They discussed the possible benefits of utilizing the Positive Peer-Group Reinforcement strategy, and brainstormed about their options until one sounded good to both of them. They agreed to play a game in class similar to "It's Academic." Mr. Carson would divide the class into teams, ask a question, and give the teams a limited time to answer. The first team to answer would receive a point. Sometimes the entire class would work together to earn points. If they earned a designated number of points in a week, everyone in the class would receive a "no homework" pass.

James showed some anxiety at first. However, once the approach caught on, James was the "main man." Students wanted him in their group, and he was encouraged to answer frequently to help meet the class goal. The frequency of anxious behavior decreased to nearly zero. Not only had James's behavior improved, but the entire class was more responsive and motivated to learn.

Summary

James's case is of particular interest for three reasons. First, anxiety may be a sign of potentially violent behavior in a youth. Most crisis situations begin because someone is in an anxious state of mind. Intervening early can prevent more serious problems in the future.

Second, this case shows how a teacher can improvise when the suggested strategies do not work. For example, when Mr. Carson had exhausted the specific strategies listed under Anxiety in Part 2 that were appropriate for James, he looked for a general strategy in chapter 3 and tailored it to meet James's needs.

Third, this case demonstrates how older students can actively participate in the problem-solving process. Mr. Carson shared the Behavior Style Checklist results with James. He also had James look in this Handbook for possible strategies. In this way, Mr. Carson communicated to James that he is a unique individual with preferred ways of learning. Moreover, Mr. Carson showed that he had confidence in James's ability to solve his own problems.

Depending upon their maturity level—and level of motivation—students as young as fourth graders can be involved in the problem-solving process. Generally, however, children in middle school and high school respond best to the participative style modeled in this case.

Handbook of Individualized Strategies for Classroom Discipline
Problem-Solving Worksheet
by W. George Selig, Ed.D. and Alan A. Arroyo, Ed.D.

Published by

WPS WESTERN PSYCHOLOGICAL SERVICES
Publishers and Distributors
12031 Wilshire Boulevard
Los Angeles, California 90025-1251

Student's Name ___James Jackson___

Age ___14___   Gender: ☑M ☐F   Grade ___9___

Date ___12/13/94___   Teacher's Name ___Mr. Carson___

Instructions

Review the list of problem behaviors in Table 5 of the *Handbook of Individualized Strategies for Classroom Discipline* (WPS Product No. W-315A), and enter the problem behavior for this student on the designated line below. Complete the Level of Motivation Checklist and the Behavior Style Checklist on the reverse side of this worksheet. Then, in the table below, place a check mark at the intersection of this student's behavior style and level of motivation. In Part 2 of the Handbook, compare this table with the coded tables that precede the intervention strategies suggested for addressing this student's problem behavior. A black square at the same intersection of behavior style and level of motivation indicates that the strategies immediately following that table are the ones with the highest probability of success for this student.

Problem Behavior ___Anxiety___

Level of Motivation	Behavior Style			
	Self-Assertive	Socially Interactive	Analytic	Accommodating
1. Self-Absorbed				
2. Approval Oriented				
3. Interpersonal Loyalty			✓	
4. Others Oriented				

Intervention Strategy ___Positive Peer-Group Reinforcement___

Page Number ___26___

Results ___James and the whole class have become more responsive and motivated. James is much less anxious and is performing in accordance with his abilities. Will continue group activities, but less often, as the situation indicates.___

W-315B

Figure 5
Final Problem-Solving Worksheet for Case Study 3

Level of Motivation Checklist

Review the levels of motivation described in Table 1 of the Handbook. Then think about a specific setting (e.g., a classroom or the hallway), and check the items below that describe this student's typical behavior in that setting. Total the check marks for each level of motivation. The level with the highest number of check marks is the one that best describes this student.

Level 1 (Self-Absorbed)	Level 2 (Approval Oriented)	Level 3 (Interpersonal Loyalty)	Level 4 (Others Oriented)
☐ Usually wants his or her own way	☐ Pursues certain subjects, activities, or hobbies in order to win approval	☑ Wants to be respected for his or her ideas	☐ Seeks opportunities to help others
☐ Has a very short attention span, and changes activities often	☐ Demands attention	☐ Is loyal and will stand up for family or friends	☐ Often praises peers, even in their absence
☐ Is very possessive of his or her belongings	☐ Completes most tasks, but seeks verbal praise for his or her efforts	☑ Is even tempered and self-controlled	☑ Is self-motivated; enjoys feeling productive
☐ Uses other people's belongings without asking permission	☐ Is considered to be a show-off	☑ Enjoys organized group activities	☐ Volunteers for necessary tasks
☐ Becomes angry or resentful if opposed	☐ Demands admiration for his or her achievements	☑ Has a healthy appreciation of rules, and likes strong adult guidance	☐ Is able to make decisions objectively
☐ Gets unusually upset when contradicted	☐ Enjoys participating in competitive activities, but is upset if his or her efforts go unrecognized	☑ Strives for competence	☑ Can converse with adults on their level
☐ Often must be told specifically what behavior is expected before he or she will comply	☐ Is quick to judge peers	☑ Enjoys being part of a particular group	☐ Is generally optimistic
☐ Has a low trust level	☐ Behaves best when he or she is the center of attention	☑ Enjoys the company of adults, both family members and others	☐ Is able to stand up for his or her beliefs, even in the face of criticism
	☐ Loses interest in a task if not given constant attention and encouragement		
_0_ Total Checked	_0_ Total Checked	_7_ Total Checked	_2_ Total Checked

Behavior Style Checklist

Review the behavior styles described in Table 2 of the Handbook. Then think about a specific setting (e.g., a classroom or the hallway), and check the items below that describe this student's typical behavior in that setting. Total the check marks for each behavior style. The style with the highest number of check marks is the one that best describes this student.

Self-Assertive	Socially Interactive	Analytic	Accommodating
☐ Is outspoken, opinionated, assertive	☐ Uses facial expressions and hand movements when talking	☑ Is systematic and well-ordered—prefers to have a plan or method	☑ Has an honest, sincere, low-key style—doesn't appear to mislead people
☐ Is active, restless—has difficulty staying in one place	☑ Expresses himself or herself well verbally	☐ Seems very organized	☑ Likes routine—is predictable and not quick to change
☐ Is persistent—keeps pushing until goal is reached	☐ Tends to be cheerful, sees the bright side of situations	☑ Seems prepared for most events or activities	☑ Seems mild tempered
☐ Is decisive—makes decisions easily and sticks with them	☐ Is persuasive—can present ideas convincingly	☑ Tries hard to avoid unwanted surprises	☑ Is humble and modest about accomplishments
☐ Usually wins arguments or debates	☐ Is open-minded—open to others' ideas	☑ Seeks details	☐ Is compassionate—tends to be one of the first to help someone who is sick or hurting
☐ Tells people what he or she thinks	☐ Is friendly and outgoing	☐ Keeps records	☐ Is reserved around new people or in new situations
☐ Gets right to the point	☐ Doesn't mind changing plans and is flexible	☑ Is restrained and usually very self-controlled, seldom loses temper	☐ Takes time to think things through and get in touch with his or her feelings
☐ Usually takes a leading role in a group	☑ Enjoys being around people most of the time	☐ Appears to be steady and calm	☑ Is tenderhearted—usually approaches people in a gentle, soft manner
☐ Is productive—works hard and gets a lot done	☐ Likes change and diversity	☑ Is often critical of self or others	☑ Is empathetic—considers other people's thoughts and feelings
☑ Does not change mind easily once he or she has formed an opinion	☐ Is usually talkative	☐ Prefers to thoroughly understand a new task or situation before trying it	☐ Prefers an organized environment that is free from unexpected change
☐ Likes to work independently and is able to do so effectively	☐ Expresses affection and appreciation for others	☑ Is analytic—approaches most problems in a logical fashion	☐ Appears ready to defend and protect others—especially those in a weaker position
☐ Is competitive—strives to be first in most things	☐ Is original—thinks of new and different ways to do things	☑ Is usually careful and tactful when communicating with others	☑ Is stable—acts sensibly and responsibly
☐ Tends to be result oriented	☐ Enjoys discussing goals and dreams	☑ Is thorough—often checks things two or three times	☐ Is usually calm, easygoing, and relaxed
_1_ Total Checked	_2_ Total Checked	_9_ Total Checked	_7_ Total Checked

Figure 5 (continued)
Final Problem-Solving Worksheet for Case Study 3

PART 2

PROBLEM BEHAVIORS AND SPECIFIC INTERVENTION STRATEGIES

ABSENTEEISM

Chronic, willful absence from school for a class period, a day, or any other length of time

Limit Setting

Level of Motivation	Behavior Style			
	Self-Assertive	Socially Interactive	Analytic	Accommodating
1. Self-Absorbed				
2. Approval Oriented			■	■
3. Interpersonal Loyalty	■	■	■	■
4. Others Oriented	■	■	■	■

▶ **Reflecting Verbal Responses**

Verbally reflect the essence of a student's argument in order to clarify his or her true feelings.

1. Engage the student in a discussion of his or her absenteeism.
2. Listen carefully to determine the student's true feelings.
3. Verbally reflect your perception of what the student is saying (e.g., "What I hear you saying is ...").
4. Assess the student's response, try to discern his or her basic message, and again reflect that verbally.
5. Repeat Steps 2–4 until no further clarification is forthcoming.
   Do not try to guess what the student means—reflect only what is actually said.

▶ **Student Self-Monitoring**

Have the student monitor his or her own behavior using charts or other means to record progress.

1. Chart the time missed; discuss individual absences and their causes with the student.
2. Analyze the student's pattern of absenteeism to determine when and how he or she decides to stay away from school.
3. Help the student to set specific goals. It may be necessary to work toward perfect attendance by first setting intermediate goals (e.g., three attendance days the first week).
   Once a goal is consistently attained, the student should set a new goal.
4. Have the student maintain a neat, handwritten chart to monitor his or her progress.
5. Establish rewards for attainment of goals.

▶ **Exchanging Information With Parents**

Work with the student's parents to gather information that might help resolve the problem.
   Note. Before using this strategy, you may want to try the less intrusive Alerting Parents to Concerns strategy (see under *Prevention* in chapter 3).

1. Determine the frequency of the student's absences, and attempt to identify a pattern.
2. Prepare a list of questions to ask the parents.
3. Contact the parents, define and describe the student's problem, and provide information about any pattern that may have emerged.
4. Ask the questions you prepared earlier.
5. Provide the parents with the information they need to assume responsibility for their child's behavior, but avoid leading them to a solution. Allow their sense of responsibility to occur naturally.
6. Write down any helpful information you receive.
7. In closing the conversation, reaffirm your support for their child's education and your willingness to communicate with them.
8. Thank them for their time and cooperation.

Reinforcement of Limits

Level of Motivation	Behavior Style			
	Self-Assertive	Socially Interactive	Analytic	Accommodating
1. Self-Absorbed		■	■	■
2. Approval Oriented	■	■		
3. Interpersonal Loyalty				
4. Others Oriented				

▶ Establishing Logical Consequences

Establish logical consequences for certain behaviors.

1. Prepare a list of classroom rules, and make sure that regular attendance is included on the list.
2. Establish consequences that correspond to the severity of the student's absenteeism. For example:
   - Have the student forfeit a break, recess, lunch period, or other free time to make up missed work.
   - Exclude the student from special activities, such as field trips, films, and so on, if there is still work to be made up.
   - When assigning grades, deduct points for missed work.
3. Rehearse the rules with the student, and explain how the consequences logically relate to his or her absenteeism.

▶ Charting Progress

Use charts to monitor misbehavior and check the student's progress.

1. Discuss with the student what precipitates his or her decision to stay home, and analyze that decision-making process.
2. Set specific attendance goals for the student.
3. Establish an accurate record keeping system to chart the student's attendance, record it consistently, and show the chart to the student.
4. Establish rewards for successful attainment of the written attendance goals. Rewards should be commensurate with the degree of improvement.

Level of Motivation	Behavior Style			
	Self-Assertive	Socially Interactive	Analytic	Accommodating
1. Self-Absorbed	■	■	■	■
2. Approval Oriented	■	■		
3. Interpersonal Loyalty				
4. Others Oriented				

▶ Suggesting Parental Intervention Strategies

Enlist the parents' help in correcting the student's behavior.

Note. Before using this strategy, you may want to try the less intrusive Alerting Parents to Concerns and/or Exchanging Information With Parents strategies (see under *Prevention* and *Limit Setting,* respectively, in chapter 3).

1. Contact the parents, review the facts concerning the student's absenteeism, and communicate your assurance that the problem is manageable.
2. Determine what measures the parents can take to insure their child's attendance. Make suggestions if needed. These may include:
   - Assuming responsibility for waking up the student and facilitating his or her morning preparations on a specific schedule
   - Insuring that the student catches the bus or at least arrives at the pickup point in a timely manner
   - Discouraging any late night activities that have been shown to precede absenteeism
3. Elicit an agreement from the parents regarding what they will do.

Control

Level of Motivation	Behavior Style			
	Self-Assertive	Socially Interactive	Analytic	Accommodating
1. Self-Absorbed		■	■	■
2. Approval Oriented	■	■		
3. Interpersonal Loyalty				
4. Others Oriented				

▶ Coordinating Outside Intervention

Coordinate help or support from an outside source
(e.g., a mental health or family service agency, the legal system, etc.).

1. Keep accurate records of the student's attendance and excuses for absence.
   Check for lack of motivation or a passive attitude toward class.
2. Call the parents if the problem seems chronic or if there seems to be a pattern.
   Suggest possible intervention by an agency outside the school.
3. Work with school officials to contact appropriate agencies if the problem seems to be beyond
   the expertise of the teacher and parents.
4. Cooperate with agency personnel and assist them in helping the student as part of a coordinated plan.

Level of Motivation	Behavior Style			
	Self-Assertive	Socially Interactive	Analytic	Accommodating
1. Self-Absorbed	■			
2. Approval Oriented				
3. Interpersonal Loyalty				
4. Others Oriented				

▶ Deducting Points for Misbehavior

Deduct points (or tokens) or withhold privileges the student has earned.
(Deduction of points should occur in conjunction with a token reinforcement system.)

1. Choose the number of points the student can earn for attending school per week
   and the number of points that will be deducted for each day he or she is absent.
2. Inform the student of these rules for earning or losing points.
   When dealing with group absenteeism, announce and post these rules.
3. Deduct points exactly as you have stipulated if absenteeism occurs that week.
4. If this strategy is not effective, consider increasing the frequency with which points are awarded
   and/or increasing the desirability of the rewards for which points can be redeemed
   (e.g., rather than 10 minutes of free reading time, substitute an opportunity to
   play an enjoyable computer game that is normally restricted).
5. If absenteeism persists, increase the number of points deducted for each day the student is absent
   (e.g., one day absent equals 10 points deducted, two days absent equals 25 points, etc.).

Control *(continued)*

	Behavior Style			
Level of Motivation	Self-Assertive	Socially Interactive	Analytic	Accommodating
1. Self-Absorbed		■	■	■
2. Approval Oriented	■	■		
3. Interpersonal Loyalty				
4. Others Oriented				

▶ **Detention**

Keep the student after school for a specified period of time. Be sure, however, that the resources are available for detention to be remedial, not punitive.

1. Make it clear to the student that detention will be used as a method of discipline.
2. Use detention time to develop a relationship with the student.
   Try to get the student to talk about his or her needs and frustrations.
3. Drill the student in areas of academic weakness, and have him or her make up missed schoolwork.
4. Work with the student to develop a plan for recognizing and improving problem behavior.
5. End the detention on a positive note if possible.
6. Increase detention time if absenteeism persists.

▶ **Having a Parent in the Classroom**

Bring one of the student's parents into the classroom to observe the student's behavior there.

Note. Before using this strategy, you may want to try one or more of the following three less intrusive strategies: Alerting Parents to Concerns, Exchanging Information With Parents, and Suggesting Parental Intervention Strategies (see under *Prevention, Limit Setting,* and *Reinforcement of Limits,* respectively, in chapter 3).

1. The goal of this strategy is to lessen the student's need for external control and increase his or her internal control. As the first step toward that goal, ask the parents to escort the student to school and to stay at school until class begins.
2. Periodically discuss the student's progress with the parents to determine the success or failure of this strategy.
3. Gradually allow the student to assume more responsibility for coming to school unattended. Switch from parental escort to some type of reward system as improvement occurs.
   A sibling or a friend may be an escort as an intermediary step.

ANGER

Sudden, keen displeasure manifested by an outburst of wrath or hostility;
a sense of resentment, unjust treatment, or injury

Prevention

Level of Motivation	Behavior Style			
	Self-Assertive	Socially Interactive	Analytic	Accommodating
1. Self-Absorbed	■	■	■	■
2. Approval Oriented	■	■	■	■
3. Interpersonal Loyalty	■	■	■	■
4. Others Oriented				

▶ **Increasing Physical Proximity**

Spend more time near the student throughout the class period.

1. Circulate throughout the classroom while lecturing, and move toward the student when he or she shows signs of frustration.
2. Walk up and down the aisles near the student without interrupting the lecture.
3. Sit on an empty desk or chair near the student.
4. Verbally encourage the student's efforts in order to counteract any built-up anger.
5. Make yourself available for a private question or discussion by standing nearby and quietly providing hints or redirection.

Limit Setting

Level of Motivation	Behavior Style			
	Self-Assertive	Socially Interactive	Analytic	Accommodating
1. Self-Absorbed				
2. Approval Oriented			■	■
3. Interpersonal Loyalty	■	■	■	
4. Others Oriented				

▶ Using Affirmative Statements

Verbally acknowledge and emphasize the student's strengths and achievements.

1. Find the student's areas of interest and design opportunities for success in those areas.
2. Emphasize the need for improvement, not perfection. Frustration is a form of anger.
3. Match the student with other students who are willing to help him or her.
4. Avoid putting the student in competitive situations.
5. Comment positively on the student's efforts
   (e.g., "I like the way you responded to Joe when he made that remark").

▶ Describing Misbehavior as It Occurs

Describe to the student what he or she has just done, is doing, or is about to do.

1. Describe to the student exactly what is happening
   (e.g., "I see you kicking the desk, and that usually means someone is angry").
2. Wait for a sign of acknowledgment from the student.
3. Allow the student to suggest a solution to the situation.
4. Describe the effect of the student's behavior on others
   (e.g., "It's difficult for those next to you to continue working when you kick the desk").
5. Reinforce alternative behavior and describe it when you see it
   (e.g., "Now your legs are relaxed and you're taking notes. Now we can all get something done.").

Limit Setting *(continued)*

Level of Motivation	Behavior Style			
	Self-Assertive	Socially Interactive	Analytic	Accommodating
1. Self-Absorbed				
2. Approval Oriented			■	
3. Interpersonal Loyalty	■	■		■
4. Others Oriented				

▶ **Reflecting Verbal Responses**

Verbally reflect the essence of a student's argument in order to clarify his or her true feelings.

1. Listen to the student, and try to determine his or her hidden message.
2. Repeat that message.
3. Continue to repeat such messages until no further clarification is forthcoming.
4. Do not try to guess what the underlying problem is—just reflect what is actually said.
   For example, consider the following dialogue.

   STUDENT: I hate this class.

   TEACHER: This class makes you unhappy?

   STUDENT: I just can't stand spelling.

   TEACHER: Spelling is something you would rather not do?

   STUDENT: I don't like spelling tests. I get nervous and I might fail.

   TEACHER: Spelling tests are difficult and unpleasant for you?

   STUDENT: I guess I need help in spelling.

   TEACHER: Help could be given.

5. Elicit as much information as possible. Hopefully, the student will then be able to recognize and resolve his or her own problem. You may need a different strategy to resolve the problem in the long run.

Reinforcement of Limits

Level of Motivation	Behavior Style			
	Self-Assertive	Socially Interactive	Analytic	Accommodating
1. Self-Absorbed		■	■	■
2. Approval Oriented	■	■		
3. Interpersonal Loyalty				
4. Others Oriented				

▶ Asking "What" Questions

Ask "what" questions until the student acknowledges his or her misbehavior; do not accept excuses.

1. Ask a "what" question regarding anger (e.g., "What are you angry about?").
2. Continue to ask "what" questions until the student describes his or her misbehavior without making excuses for it.
3. Ask a "how" question (e.g., "How did this angry outburst help you solve the math problem?").
4. Ask another "what" question regarding future action (e.g., "What would be a better way to express frustration next time?").
5. Reach a verbal agreement with the student regarding appropriate behavior in the future.

▶ Token Rewards

Over a period of time, reward students who demonstrate appropriate behavior with tokens that can be redeemed for a prize.

1. Brainstorm with the student to determine what rewards should be offered. Make sure rewards are appropriate.
2. Establish goals (e.g., a specific number of days with no angry outbursts or a reduced occurrence of outbursts per day or week).
3. Teach coping skills (e.g., positive self-talk or social skills training) as alternatives to angry outbursts, and discuss signs that would indicate when these skills should be employed.
4. Make a verbal or written contract with the student, and make sure that he or she understands that agreement. The contract should be positive, fair, and systematic.
5. Gradually reduce the number of tokens earned until the strategy can be phased out altogether.

▶ Suggesting Parental Intervention Strategies

Enlist the parents' help in correcting the student's behavior.

   Note. Before using this strategy, you may want to try the less intrusive Alerting Parents to Concerns and/or Exchanging Information With Parents strategies (see under *Prevention* and *Limit Setting,* respectively, in chapter 3).

1. Contact the parents, and review the facts concerning the problem.
2. Describe the student's behavior as objectively as possible. Refrain from making any judgments regarding his or her character.
3. Discuss with the parents any possible solutions they may have, and also suggest your own. Write them down.
4. Elicit an agreement from the parents regarding what measures they will take at home and how you will keep each other informed of the student's progress.

Control

Level of Motivation	Behavior Style			
	Self-Assertive	Socially Interactive	Analytic	Accommodating
1. Self-Absorbed		■	■	■
2. Approval Oriented	■	■		
3. Interpersonal Loyalty				
4. Others Oriented				

▶ Isolation Within the Classroom

Temporarily move the student to an isolated area of the classroom where he or she can continue to work.

1. Tell the class ahead of time that outbursts of anger will result in temporary removal to an isolated area of the classroom.
2. Designate a readily available area where the student can cool down without bothering others.
3. Discuss the purpose of the strategy and the requirements for rejoining the class.
4. Follow through exactly as promised.
5. Praise students when they handle situations appropriately and do not display anger.

Control *(continued)*

Level of Motivation	Behavior Style			
	Self-Assertive	Socially Interactive	Analytic	Accommodating
1. Self-Absorbed	■			
2. Approval Oriented				
3. Interpersonal Loyalty				
4. Others Oriented				

▶ **Coordinating Outside Intervention**
Coordinate help or support from an outside source (e.g., a mental health or family service agency, the legal system, etc.).

1. Keep accurate records of the student's angry behavior patterns, especially the antecedent events or consequences of anxiety.
2. Call the parents if the problem requires more attention than you are able to give.
3. Confer with the principal and other support personnel to decide whether the student's behavior warrants agency intervention.
4. Once the outside agency or agencies have been decided upon and contacted, cooperate with agency personnel, and assist them in helping the student as part of a coordinated plan.

▶ **Time Out**
Move the student to a nonstimulating environment so that he or she can cool down and regain the ability to think rationally.

1. Move the student to a designated relocation area.
2. Allow the student to rejoin the class only after he or she has cooled down or after a fixed period of time. Relocation periods longer than 15 minutes are generally not effective.
3. Try to resolve the problem that caused the anger, and discuss appropriate ways to handle frustration.
4. Increase the amount of time spent in isolation for each subsequent offense throughout the day, up to a reasonable limit.
5. Consider combining another strategy with Time Out if this strategy is not successful by itself.

▶ **Requiring a Plan for Improvement**
Separate the student from the rest of the class, and have him or her prepare a plan for improved behavior. Do not allow the student to return to the classroom until he or she presents an acceptable plan.

1. Designate a relocation area away from stimulating objects or people.
2. Have the student submit a plan that addresses the following questions: What did I do? What rule did I break? Why is this a problem? How do I plan to avoid this problem?
3. Discuss the plan with the student and encourage him or her to consider it carefully.
4. Have the student sign the plan. Have the student rewrite the plan if it is obviously not being adhered to.
5. Continue this process until a workable plan is devised and successfully implemented.

▶ **Detention**
Keep the student after school for a specified period of time.

1. Make it clear to the class that you will use detention in response to disturbances such as angry outbursts.
2. Use the detention time to develop a relationship with the student, to probe for underlying problems, to ask questions and address frustrations, and to drill the student in areas of academic weakness.
3. Work out a plan to help the student see how his or her angry outbursts have been counterproductive, and help him or her consider alternatives.
4. End detention on a positive note if at all possible.

ANXIETY

Worry or uneasiness about a situation

Prevention

Level of Motivation	Behavior Style			
	Self-Assertive	Socially Interactive	Analytic	Accommodating
1. Self-Absorbed				
2. Approval Oriented				
3. Interpersonal Loyalty			■	■
4. Others Oriented	■	■	■	■

▶ Checking for Understanding

To avoid misbehavior caused by frustration, have the student repeat instructions to make sure that he or she clearly understands what is expected.

1. Ask the student to repeat or rephrase your questions, assignments, directions, or rules.
2. If the student still fails to understand, ask another student to give the directions, or repeat them yourself. Try not to draw attention to the target student if it will increase his or her anxiety.
3. Ask the student again to answer questions about the assignment or to repeat the directions.
4. Continue until you are sure the student understands what is expected.

▶ Increasing Physical Proximity

Spend more time near the student throughout the class period.

1. Circulate throughout the classroom, especially while lecturing.
2. Walk up and down the aisles near the student, without interrupting the lecture, to gauge his or her anxiety.
3. Sit on an empty desk or chair near the student.
4. Make yourself available for questions from the student, and ask questions quietly, without drawing attention to the student.

▶ Using Humor to Relieve Stress

Use humor to lighten a stressful situation.

1. Do not use mean or sarcastic humor. Try to lighten the situation in a way that makes the real problem less imposing (e.g., "When that happened to me, I thought the earth was going to crash in around me, but it didn't" or "What do you think your parents will do? Throw you in jail?").
2. Use humor when a student is about to panic, is becoming too serious or negative, is on the verge of misbehaving, or is trying very hard but becoming frustrated.
3. Use humor that the student will understand.

Prevention *(continued)*

Level of Motivation	Behavior Style			
	Self-Assertive	Socially Interactive	Analytic	Accommodating
1. Self-Absorbed				
2. Approval Oriented				
3. Interpersonal Loyalty			■	■
4. Others Oriented	■		■	■

▶ Probing for Values

Listen for and encourage the student to express closely held values.

1. Listen to the student during situations in which he or she seems to be revealing deeply held beliefs (e.g., a class discussion relating to history or literature, in which the student refers to the importance of honesty or responsibility).

2. Look for consistent, repetitive responses to make sure that the values expressed are not simply the student's mood of the moment.

3. When anxiety occurs, ask the student about the cause of his or her anxiety and discuss related values. Help the student to put anxiety in perspective and encourage him or her to act in accordance with those values if the results will be positive for all concerned (e.g., resisting peer pressure inside or outside of school to do something potentially harmful).

Limit Setting

Level of Motivation	Behavior Style			
	Self-Assertive	Socially Interactive	Analytic	Accommodating
1. Self-Absorbed				
2. Approval Oriented			■	■
3. Interpersonal Loyalty	■	■		
4. Others Oriented				

▶ Using Affirmative Statements

Verbally acknowledge and emphasize the student's strengths and achievements.

1. Avoid placing the student in competition with other students.
2. Match the student with others who are willing to help him or her.
3. Emphasize the need for improvement, not perfection.
4. Find the student's areas of interest or ability.
   Design activities that encourage the use of those interests and abilities.
5. Remind the student of his or her past accomplishments and successes, and try to instill the idea that, having succeeded in one tough situation, he or she can succeed in another.
6. Praise the student's efforts in anxiety-producing situations (e.g., "I like the way you went right to work after I gave the assignment" or "I see you have approached this in a systematic way; that's good").

Level of Motivation	Behavior Style			
	Self-Assertive	Socially Interactive	Analytic	Accommodating
1. Self-Absorbed				
2. Approval Oriented				■
3. Interpersonal Loyalty			■	
4. Others Oriented	■	■	■	

▶ Modeling Expected Behavior

Demonstrate by example the behavior you want the student to exhibit.

1. Explain how the student's anxious behavior may be counterproductive and distracting.
2. Model alternative behaviors that can be beneficial when someone is feeling anxious (e.g., deep breathing, or talking to someone about a problem).
3. Have the student imitate your modeled behavior.
4. Verbally reinforce the student when he or she uses the modeled behavior(s) successfully in natural situations.

Limit Setting *(continued)*

Level of Motivation	Behavior Style			
	Self-Assertive	Socially Interactive	Analytic	Accommodating
1. Self-Absorbed				
2. Approval Oriented			■	■
3. Interpersonal Loyalty	■	■		
4. Others Oriented				

▶ **Reflecting Verbal Responses**

Verbally reflect the essence of a student's argument in order to clarify his or her true feelings.

1. Engage the student in a discussion about his or her anxiety.

2. Listen to what the student says and attempt to determine his or her hidden message.

3. Repeat your perception of that message
   (e.g., "What I hear you saying is..." or "I can see that you're concerned about...").

4. Continue to repeat such messages until no further clarification is forthcoming.

5. Do not try to guess at what the student may mean.
   Limit feedback to what is actually stated or observed.

Reinforcement of Limits

Level of Motivation	Behavior Style			
	Self-Assertive	Socially Interactive	Analytic	Accommodating
1. Self-Absorbed		■	■	■
2. Approval Oriented	■	■		
3. Interpersonal Loyalty				
4. Others Oriented				

▶ **Stopping and Redirecting**

Stop the student's inappropriate behavior, and redirect his or her attention to the task at hand.

1. Determine which activities or expectations may be causing the student to be anxious.
2. Ask the student to stop that behavior.
3. Redirect the student to an activity that does not produce anxiety, or restate your expectations in order to reduce the student's anxiety.
4. Check shortly thereafter to see if the student's anxiety has been reduced.

▶ **Suggesting Parental Intervention Strategies**

Enlist the parents' help in correcting the student's behavior.

Note. Before using this strategy, you may want to try the less intrusive Alerting Parents to Concerns and/or Exchanging Information With Parents strategies (see under *Prevention* and *Limit Setting,* respectively, in chapter 3).

1. Think of ways that the parents could help the student.
2. Engage in brainstorming with the parents to come up with a list of possible ways to relieve the student's anxiety.
3. Reach an agreement as to what the parents and the school can do together to improve the student's behavior.
4. Explain to the parents that they should not expect changes to occur overnight. Encourage them to keep records so that even slight improvements can be noted and appreciated.

Control

Level of Motivation	Behavior Style			
	Self-Assertive	Socially Interactive	Analytic	Accommodating
1. Self-Absorbed		■	■	■
2. Approval Oriented	■	■		
3. Interpersonal Loyalty				
4. Others Oriented				

▶ **Coordinating Outside Intervention**
Coordinate help or support from an outside source
(e.g., a mental health or family service agency, the legal system, etc.).

1. Keep accurate records of the student's behavior patterns,
   especially the antecedent events or consequences of anxiety.
2. Call the parents if the problem needs more attention than you are able to give it.
3. Contact an agency or the principal if it appears that the severity of the problem is beyond
   the expertise of the parents or the school.
4. Cooperate with agency personnel, and assist them in helping the student as part of a coordinated plan.

Level of Motivation	Behavior Style			
	Self-Assertive	Socially Interactive	Analytic	Accommodating
1. Self-Absorbed	■			
2. Approval Oriented				
3. Interpersonal Loyalty				
4. Others Oriented				

▶ **Requiring a Plan for Improvement**
Separate the student from the rest of the class, and have him or her prepare a plan for improved behavior.
Do not allow the student to return to the classroom until he or she presents an acceptable plan.

1. Designate a readily available relocation area, away from others. Relocation should not be used
   as punishment, but as an opportunity for the student to calmly approach problems in a logical,
   rational manner.
2. Have the student complete a plan that addresses the following questions: What did I do?
   Why is it a problem? What rule did I break? How do I plan to avoid this problem?
3. Discuss the plan and assure the student that, if he or she sticks with it, anxiety will decrease.
4. Have the student rewrite the plan if anxiety continues to be a problem.

ARGUING

Disputing, quarreling

Prevention

Level of Motivation	Behavior Style			
	Self-Assertive	Socially Interactive	Analytic	Accommodating
1. Self-Absorbed				
2. Approval Oriented				
3. Interpersonal Loyalty			■	■
4. Others Oriented	■	■	■	■

▶ Nonverbal Communication

Use eye contact, body movements, or hand signals to gain the student's attention.

1. Acknowledge arguing in the following ways: raise your eyebrows, scowl or frown, roll your eyes, shake your head, or stare menacingly.

2. Acknowledge appropriate behavior by smiling, nodding to show approval, or gesturing to indicate satisfaction (e.g., thumbs-up).

Level of Motivation	Behavior Style			
	Self-Assertive	Socially Interactive	Analytic	Accommodating
1. Self-Absorbed				
2. Approval Oriented				
3. Interpersonal Loyalty			■	■
4. Others Oriented	■		■	■

▶ Probing for Values

Listen for and encourage the student to express closely held values.

1. Watch for situations in which the student seems to be revealing his or her values.

2. If the student does not express positive values concerning keeping the peace, bring up the issue in a nonthreatening way during an open discussion (i.e., by describing a real example or a hypothetical scenario).

3. Look for consistent, repetitive responses to make sure that the values expressed are not simply the student's mood of the moment.

4. If arguing begins again later, ask the student to restate his or her position on arguing.

5. Ask the student to discuss the discrepancy between his or her behavior and his or her beliefs.

Prevention *(continued)*

Level of Motivation	Behavior Style			
	Self-Assertive	Socially Interactive	Analytic	Accommodating
1. Self-Absorbed				
2. Approval Oriented				
3. Interpersonal Loyalty			■	■
4. Others Oriented	■	■	■	■

▶ Alerting Parents to Concerns

Contact parents to express your concern about the student's attitude or behavior.

1. Determine and define the student's problem when planning how to approach the parents (e.g., "Sarah has been tardy 2 out of 5 days this week" or "When she's in class, she lays her head on the desk and does not enter into class discussions").

2. Describe the student's behavior as objectively as possible. Do not comment on the student's character.

3. Write down any information the parents provide that might be helpful in solving or understanding the student's problem.

4. Avoid suggesting a solution.

5. In closing the conversation, reaffirm your support for their child's education and your willingness to keep them informed as you work together for the student's benefit.

6. Thank them for their time and cooperation.

Limit Setting

Level of Motivation	Behavior Style			
	Self-Assertive	Socially Interactive	Analytic	Accommodating
1. Self-Absorbed				
2. Approval Oriented			■	■
3. Interpersonal Loyalty	■	■		
4. Others Oriented				

▶ Disguising Directives

Disguise verbal directives to stop the arguing behavior and to avoid confrontations.

1. Give the class as a whole a hint that the student who is arguing is sure to notice (e.g., "Are we discussing or arguing?").
2. Give a disguised verbal directive to the target student if he or she does not respond to the hint (e.g., "Is this discussion helping you meet your goal?").
3. Try to avoid unintentionally inviting a confrontation.

▶ Direct Commands

Make specific demands, spoken with authority, concerning the student's behavior.

1. Think of a positive way to state the command. What do you want the student to do?
2. Anticipate situations where the command must be given, and practice your tone and posture.
3. State the command assertively, firmly, and without anger (e.g., "Stop arguing").
4. Assess its effect. Did it work?
5. If there is no response, ask the student to repeat what you just said.
   If this does not achieve the desired response, move immediately to a more intrusive strategy.

▶ Probing for Motives

Ask yourself questions to determine the goal behind the student's misbehavior.

1. Consider the following questions immediately after the student's misbehavior.
   - Do I feel annoyed? Attention-getting may be or is likely the goal.
   - Do I feel beaten or intimidated? Power may be or is likely the goal.
   - Do I feel wronged or hurt? Revenge may be or is likely the goal.
   - Do I feel incapable of reaching this student? Helplessness may be or is likely the goal.
2. Respond to the appropriate motive as follows:
   - *Attention-getting.* Deprive the student of attention by quickly directing others to another task without recognizing the misbehavior.
   - *Power.* Do not allow open conflict. State the rules and consequences, and then move on.
   - *Revenge.* Find out why the student feels hurt.
   - *Helplessness.* Help the student succeed by emphasizing his or her strengths.

   Once you have determined the reason for the student's argumentativeness, you may want to try a strategy that addresses that problem directly.

Reinforcement of Limits

Level of Motivation	Behavior Style			
	Self-Assertive	Socially Interactive	Analytic	Accommodating
1. Self-Absorbed		■	■	■
2. Approval Oriented	■	■		
3. Interpersonal Loyalty				
4. Others Oriented				

▶ Asking "What" Questions

Ask "what" questions until the student acknowledges his or her misbehavior; do not accept excuses.

1. Ask a "what" question that addresses the misbehavior
   (e.g., "What are you doing now that is keeping you from your work?").
2. Continue asking "what" questions until the student describes his or her misbehavior
   without making excuses.
3. Ask, "What should you be doing?"
4. Establish a verbal plan for improvement that includes consequences for continued arguing.

▶ Positive Peer-Group Reinforcement

Provide incentives for peers to motivate students to behave appropriately.

1. Determine whether the overall maturity level of the class is sufficient to support this strategy.
2. Set an achievable goal for the class (e.g., less than three occurrences of arguing per day or week).
3. Closely monitor progress toward the goal.
   Praise the students when they handle a difficult situation appropriately.
4. Reward the class if the goal is met.
5. As arguing decreases, increase requirements for achieving the goal until the strategy
   is no longer necessary.

▶ Suggesting Parental Intervention Strategies

Enlist the parents' help in correcting the student's behavior.

   Note. Before using this strategy, you may want to try the less intrusive Alerting Parents to
Concerns and/or Exchanging Information With Parents strategies (see under *Prevention* and
Limit Setting, respectively, in chapter 3).

1. Meet with the student's parents. Share with them the facts concerning the problem, then suggest ways
   that they can help their child.
2. Focus on the least disruptive things that the parents could do.
3. Reach an agreement with the parents that includes a process by which you can monitor progress.
4. Serve as a consultant to the parents in determining whether to modify or adjust the plan.

Control

Level of Motivation	Behavior Style			
	Self-Assertive	Socially Interactive	Analytic	Accommodating
1. Self-Absorbed	■			
2. Approval Oriented				
3. Interpersonal Loyalty				
4. Others Oriented				

▶ Isolation Within the Classroom

Temporarily move the student to an isolated area of the classroom where he or she can continue to work.

1. Designate a readily available relocation area where the student cannot be bothered or noticed by others.
2. Discuss with the class why arguing will result in removal to the designated area.
3. Use the strategy exactly as promised.
4. Praise students who do not argue.
5. If isolation is not sufficient to stop the problem, consider additional strategies.

▶ Time Out

Move the student to a nonstimulating environment so that he or she can cool down and regain the ability to think rationally.

1. Determine whether the student has lost the ability to think rationally.
2. Move the student to a designated relocation area, away from stimulating objects or people.
3. Bring the student back into class once he or she has cooled down or after a designated period of time.
4. Have the student complete all assignments missed while away.

▶ Requiring a Plan for Improvement

Separate the student from the rest of the class, and have him or her prepare a plan for improved behavior. Do not allow the student to return to the classroom until he or she presents an acceptable plan.

1. Designate an isolated relocation area that is readily available.
2. Have the student submit a written plan that addresses the following questions: What did I do? Why is it a problem? What rule did I break? How do I plan to correct this behavior and avoid arguing?
3. Discuss the plan, and encourage the student to adhere to it as closely as possible.
4. Have the student sign the plan.

ATTENTION SPAN PROBLEMS

Not focusing on a task or activity for an appropriate length of time

Prevention

Level of Motivation	Behavior Style			
	Self-Assertive	Socially Interactive	Analytic	Accommodating
1. Self-Absorbed				
2. Approval Oriented				
3. Interpersonal Loyalty			■	■
4. Others Oriented		■	■	■

▶ Checking for Understanding

To avoid misbehavior caused by frustration, have the student repeat instructions to make sure that he or she clearly understands what is expected.

1. Ask questions frequently throughout the lesson.
2. Call on inattentive students to answer specific questions.
3. Vary the order in which students are chosen so that no one knows who will be called on next.
4. Reward correct answers.

▶ Increasing Physical Proximity

Spend more time near the student throughout the class period.

1. Circulate throughout the classroom.
2. Sit near the student for short periods of time.
3. Walk up and down the aisles near the student.
4. Ask the student questions or focus discussion near him or her.

▶ Introducing Role Models

Acknowledge positive behavior that the student should model.

1. Praise a student who is attending to the task (e.g., say, "Jackie is sitting quietly with her math book open, ready to listen. I like to see that. Thank you, Jackie.").
2. Closely monitor inattentive students after praising the model student's behavior.
3. Praise students who imitate the model student's behavior.
4. Reward those who stay on task.

Limit Setting

Level of Motivation	Behavior Style			
	Self-Assertive	Socially Interactive	Analytic	Accommodating
1. Self-Absorbed				
2. Approval Oriented			■	■
3. Interpersonal Loyalty		■		
4. Others Oriented				

▶ Using Affirmative Statements

Verbally acknowledge and emphasize the student's strengths and achievements.

1. Determine the student's areas of interest and abilities.
2. Design activities that capitalize on those abilities.
3. Emphasize to the student that you would like to see increased attention, not overnight perfection.
4. Avoid placing the student in a distracting or competitive situation.

▶ Disguising Directives

Disguise verbal directives to get the student to attend to the task at hand and to avoid confrontation.

1. Give the class as a whole a hint about getting back on task.
2. Give a disguised verbal directive to the student if he or she does not respond to the hint (e.g., "Remember, we have to look carefully at the sign in order to know how to solve the problem").
3. Watch the student's reaction to see if the statement was taken negatively.
4. If it was, talk to the student individually.

▶ Student Self-Monitoring

Have the student monitor his or her own behavior using charts or other means to record progress.

1. Analyze the student's short attention span: When does it happen? How often? In which subjects?
2. Record the frequency of the student's off-task behavior for a week.
3. Discuss the results and help the student to set goals for increasing his or her attention span.
4. Devise a chart to be kept by the student. Provide instruction about when and how to check whether he or she is paying attention (e.g., setting a timer for 10-minute intervals and marking the chart if he or she is on-task when the timer sounds, or looking at the clock periodically and marking the chart every 15 minutes).
5. Frequently monitor the student's progress and recording accuracy, and examine the chart with the student to see if his or her goals are being accomplished.
6. Reward attainment of the goals.

Reinforcement of Limits

Level of Motivation	Behavior Style			
	Self-Assertive	Socially Interactive	Analytic	Accommodating
1. Self-Absorbed	■	■	■	■
2. Approval Oriented		■		
3. Interpersonal Loyalty				
4. Others Oriented				

▶ Stopping and Redirecting

Stop the student's inappropriate behavior, and redirect his or her attention to the task at hand.

1. Determine why the student is not paying attention.
2. Tell the student exactly what he or she should be concentrating on.
3. Shortly thereafter, check to see if he or she is back on task.
4. Redirect the student if necessary.

▶ Asking "What" Questions

Ask "what" questions until the student acknowledges his or her misbehavior; do not accept excuses.

1. Ask a "what" question that addresses the student's misbehavior
   (e.g., "What are you doing?" or "What are you working on?").
2. Get the student to describe his or her misbehavior without making excuses.
3. Ask a "how" question
   (e.g., "How did talking to your neighbor help you with your reading assignment?").
4. Ask another "what" question
   (e.g., "What would be a better way to get your reading assignment done?").
5. Work with the student to establish a verbal or, if necessary, a written plan for improvement.
   (See Requiring a Plan for Improvement under *Control* in chapter 3.)

Control

Level of Motivation	Behavior Style			
	Self-Assertive	Socially Interactive	Analytic	Accommodating
1. Self-Absorbed	■	■	■	■
2. Approval Oriented		■		
3. Interpersonal Loyalty				
4. Others Oriented				

▶ Relocation Within the Classroom

Move the misbehaving student to a less problematic location within the classroom.

1. Identify the object or person that is causing the student to get off task.
2. Move the student to another spot in the classroom that is closer to the teacher.
3. Try to move the student without disrupting the lesson.
4. Leave the student in the new location for a specified time or until you see some improvement in his or her concentration and attentiveness.

Level of Motivation	Behavior Style			
	Self-Assertive	Socially Interactive	Analytic	Accommodating
1. Self-Absorbed	■			
2. Approval Oriented				
3. Interpersonal Loyalty				
4. Others Oriented				

▶ Requiring a Plan for Improvement

Separate the student from the rest of the class, and have him or her prepare a plan for improved behavior. Do not allow the student to return to the classroom until he or she presents an acceptable plan.

1. Designate a readily available relocation area.
2. While isolated, have the student complete a written plan that addresses the following questions: What did I do? Why is it a problem? What rule did I break? How do I plan to avoid this problem?
3. Discuss the plan with the student.
4. Refer to the plan often, and enforce the student's adherence to it.

Control *(continued)*

Level of Motivation	Behavior Style			
	Self-Assertive	Socially Interactive	Analytic	Accommodating
1. Self-Absorbed				
2. Approval Oriented	■			
3. Interpersonal Loyalty				
4. Others Oriented				

▶ Deducting Points for Misbehavior

Deduct points (or tokens) or withhold privileges the student has earned.
(Deduction of points should occur in conjunction with a token reinforcement system.)

1. Choose the number of points that will be deducted for not paying attention.
2. Inform the student that although he or she will earn points for appropriate behavior, the number of points you have chosen will be deducted when he or she fails to pay attention.
3. Initially, a nonverbal signal could be given as a warning when you observe the student not paying attention.
4. Deduct points exactly as you have stipulated if the misbehavior continues.
5. If this strategy is not effective, consider increasing the frequency with which points are awarded and/or increasing the desirability of the rewards for which points can be redeemed (e.g., rather than 10 minutes of free reading time, substitute an opportunity to play a game with a friend).
6. If the problem persists, increase the number of points deducted for each subsequent offense (e.g., 10 points for the first time, 25 points for the second time, etc.).

Level of Motivation	Behavior Style			
	Self-Assertive	Socially Interactive	Analytic	Accommodating
1. Self-Absorbed	■			
2. Approval Oriented				
3. Interpersonal Loyalty				
4. Others Oriented				

▶ Having a Parent in the Classroom

Bring one of the student's parents into the classroom to observe the student's lack of attention to tasks, and the subsequent problems that result.

Note. Before using this strategy, you may want to try one or more of the following three less intrusive strategies: Alerting Parents to Concerns, Exchanging Information With Parents, and Suggesting Parental Intervention Strategies (see under *Prevention, Limit Setting,* and *Reinforcement of Limits,* respectively, in chapter 3).

1. Ask one or both parents to attend a typical class session for at least one hour.
2. Notify the student that his or her parent(s) will be coming to class to observe.
3. Have the parent(s) sit near the back of the room.
4. Schedule some time after class to talk with the parent(s) about what went on and to discuss ways to remedy the situation.

BABY TALK

Use of verbal conversation that is significantly below age or maturity level

Prevention

Level of Motivation	Behavior Style			
	Self-Assertive	Socially Interactive	Analytic	Accommodating
1. Self-Absorbed				
2. Approval Oriented				
3. Interpersonal Loyalty			■	■
4. Others Oriented		■	■	■

▶ Ignoring Misbehavior

Eliminate the student's payoff for inappropriate attention-getting behavior by refusing to acknowledge it.

1. Determine whether the student's baby talk is being used to gain attention.
2. Decide whether the baby talk can be allowed to continue for short intervals without disturbing other students.
3. Choose to ignore the baby talk the next time it occurs.
4. Although there may be a temporary increase in the misbehavior, baby talk should decrease or disappear within 2 to 3 weeks.
5. Praise significant attempts to avoid using baby talk
   (e.g., say, "I really like the way you answer my questions in such a grown-up way").

▶ Nonverbal Communication

Use eye contact, body movements, or hand signals to gain the student's attention.

1. Acknowledge positive behavior by smiling, nodding your head, and so on.
2. Acknowledge baby talk by raising your eyebrows, scowling, or shaking your head.
3. Record the ratio of negative to positive gestures throughout the day to assess the effectiveness of this approach.

▶ Asking Adult Questions

Use adult-oriented questions to appeal to the student's rational abilities.

1. Assume that the student is rational in spite of his or her use of baby talk.
2. Ask an adult-oriented question that appeals to the student's rational state
   (e.g., "What are some other ways that you could say this?" or "When people make fun of the way you talk, what are you going to do?").
3. Avoid judgmental questions or comments (e.g., do not say, "Why do you always have to talk like a baby?" or "Stop acting like a baby. You're an embarrassment to be around.").

Limit Setting

Level of Motivation	Behavior Style			
	Self-Assertive	Socially Interactive	Analytic	Accommodating
1. Self-Absorbed				
2. Approval Oriented			■	■
3. Interpersonal Loyalty		■		
4. Others Oriented				

▶ Announcing/Rehearsing the Rules

Establish rules regarding behavior in the classroom in order to define boundaries, expectations, and the consequences for misbehavior. Review them regularly.

1. Establish clear expectations and rules for appropriate speech in the classroom.
2. Be sure the students understand the consequences for breaking the rules.
3. Post the rules in a conspicuous place at the front of the classroom.
4. Repeat the rules and the consequences for breaking them, until students can recite and follow them automatically, and can paraphrase the reasons behind them.
5. Have the target student repeat the rules aloud.
6. Enforce the rules without fail. Be consistent.

▶ Disguising Directives

Disguise verbal directives to get the student to behave and to avoid confrontation.

1. Make a general statement or give the class as a whole a hint regarding the type of speech expected (e.g., "Remember, people like being able to understand what someone is saying").
2. Do not address any particular individual when giving the hint.
3. If the student does not respond to the classroom hint, use a disguised verbal directive (e.g., "Would you like to repeat what you just said so that everyone can hear and understand?").

▶ Modeling Expected Behavior

Demonstrate by example the behavior you want the student to exhibit.

1. Do not respond to baby talk with laughter, smiles, anger, or verbal reprimands.
2. When baby talk occurs, restate what the student has said in a more age-appropriate manner.
3. Expect the student to model the correct manner of speaking.
4. Consistently speak as you would like to have the student speak.

Reinforcement of Limits

Level of Motivation	Behavior Style			
	Self-Assertive	Socially Interactive	Analytic	Accommodating
1. Self-Absorbed		■	■	■
2. Approval Oriented	■	■		
3. Interpersonal Loyalty				
4. Others Oriented	■			

▶ Establishing Logical Consequences

Establish logical consequences for certain behaviors.

1. Make a list of classroom rules. Be sure the students understand what is meant by the term *baby talk*.
2. Remember to keep the rules positive and not demeaning
   (e.g., "Fourth graders should speak so that everyone can understand them").
3. Rehearse expected responses with the students.
4. Establish logical consequences for baby talk (e.g., having the student remain in the classroom during recess or lunch in order to practice more effective ways of communicating).
5. Make sure that the punishment and rewards fit the behavior.

Level of Motivation	Behavior Style			
	Self-Assertive	Socially Interactive	Analytic	Accommodating
1. Self-Absorbed		■	■	■
2. Approval Oriented	■	■		
3. Interpersonal Loyalty	■			
4. Others Oriented	■			

▶ Setting Achievable Goals

Establish achievable goals to improve behavior step-by-step.

1. Assess the student's baby talk to determine which words are used most frequently and how they are used in sentences. Determine specifically what elements of speech you need to concentrate on.
2. Decide on a specific, realistic goal that would increase the student's positive speech patterns.
   For example, have the student concentrate on the first three words of each response to the teacher.
3. Verbally encourage the student each time the goal is achieved.
4. Once a goal is mastered, set a new, more challenging goal.
5. Work on one problem at a time, and look for successful correction of a problem before moving on.

Reinforcement of Limits *(continued)*

Level of Motivation	Behavior Style			
	Self-Assertive	Socially Interactive	Analytic	Accommodating
1. Self-Absorbed		■	■	■
2. Approval Oriented	■	■		
3. Interpersonal Loyalty				
4. Others Oriented	■			

▶ Using Written Contracts

Have the student agree, in writing, to follow a plan for improved behavior.

1. Prepare a list of rules regarding the use of a baby talk, and a list of the consequences for both breaking and following those rules. Put the word *contract* at the top of the list.
2. Discuss the contract with the student.
3. Agree on the exact details of the contract, including how you will chart and evaluate the student's progress. Have the student sign the contract along with you.
4. Enthusiastically reward the first signs of progress.

Control

Level of Motivation	Behavior Style			
	Self-Assertive	Socially Interactive	Analytic	Accommodating
1. Self-Absorbed	■			
2. Approval Oriented				
3. Interpersonal Loyalty				
4. Others Oriented				

▶ Exclusion From Fun Activities
Exclude the student from an activity he or she enjoys.
1. Warn students that any baby talk during an enjoyable activity will result in exclusion from that activity.
2. Remove any student who resorts to baby talk.
3. Verbally encourage those who speak correctly during the activity.
4. Follow through consistently every time an offense occurs. Be sure the student understands the offense.
5. Allow the student to observe the forfeited activity from a distance.

▶ Time Out for a Specified Period or Activity
Establish rules in advance for the use of specified periods of time out in response to inappropriate behavior.
1. Tell the class that continued use of baby talk will not be tolerated in the classroom.
2. Explain the Time Out strategy (see Time Out under *Control* in chapter 3).
3. Follow through exactly as promised.
4. Establish a specific amount of time that the student will be removed from the classroom for baby talk, and require him or her to make up any assignments missed.
5. Increase the amount of time spent in isolation for each subsequent offense.

▶ Deducting Points for Misbehavior
Deduct points (or tokens) or withhold privileges the student has earned.
(Deduction of points should occur in conjunction with a token reinforcement system.)
1. Choose the number of points that will be deducted for engaging in baby talk.
2. Inform the student that although he or she will earn points for appropriate behavior, the number of points you have chosen will be deducted when he or she engages in baby talk.
3. Give the student one warning before actually beginning to deduct points.
4. Deduct points exactly as you have stipulated if the baby talk continues.
5. If this strategy is not effective, consider increasing the frequency with which points are awarded and/or increasing the desirability of the rewards for which points can be redeemed (e.g., rather than 10 minutes of free reading time, substitute an opportunity to play an enjoyable computer game that is normally restricted).
6. If the problem persists, increase the number of points deducted for each subsequent offense (e.g., 10 points for the first time, 25 points for the second time, etc.).

BOSSINESS

Inappropriate use of physical or verbal communication to manipulate or control others

Prevention

Level of Motivation	Behavior Style			
	Self-Assertive	Socially Interactive	Analytic	Accommodating
1. Self-Absorbed				
2. Approval Oriented				
3. Interpersonal Loyalty	■		■	
4. Others Oriented	■	■	■	

▶ Introducing Role Models

Acknowledge positive behavior that the student should model.

1. Identify a student who is admired by the misbehaving student.

2. Praise the idealized student for behavior that you want the misbehaving student to emulate. Praise other students who accept help or directions and are able to work cooperatively.

3. Give group leadership tasks to students with cooperative attitudes, and make it clear that it is because they are cooperative that you trust them with responsibility (e.g., say, "I noticed that you are very cooperative, and I want you to be the group leader for this project").

4. Reward noticeably improved behavior.

Limit Setting

Level of Motivation	Behavior Style			
	Self-Assertive	Socially Interactive	Analytic	Accommodating
1. Self-Absorbed				
2. Approval Oriented	■		■	■
3. Interpersonal Loyalty		■	■	■
4. Others Oriented				

▶ Disguising Directives

Disguise verbal directives to get the student to behave and to avoid confrontation.

1. Give the class as a whole a hint that those who are misbehaving are sure to notice
   (e.g., "People like to be around those who are considerate of them and who do not boss them around").
2. Give a disguised verbal directive to the target student
   (e.g., "Would you like to put that in the form of a question?").
3. Try to avoid inviting a confrontation.

Level of Motivation	Behavior Style			
	Self-Assertive	Socially Interactive	Analytic	Accommodating
1. Self-Absorbed				
2. Approval Oriented			■	■
3. Interpersonal Loyalty	■	■	■	■
4. Others Oriented				

▶ Describing Misbehavior as It Occurs

Describe to the student what he or she has just done, is doing, or is about to do.

1. Privately describe to the student exactly what is occurring
   (e.g., "When you are in a group, you tell the others what to do rather than discussing it with them").
2. Wait for a sign that the student understands that his or her behavior is wrong,
   then allow the student to suggest a solution.
3. Describe to the student the reaction of other students when he or she bosses them
   (e.g., "When you tell other students what to do, they argue with you or ignore you").

▶ Direct Commands

Make specific demands, spoken with authority, concerning the student's behavior.

1. Anticipate situations where commands must be given, and practice your tone and posture.
2. State the command in a positive way (e.g., "Bill, please allow Robert to do his own work").
3. Assess the student's response: Did the bossiness stop? For how long?
   What were the positive and negative results?

Reinforcement of Limits

Level of Motivation	Behavior Style			
	Self-Assertive	Socially Interactive	Analytic	Accommodating
1. Self-Absorbed		■	■	■
2. Approval Oriented	■	■		
3. Interpersonal Loyalty				
4. Others Oriented				

▶ Stopping and Redirecting
Stop the student's inappropriate behavior, and redirect his or her attention to the task at hand.
1. Identify the circumstances that result in the student's bossiness.
2. Ask the student to stop that particular behavior (e.g., say, "Please do not boss your group around").
3. Tell the student exactly what he or she should be concentrating on
   (e.g., say, "Ask nicely when you want to get your group's cooperation").
4. Shortly thereafter, check to see if the student has obeyed your directive.

▶ Positive Peer-Group Reinforcement
Provide incentives for peers to motivate students to behave appropriately.
1. Determine the maturity level of the class as a whole, and devise a motivation method commensurate with their ability to respond positively.
2. Establish an obtainable goal for the class.
3. Closely monitor the students' progress toward their goal.
4. Model ways to achieve the goal.
5. Reward the students for the achievement of their goal.

▶ Charting Progress
Use charts to monitor misbehavior and check the student's progress.
1. Define for the student exactly what words or actions are considered bossy.
2. Set specific goals designed to eliminate such bossiness.
3. Maintain a chart showing occurrences of bossiness. Reward reductions in bossiness until it is eliminated.
4. Intermittently reward students with verbal praise after bossiness has been effectively eliminated.

▶ Suggesting Parental Intervention Strategies
Enlist the parents' help in correcting the student's behavior.
   Note. Before using this strategy, you may want to try the less intrusive Alerting Parents to Concerns and/or Exchanging Information With Parents strategies (see under *Prevention* and *Limit Setting,* respectively, in chapter 3).
1. Contact the parents, and review the facts concerning the problem.
2. Describe the student's behavior as objectively as possible.
   Refrain from making any judgments regarding his or her character.
3. Discuss with the parents any possible solutions they may have, and also suggest your own. Write them down.
4. Elicit an agreement from the parents regarding what measures they will take at home and how you will keep each other informed of the student's progress.

Control

Level of Motivation	Behavior Style			
	Self-Assertive	Socially Interactive	Analytic	Accommodating
1. Self-Absorbed	■			
2. Approval Oriented				
3. Interpersonal Loyalty				
4. Others Oriented				

▶ ### Exclusion From Fun Activities

Exclude the student from an activity he or she enjoys.

1. Inform the student that cooperative behavior is a prerequisite for participation in a particular enjoyable activity.
2. Remove the student if he or she attempts to manipulate or control others verbally or physically.
3. Let the student observe others working cooperatively from a distance if he or she can do so without causing a disturbance.
4. Establish a plan or procedure that the student must follow before being allowed to return to the activity.

▶ ### Requiring a Plan for Improvement

Separate the student from the rest of the class, and have him or her prepare a plan for improved behavior. Do not allow the student to return to the classroom until he or she presents an acceptable plan.

1. Designate a relocation area away from any stimulating persons, objects, or activities.
2. Have the student complete a written plan that addresses the following questions: What did I do? Why is it a problem? What rule did I break? How do I plan to avoid being bossy in the future?
3. Discuss the plan, and encourage the student to rethink problem areas.
4. Enforce the student's adherence to the plan, and refer to it often when dealing with subsequent occurrences of bossiness.
5. If the plan does not work, require the student to develop another plan. Do not accept a simple vow to do better.

CALLING OUT ANSWERS

Responding to questions without waiting to be called on
(especially troublesome in large group discussions)

Prevention

Level of Motivation	Behavior Style			
	Self-Assertive	Socially Interactive	Analytic	Accommodating
1. Self-Absorbed				
2. Approval Oriented				
3. Interpersonal Loyalty			■	■
4. Others Oriented		■	■	■

▶ Using a Businesslike Teaching Style
Maintain a productive, businesslike atmosphere in the classroom.
1. If student interaction and participation become disorderly and interfere with learning, plan well-organized lessons and activities with clear expectations of on-task behavior.
2. Maintain a productive, yet supportive and caring, atmosphere in the classroom.
3. Make it clear that a student must always raise his or her hand before giving an answer in large group discussions.
4. Ignore students who call out answers; allow responses only from those who raise their hand. If necessary, use a direct command to tell a student to raise his or her hand before talking.

▶ Introducing Role Models
Acknowledge positive behavior that the student should model.
1. Praise students who raise their hand before answering in large group discussions.
2. Ignore answers called out without permission.
3. Point out and praise behavior you want the students to emulate (e.g., say, "I like the way you raised your hand before answering").
4. Reward students who raise their hand and who are held in high esteem by students who seldom raise their hand.

▶ Sharing Authority and Decision Making
Give peers some authority to help stop a student's misbehavior.
1. Establish and discuss the rule that students are to raise their hand and wait to be called on before answering a question.
2. Emphasize the need for a cooperative class effort to help stop students who call out answers in class without first raising their hand and getting permission to speak.
3. Develop a nonverbal signal to be given by a dependable student near the target student.
4. Praise both the target student and the student helper each time they behave as directed.

Limit Setting

Level of Motivation	Behavior Style			
	Self-Assertive	Socially Interactive	Analytic	Accommodating
1. Self-Absorbed				
2. Approval Oriented			■	■
3. Interpersonal Loyalty		■		
4. Others Oriented				

▶ Announcing/Rehearsing the Rules

Establish rules regarding behavior in the classroom in order to define boundaries, expectations, and the consequences for misbehavior. Review them regularly.

1. Be sure that a rule requiring students to raise their hand before speaking is prominently posted with other classroom rules.
2. When a student calls out an answer without first raising his or her hand and getting permission to speak, calmly restate the rule regarding such behavior (e.g., say, "Rule 2 for our classroom is that you must raise your hand before answering").
3. Repeat the question that elicited the student's unauthorized response, and call on the same student if his or her hand is raised. Otherwise, call on a different student whose hand is raised.

▶ Describing Misbehavior as It Occurs

Describe to the student what he or she has just done, is doing, or is about to do.

1. When a student calls out an answer without permission, describe to that student exactly what he or she has just done (e.g., "Jane was given permission to answer, and you called out the answer without permission").
2. Wait for some sign that the student understands that his or her behavior is wrong.
3. Describe how calling out answers without permission affects the other students.
4. Repeat the question that elicited the student's unauthorized response. If the same student raises his or her hand, be sure to call on that student.

▶ Student Self-Monitoring

Have the student monitor his or her own behavior using charts or other means to record progress.

1. Observe and record the number of times the student calls out answers without permission within a specified time period (e.g., within 10 minutes or during the language lesson).
2. Present that information to the student and discuss the results.
3. Work with the student to establish realistic goals for improvement (e.g., reduce unauthorized answers to three per language class the first day, two the second day, and so on).
4. Show the student how and when to record his or her behavior.
5. Establish incentives for meeting goals on schedule.
6. If the student has difficulty reducing misbehavior beyond a certain point, consider changing the consequences for not meeting goals on schedule.

Reinforcement of Limits

Level of Motivation	Behavior Style			
	Self-Assertive	Socially Interactive	Analytic	Accommodating
1. Self-Absorbed		■	■	■
2. Approval Oriented	■	■		
3. Interpersonal Loyalty	■			
4. Others Oriented				

▶ Stopping and Redirecting

Stop the student's inappropriate behavior, and redirect his or her attention to the task at hand.

1. When misbehavior occurs, stop it with a direct statement (e.g., "Stop calling out answers").
2. Redirect the student to the appropriate behavior
   (e.g., say, "If you want to speak, please raise your hand").
3. If the student then raises his or her hand, respond positively
   (e.g., say, "Good. That's the way I want you to respond when I ask a question of the class.").

▶ Asking "What" Questions

Ask "what" questions until the student acknowledges his or her misbehavior; do not accept excuses.

1. When the student calls out an answer without permission, ask "What are you doing?"
2. Get the student to describe his or her misbehavior without making excuses for it.
3. Ask a "how" question (e.g., "How do you think other students feel when you call out an answer that they wanted to give?").
4. Ask another "what" question (e.g., "What would be a better way to respond next time?").
5. Obtain a verbal commitment from the student to change his or her behavior.

▶ Tangible Reinforcement

Give students tangible, immediately satisfying rewards for appropriate behavior.

1. Observe the student to see how many times he or she calls out answers during a specific class session.
2. Discuss the problem with the student and set up a system by which he or she will be rewarded with prizes for improved behavior.
3. Reward the student as soon as possible after he or she behaves appropriately.
4. Switch to the Token Rewards strategy once behavior is within acceptable limits.

Control

Level of Motivation	Behavior Style			
	Self-Assertive	Socially Interactive	Analytic	Accommodating
1. Self-Absorbed	■			
2. Approval Oriented				
3. Interpersonal Loyalty				
4. Others Oriented				

▶ Time Out for a Specified Period or Activity

Establish rules in advance for the use of specified periods of time out in response to angry outbursts.

1. Designate an isolation area within the classroom.
2. Discuss with the class what will happen if someone calls out an answer without permission.
3. Praise students who respond appropriately, and occasionally remind them to be sure to raise their hand before speaking.
4. Increase the time in the isolation area for each subsequent infraction.
5. Follow through exactly as promised.

▶ Requiring a Plan for Improvement

Separate the student from the rest of the class, and have him or her prepare a plan for improved behavior. Do not allow the student to return to the classroom until he or she presents an acceptable plan.

1. Designate an isolated relocation area that is readily available (e.g., another classroom or a separate area of the classroom).
2. Have the student submit a written plan that addresses the following questions: What did I do? Why is it a problem? What rule did I break? How do I plan to correct this behavior and avoid calling out without permission?
3. Discuss the plan and encourage the student to adhere to it as closely as possible.
4. Have the student sign the written plan.
5. Praise the student's improved behavior.

▶ Deducting Points for Misbehavior

Deduct points (or tokens) or withhold privileges the student has earned.
(Deduction of points should occur in conjunction with a token reinforcement system.)

1. Choose the number of points that will be deducted for calling out answers.
2. Inform the student that although he or she will earn points for appropriate behavior, the number of points that you have chosen will be deducted for calling out answers. When dealing with a group behavior problem, announce and post the terms of this rule.
3. Deduct points exactly as you have stipulated when the offense occurs, after one warning per each class discussion period.
4. If this strategy is not effective, consider increasing the frequency with which points are awarded and/or increasing the desirability of the rewards for which points can be redeemed (e.g., rather than 10 minutes of free reading time, substitute an opportunity to play a game with a friend).
5. After the warning and the first deduction of points, increase the number of points deducted for each subsequent offense during a single class discussion period (e.g., 10 points for the first time, 25 points for the second time, etc.).

CHEATING

Copying other students' answers, taking credit for other students' work,
or inappropriately accessing information

Prevention

Level of Motivation	Behavior Style			
	Self-Assertive	Socially Interactive	Analytic	Accommodating
1. Self-Absorbed				
2. Approval Oriented				
3. Interpersonal Loyalty			■	■
4. Others Oriented			■	■

▶ Checking for Understanding
To avoid misbehavior caused by frustration, have the student repeat instructions to make sure that he or she clearly understands what is expected.

1. Ask questions frequently throughout the lesson or activity.
2. Explain directions or present information in a number of ways. Check for understanding frequently.
3. Have students explain how to solve a problem or how they arrived at their answer.

Level of Motivation	Behavior Style			
	Self-Assertive	Socially Interactive	Analytic	Accommodating
1. Self-Absorbed				
2. Approval Oriented				
3. Interpersonal Loyalty			■	■
4. Others Oriented	■	■	■	■

▶ Alerting Parents to Concerns
Contact parents to express your concern about the student's attitude or behavior.

1. Determine whether the student's cheating is severe enough to be of concern to the parents.
2. Decide in advance which specific observations you will share with the parents so that no misunderstandings occur.
3. Avoid leading the parents to a solution. Simply bring the problem to their attention.
4. Write down any information the parents provide that might be helpful in solving the student's problem.
5. In closing the conversation, reaffirm your support for their child's education and your willingness to work with them.
6. Thank them for their time and cooperation.

Limit Setting

Level of Motivation	Behavior Style			
	Self-Assertive	Socially Interactive	Analytic	Accommodating
1. Self-Absorbed				
2. Approval Oriented			■	■
3. Interpersonal Loyalty	■	■	■	■
4. Others Oriented				

▶ Announcing/Rehearsing the Rules

Establish rules regarding behavior in the classroom in order to define boundaries, expectations, and the consequences for misbehavior. Review them regularly.

1. Talk with the students about honesty and obedience. Explain how cheating violates these ethics.
2. Make the rules and consequences regarding cheating very clear, and post those rules conspicuously.
3. Repeat the rules and the consequences for breaking them, until students can recite and follow them automatically, and can paraphrase the reasons behind them.
4. Evaluate whether the rules and the consequences for breaking them are effective and clearly understood.
5. Enforce the rules consistently.

▶ Disguising Directives

Disguise verbal directives to get the student to behave and to avoid confrontation.

1. When cheating is detected, respond verbally (e.g., say, "What might I think if I see your eyes wandering?" or "There is no reason why anyone should have another person's assignment").
2. Wait a minute to see if the suspicious behavior has ceased.
3. If cheating continues, use a more intrusive strategy.

▶ Student Self-Monitoring

Have the student monitor his or her own behavior using charts or other means to record progress.

1. Discuss his or her cheating with the student.
2. Identify the events leading up to cheating (e.g., not studying the night before a test, improper note taking, not listening during class discussions, etc.).
3. Establish a goal to increase behavior that would likely decrease the temptation to cheat (e.g., proper study habits, improved note taking and listening).
4. Break down the behaviors into workable steps on a chart or checklist.
5. Teach the student to check the appropriate space every time he or she performs the desired behavior.
6. Establish a reward for successfully meeting the goal.

▶ Exchanging Information With Parents

Work with the student's parents to gather information that might help resolve the problem.
   Note. Before using this strategy, you may want to try the less intrusive Alerting Parents to Concerns strategy (see under *Prevention* in chapter 3).

1. Before calling the parents, write down any unanswered questions about the student's study habits or activities outside school that may be contributing to the misbehavior.
2. Contact the parents and frankly describe the student's cheating. Be as specific as possible.
3. At this point, avoid suggesting solutions to the parents.
4. Write down any information that might be helpful in solving the problem.
5. In closing the conversation, reaffirm your support for their child's education and your willingness to communicate with them.
6. Thank them for their time and cooperation.

Reinforcement of Limits

Level of Motivation	Behavior Style			
	Self-Assertive	Socially Interactive	Analytic	Accommodating
1. Self-Absorbed		■	■	■
2. Approval Oriented	■	■		
3. Interpersonal Loyalty				
4. Others Oriented				

▶ **Stopping and Redirecting**

Stop the student's inappropriate behavior, and redirect his or her attention to the task at hand.

1. When you suspect cheating, ask the student to stop it (e.g., say, "Stop looking at Gary's paper").
2. Redirect the student to the appropriate behavior
   (e.g., say, "Look at your own paper, and complete the test").
3. Shortly thereafter, ask the student another question to see if he or she has complied
   (e.g., "Are you working on your paper?").

▶ **Asking "What" Questions**

Ask "what" questions until the student acknowledges his or her misbehavior; do not accept excuses.

1. Ask a "what" question when you suspect the student of cheating (e.g., "What are you doing?").
2. Continue to ask "what" questions until the student describes his or her behavior
   without making excuses.
3. If the student denies cheating, have him or her describe exactly what was happening.
4. Ask a "how" question next
   (e.g., "How could looking at your neighbor's paper during the test cause you problems?").
5. Ask another "what" question
   (e.g., "What can you do to avoid cheating or the appearance of cheating in the future?").
6. Establish a verbal agreement with the student, and monitor his or her progress closely.

▶ **Suggesting Parental Intervention Strategies**

Enlist the parents' help in correcting the student's behavior.

   Note. Before using this strategy, you may want to try the less intrusive Alerting Parents to Concerns and/or Exchanging Information With Parents strategies (see under *Prevention* and *Limit Setting,* respectively, in chapter 3).

1. Think of things that the parents could do to help the student solve his or her cheating problem.
2. Contact the parents, inform them of the problem, and recommend some solutions.
3. Reach agreement with the parents regarding each person's role in ending the student's cheating.
4. Establish checkpoints, and plan to discuss the student's progress.
5. Adapt the plan as needed.

Control

Level of Motivation	Behavior Style			
	Self-Assertive	Socially Interactive	Analytic	Accommodating
1. Self-Absorbed	■			
2. Approval Oriented				
3. Interpersonal Loyalty				
4. Others Oriented				

▶ Deducting Points for Misbehavior

Deduct points (or tokens) or withhold privileges the student has earned.
(Deduction of points should occur in conjunction with a token reinforcement system.)

1. Announce that cheating will result in the loss of points or privileges, and post a reminder.

2. Deduct a specified number of points if the student is on a token reinforcement system, or deduct points from his or her score on a test or other assignment.

3. If this strategy is not effective, consider increasing the frequency with which points are awarded and/or increasing the desirability of the rewards for which points can be redeemed (e.g., rather than 10 minutes of free time, substitute an opportunity to play an enjoyable computer game that is normally restricted).

4. If the problem persists, increase the number of points deducted for each subsequent offense (e.g., 10 points for the first time, 25 points for the second time, etc.).

▶ Detention

Keep the student after school for a specified period of time.

1. Before a test or some other activity where cheating may occur, announce that the consequence for cheating is detention.

2. Use detention time to have the student redo work done by cheating.

3. If that work is not acceptable, have the student spend additional time in detention to study or do homework for a specified period (e.g., 3 days).

4. At the end of that period, have the student do the work again.

▶ Having a Parent in the Classroom

Bring one of the student's parents into the classroom to observe the student's behavior there.

   Note. Before using this strategy, you may want to try one or more of the following three less intrusive strategies: Alerting Parents to Concerns, Exchanging Information With Parents, and Suggesting Parental Intervention Strategies (see under *Prevention, Limit Setting,* and *Reinforcement of Limits,* respectively, in chapter 3).

1. Ask one of the student's parents to attend the next test-taking session.

2. Let the student know that his or her parent will be coming to class to observe. Explain that this is the only way you know to keep him or her from cheating, as other attempts have not worked.

3. Have the parent sit where he or she has a clear view of the student.

4. Schedule time afterward to meet with the parent and the student to discuss the experience. A less intrusive plan could be developed at that time. Make it clear to the student that the parent and you are willing to take this measure again to stop the cheating behavior.

CUTTING IN LINE

Stepping into a waiting line of students inappropriately

Prevention

Level of Motivation	Behavior Style			
	Self-Assertive	Socially Interactive	Analytic	Accommodating
1. Self-Absorbed				
2. Approval Oriented				
3. Interpersonal Loyalty			■	■
4. Others Oriented		■	■	■

▶ Sharing Authority and Decision Making

Give peers some authority to help stop a student's misbehavior.

1. Schedule a formal or informal class meeting or discussion group, preferably as part of a regularly scheduled meeting, to review the rules regarding cutting in line.
2. Allow students to express their feelings about cutting in line.
3. Discuss the consequences for cutting in line.
4. Try to bring the group to a consensus, but do not allow a decision by vote. Retain veto power, but use it only if absolutely necessary.
5. Have students help enforce the new rule. Acknowledge and praise acceptable behavior as it occurs.

Limit Setting

Level of Motivation	Behavior Style			
	Self-Assertive	Socially Interactive	Analytic	Accommodating
1. Self-Absorbed				
2. Approval Oriented			■	■
3. Interpersonal Loyalty	■	■	■	■
4. Others Oriented				

▶ Modeling Expected Behavior

Demonstrate by example the behavior you want the student to exhibit.

1. Discuss with the student the need for orderly conduct in line.
2. Model appropriate "standing in line" behavior.
3. Have the student demonstrate the appropriate behavior in your presence.
4. Remind the student periodically of the appropriate behavior.

▶ Probing for Motives

Ask yourself questions to determine the goal behind the student's misbehavior.

1. Consider the following questions immediately after the student's misbehavior:
   • Do I feel annoyed? Attention-getting may be or is likely the goal.
   • Do I feel beaten or intimidated? Power may be or is likely the goal.
   • Do I feel wronged or hurt? Revenge may be or is likely the goal.
   • Do I feel incapable of reaching this student? Helplessness may be or is likely the goal.
2. Respond to the appropriate motive as follows:
   • *Attention-getting.* Deprive the student of attention.
   • *Power.* Do not allow open conflict. State the rules and consequences, and then move on.
   • *Revenge.* Find out why the student feels hurt.
   • *Helplessness.* Provide opportunities for the student to succeed.

   Depending on the student's motives, more intrusive strategies may be necessary.

Limit Setting (continued)

Level of Motivation	Behavior Style			
	Self-Assertive	Socially Interactive	Analytic	Accommodating
1. Self-Absorbed		■	■	■
2. Approval Oriented	■	■		
3. Interpersonal Loyalty				
4. Others Oriented				

▶ **Student Self-Monitoring**

Have the student monitor his or her own behavior using charts or other means to record progress.

1. Analyze the student's pattern of cutting in line, and determine how and when he or she decides to do so.

2. Chart the instances of cutting in line. Discuss with the student the frequency of his or her behavior.

3. Work with the student to set specific, realistic goals (e.g., no cutting in line at lunch for one week).

4. Once a goal is consistently attained, a new goal should be set.

5. Establish rewards for the completion of goals.

6. Have the student maintain a neat, handwritten chart to monitor his or her progress (e.g., the student records a point for every instance of waiting his or her turn).

7. Monitor the student's accuracy in recording his or her behavior.

Reinforcement of Limits

Level of Motivation	Behavior Style			
	Self-Assertive	Socially Interactive	Analytic	Accommodating
1. Self-Absorbed		■	■	■
2. Approval Oriented	■	■		
3. Interpersonal Loyalty				
4. Others Oriented				

▶ Establishing Logical Consequences

Establish logical consequences for certain behaviors.

1. Make a list of classroom rules, and make sure the students know the rules concerning cutting in line.

2. Rehearse the rules and the consequences for breaking them until each student fully understands the cause-and-effect relationships.

3. When misbehavior occurs, choose the appropriate logical consequence and explain the cause-and-effect relationship to the student (e.g., say, "The penalty for cutting in line is moving to the end of the line").

▶ Positive Peer-Group Reinforcement

Provide incentives for peers to motivate students to behave appropriately.

1. Determine the overall maturity level of the class, and use the reinforcement method that seems most appropriate for that level.

2. Set an obtainable goal for the class (e.g., walking in their assigned order to and from lunch for a whole week).

3. Monitor the students' progress closely.

4. Model ways to achieve the goal and encourage students as they line up properly.

5. Reward accomplishment of the goal.

▶ Tangible Reinforcement

Give students tangible, immediately satisfying rewards for appropriate behavior.

1. See how often the student cuts in line during a specific activity (e.g., lunch).

2. Discuss the issue with the student, and establish a reward to be given each time he or she does not cut in line during that activity.

3. Reward the student as soon as possible after each time he or she behaves appropriately in line.

Control

Level of Motivation	Behavior Style			
	Self-Assertive	Socially Interactive	Analytic	Accommodating
1. Self-Absorbed	■			
2. Approval Oriented				
3. Interpersonal Loyalty				
4. Others Oriented				

▶ Exclusion From Fun Activities

Exclude the student from an activity he or she enjoys.

1. Determine which activity or privilege the student would most hate to be excluded from.
2. After the student cuts in line, issue a warning that if it happens again, his or her participation in the activity or privilege will be forfeited.
3. If cutting in line occurs again, follow through exactly as promised.
4. Allow the student to observe the activity from a distance, as long as he or she is not disruptive.
5. Each time cutting in line occurs, increase the time away from the preferred activity or privilege.

▶ Time Out for a Specified Period or Activity

Establish rules in advance for the use of specified periods of time out in response to angry outbursts.

1. Designate a relocation area away from class activity.
2. Establish a rule that students who cut in line will go to that area for a specified length of time (e.g., send a student who cuts in the lunch line to the relocation area for a period of time, allowing enough remaining lunch time to eat lunch, but not to socialize).
3. Discuss the reasons for time out with the class and the consequences for repeated misbehavior.
4. Carry out the time-out procedure exactly as it was described to the students.
5. If the behavior continues, increase the duration of time out or have the student develop a plan to change his or her behavior.

▶ Requiring a Plan for Improvement

Separate the student from the rest of the class, and have him or her prepare a plan for improved behavior. Do not allow the student to return to the classroom until he or she presents an acceptable plan.

1. Designate an isolated relocation area away from stimulating objects or people.
2. Have the student who cut in line prepare a written plan that addresses the following questions: What did I do? What rule did I break? Why is this a problem? How do I plan to avoid this behavior?
3. Discuss the plan with the student and reach an agreement on how to improve his or her behavior.
4. Have the student sign the plan, and enforce his or her adherence to it. Rewrite the plan if the student does not adhere to it.
5. Continue this process until a workable plan is devised.

DEFIANCE

Refusing to obey a person in authority

Limit Setting

Level of Motivation	Behavior Style			
	Self-Assertive	Socially Interactive	Analytic	Accommodating
1. Self-Absorbed				
2. Approval Oriented			■	■
3. Interpersonal Loyalty	■	■	■	■
4. Others Oriented				

▶ Probing for Motives

Ask yourself questions to determine the goal behind the student's misbehavior.

1. Ask the following questions immediately after the misbehavior:
    *   Do I feel annoyed? Attention-getting may be or is likely the goal.
    *   Do I feel beaten or intimidated? Power may be or is likely the goal.
    *   Do I feel wronged or hurt? Revenge may be or is likely the goal.
    *   Do I feel incapable of reaching this student? Helplessness may be or is likely the goal.

2. Respond to the appropriate motive as follows:
    *   *Attention-getting.* Deprive the student of attention.
    *   *Power.* Do not allow open conflict. State the rules and consequences, and then move on.
    *   *Revenge.* Determine the reason for the student's hurt feelings.
    *   *Helplessness.* Provide opportunities for the student to succeed.

    Depending on the reaction of the student, more intrusive strategies may be necessary.

Reinforcement of Limits

Level of Motivation	Behavior Style			
	Self-Assertive	Socially Interactive	Analytic	Accommodating
1. Self-Absorbed	■	■	■	■
2. Approval Oriented	■	■	■	■
3. Interpersonal Loyalty				
4. Others Oriented				

▶ Stopping and Redirecting

Stop the student's inappropriate behavior, and redirect his or her attention to the task at hand.

1. Determine the specific behavior that is indicative of the student's defiance.
2. Instruct the student to stop that behavior and begin a new task
(e.g., say, "Put away that comic book and begin your math").
3. Check within a very short time to see if the student has obeyed the directive.
4. Repeat the process again as necessary. If it is still not successful, try a more intrusive strategy.

▶ Setting Achievable Goals

Establish achievable goals to improve behavior step-by-step.

1. Analyze the student's behavior, and try to isolate the components of that behavior that result in defiance.
2. Decide which elements of the misbehavior you will address first (e.g., clenched fists, raised voice, angry look, etc.). Set obtainable goals for improving each behavioral component leading to defiance, and reward improvement continually.
3. Once the student accomplishes a goal consistently, set a new goal that is the next step toward ending the defiant behavior.

▶ Charting Progress

Use charts to monitor misbehavior and check the student's progress.

1. Focus on the specific behaviors you identify as defiant, and discuss them with the student.
2. Set specific goals to eliminate instances of defiance.
3. Chart the student's behavior, and review it with the student daily. Adjust goals regularly as behavior improves.
4. Reward accomplishment of the goals.

Control

Level of Motivation	Behavior Style			
	Self-Assertive	Socially Interactive	Analytic	Accommodating
1. Self-Absorbed	■	■	■	■
2. Approval Oriented	■	■	■	■
3. Interpersonal Loyalty				
4. Others Oriented				

▶ Isolation Within the Classroom

Temporarily move the student to an isolated area of the classroom where he or she can continue to work.

1. Decide which defiant behavior will be treated in this way.
2. Designate a nonstimulating relocation area for the student.
3. Discuss the isolation procedure with the class and the student.
4. When misbehavior occurs, follow through exactly as promised.

▶ Requiring a Plan for Improvement

Separate the student from the rest of the class, and have him or her prepare a plan for improved behavior. Do not allow the student to return to the classroom until he or she presents an acceptable plan.

1. Designate an isolated relocation area.
2. Have the student complete a written plan that addresses the following questions: What did I do? Why is it a problem? What rule did I break? How do I plan to avoid this problem?
3. Discuss the plan with the student.
4. Enforce the student's adherence to the plan. Rewrite the plan if the student does not adhere to it.

▶ Deducting Points for Misbehavior

Deduct points (or tokens) or withhold privileges the student has earned.
(Deduction of points should occur in conjunction with a token reinforcement system.)

1. Determine which types of defiant behavior will result in the loss of points, and choose the number of points to be deducted.
2. Inform the student that although he or she will earn points for appropriate behavior, the number of points you have chosen will be deducted for each instance of defiant behavior. When dealing with a group behavior problem, announce and post the terms of this rule.
3. Deduct points exactly as you have stipulated when defiant behavior occurs.
4. If this strategy is not effective, consider increasing the frequency with which points are awarded and/or increasing the desirability of the rewards for which points can be redeemed (e.g., rather than 10 minutes of free time, substitute an opportunity to play an enjoyable computer game that is normally restricted).
5. If defiant behavior persists, increase the number of points deducted for each subsequent offense (e.g., 10 points for the first time, 25 points for the second time, etc.).

Control *(continued)*

Level of Motivation	Behavior Style			
	Self-Assertive	Socially Interactive	Analytic	Accommodating
1. Self-Absorbed	■			
2. Approval Oriented				
3. Interpersonal Loyalty				
4. Others Oriented				

▶ Having a Parent in the Classroom

Bring one of the student's parents into the classroom to observe the student's behavior there.

Note. Before using this strategy, you may want to try one or more of the following three less intrusive strategies: Alerting Parents to Concerns, Exchanging Information With Parents, and Suggesting Parental Intervention Strategies (see under *Prevention, Limit Setting,* and *Reinforcement of Limits,* respectively, in chapter 3).

1. Ask one or both parents to attend school during the time that the student's defiant behavior usually occurs.
2. Notify the student that his or her parent(s) will be coming to class to observe.
3. Schedule time afterward to talk about what went on and to discuss ways to remedy the situation.
4. Continue with this strategy or devise a less intrusive plan if you think that having the parent(s) in class was a powerful signal to the student.

DEPENDENCE ON OTHERS

Reluctance to engage in an activity without an overdependence
on help from the teacher or from peers

Prevention

Level of Motivation	Behavior Style			
	Self-Assertive	Socially Interactive	Analytic	Accommodating
1. Self-Absorbed	■	■	■	■
2. Approval Oriented	■	■	■	■
3. Interpersonal Loyalty				
4. Others Oriented				

▶ Ignoring Misbehavior

Eliminate the student's payoff for inappropriate attention-getting behavior by refusing to acknowledge it.

1. Determine whether the student is aware of his or her behavior.
2. Ignore the behavior.
3. Acknowledge and praise the student when he or she demonstrates more independent behavior.

Level of Motivation	Behavior Style			
	Self-Assertive	Socially Interactive	Analytic	Accommodating
1. Self-Absorbed	■	■	■	■
2. Approval Oriented	■	■	■	■
3. Interpersonal Loyalty	■	■	■	■
4. Others Oriented				

▶ Increasing Physical Proximity

Spend more time near the student throughout the class period.

1. Move closer to the student at times when dependent behavior usually occurs.
2. As the student begins to work more independently, move a little farther away.
3. Adjust your distance from the student according to the degree of dependency being demonstrated.
4. Be sure to verbally acknowledge and praise the student for working independently on a regular basis, particularly when you are farther away.

▶ Nonverbal Communication

Use eye contact, body movements, or hand signals to gain the student's attention.

1. Determine the degree of dependency to be controlled by this method.
2. Approach the student during such behavior or right before it occurs.
3. Use positive nonverbal communication, such as thumbs-up, smiles, or an encouraging nod, to reinforce desired behavior.
4. Use negative nonverbal communication to make the student aware of his or her misbehavior (e.g., shake your head, frown, or raise your eyebrows).

Limit Setting

Level of Motivation	Behavior Style			
	Self-Assertive	Socially Interactive	Analytic	Accommodating
1. Self-Absorbed	■	■	■	■
2. Approval Oriented	■	■	■	■
3. Interpersonal Loyalty	■	■	■	■
4. Others Oriented				

▶ Using Affirmative Statements

Verbally acknowledge and emphasize the student's strengths and achievements.

1. Identify areas of interest to the student.
2. Plan activities that will engage the student's abilities in these areas of interest despite the fact that he or she still may not feel confident about working independently.
3. Encourage the student with positive, affirmative statements.
4. As the student becomes better able to work independently in areas where he or she feels competent, you should begin to see an increased willingness to attempt more challenging tasks.
5. Praise the student's efforts, even if he or she is not able to complete a task without demonstrating some dependency.

Level of Motivation	Behavior Style			
	Self-Assertive	Socially Interactive	Analytic	Accommodating
1. Self-Absorbed	■	■	■	■
2. Approval Oriented	■	■	■	■
3. Interpersonal Loyalty				
4. Others Oriented				

▶ Student Self-Monitoring

Have the student monitor his or her own behavior using charts or other means to record progress.

1. Record the number of times the student demonstrates dependency within a specified time period (e.g., within 10 minutes, or during the language lesson).
2. Present that information to the student and come to an agreement regarding how the student will monitor his or her own behavior and how the teacher can assist.
3. Establish obtainable step-by-step goals for changing the behavior (e.g., reduce dependent behavior to three times per language lesson the first day and two times per language lesson the second day).
4. Set a reward for staying on schedule, and offer a better reward for being ahead of schedule. Modify goals or rewards as necessary.

Limit Setting *(continued)*

Level of Motivation	Behavior Style			
	Self-Assertive	Socially Interactive	Analytic	Accommodating
1. Self-Absorbed	■	■	■	■
2. Approval Oriented	■	■	■	■
3. Interpersonal Loyalty	■	■	■	■
4. Others Oriented				

▶ Exchanging Information With Parents

Work with the student's parents to gather information that might help resolve the problem.

Note. Before using this strategy, you may want to try the less intrusive Alerting Parents to Concerns strategy (see under *Prevention* in chapter 3).

1. Determine the severity of the problem.
2. Contact the parents, and discuss the student's behavior objectively based on your prior data collection.
3. Prepare a list of questions to ask the parents to elicit possible explanations for the student's behavior. Be careful not to offend the parents or make them feel inadequate.
4. Write down any helpful information you receive.
5. In closing the conversation, reaffirm your support for their child's education and your willingness to communicate with them.
6. Thank them for their time and cooperation.

Reinforcement of Limits

Level of Motivation	Behavior Style			
	Self-Assertive	Socially Interactive	Analytic	Accommodating
1. Self-Absorbed	■	■		
2. Approval Oriented	■	■		
3. Interpersonal Loyalty				
4. Others Oriented				

▶ Stopping and Redirecting

Stop the student's inappropriate behavior, and redirect his or her attention to the task at hand.

1. Ask the student to stop his or her dependent behavior
   (e.g., say, "Stop checking your answers with Mary, and go on to the next problem").
2. Tell the student exactly what he or she should be doing
   (e.g., say, "Complete all 10 problems without checking with anyone").
3. Check back later to make sure that the student is maintaining the desired behavior.

Level of Motivation	Behavior Style			
	Self-Assertive	Socially Interactive	Analytic	Accommodating
1. Self-Absorbed	■	■	■	■
2. Approval Oriented	■	■	■	■
3. Interpersonal Loyalty				
4. Others Oriented				

▶ Setting Achievable Goals

Establish achievable goals to improve behavior step-by-step.

1. Decide what behavior you consider to be dependent.
2. Identify the student's most frequent or troublesome dependent behavior
   (e.g., chronically raising his or her hand to ask a question before attempting a simple task).
3. Discuss the identified behavior with the student.
4. Work with the student toward eliminating that behavior step-by-step through goal-setting and rewards
   (e.g., establish a system whereby the student can earn points for each time that he or she
   reads directions or attempts to solve a problem before asking for assistance).
5. Once a goal has been attained, move to the next step.

▶ Tangible Reinforcement

Give students tangible, immediately satisfying rewards for appropriate behavior.

1. Define the dependent behavior you want to eliminate.
2. Select tangible rewards that have real interest for the student.
3. Decide on a schedule for rewards.
4. Consistently reward correct behavior as promised.

DISORGANIZATION

Inability or unwillingness to organize work habits, school materials, notes, supplies, and so on

Limit Setting

Level of Motivation	Behavior Style			
	Self-Assertive	Socially Interactive	Analytic	Accommodating
1. Self-Absorbed				
2. Approval Oriented			■	■
3. Interpersonal Loyalty	■	■	■	■
4. Others Oriented	■	■	■	■

▶ **Direct Commands**
Make specific demands, spoken with authority, concerning the student's behavior.
1. Identify specific disorganized behavior that needs to be changed.
2. Discuss with the student the negative consequences of being disorganized.
3. State specific ways to change the behavior (e.g., say, "Clean off your desk").
4. Consistently remind the student of the need to be organized, until improved behavior becomes a habit.

▶ **Modeling Expected Behavior**
Demonstrate by example the behavior you want the student to exhibit.
1. Analyze the situation to determine whether the student knows how to be organized.
2. Discuss with the student the advantages of being organized.
3. Model organizational techniques (e.g., how to arrange a desk, take notes, keep a notebook, etc.).
4. Consistently model the correct behavior, and remind the student of the need to be organized.

Level of Motivation	Behavior Style			
	Self-Assertive	Socially Interactive	Analytic	Accommodating
1. Self-Absorbed	■			
2. Approval Oriented			■	■
3. Interpersonal Loyalty		■		
4. Others Oriented				

▶ **Student Self-Monitoring**
Have the student monitor his or her own behavior using charts or other means to record progress.
1. Discuss with the student the benefits of being organized, and point out the steps that must be taken to achieve that goal.
2. Devise a realistic, step-by-step plan to improve the student's organizational skills.
3. Have the student maintain a neat, handwritten chart to monitor his or her progress (e.g., recording a point each time he or she performs an organizational task).
4. At the end of each day, meet with the student to review his or her progress. Establish a reward for completion of each step toward achievement of the goal.
5. Monitor the student's recording accuracy.

Limit Setting *(continued)*

Level of Motivation	Behavior Style			
	Self-Assertive	Socially Interactive	Analytic	Accommodating
1. Self-Absorbed				
2. Approval Oriented			■	■
3. Interpersonal Loyalty	■	■	■	■
4. Others Oriented				

▶ **Exchanging Information With Parents**

Work with the student's parents to gather information that might help resolve the problem.

   Note. Before using this strategy, you may want to try the less intrusive Alerting Parents to Concerns strategy (see under *Prevention* in chapter 3).

1. Determine the severity of the problem.

2. Contact the parents, and discuss the student's disorganized behavior objectively.

3. Prepare a list of questions to ask the parents to elicit possible explanations for the student's behavior. Be careful not to offend the parents or make them feel inadequate.

4. Write down any helpful information you receive.

5. In closing the conversation, reaffirm your support for their child's education and your willingness to communicate with them.

6. Thank them for their time and cooperation.

Reinforcement of Limits

Level of Motivation	Behavior Style			
	Self-Assertive	Socially Interactive	Analytic	Accommodating
1. Self-Absorbed		■	■	■
2. Approval Oriented	■	■		
3. Interpersonal Loyalty				
4. Others Oriented				

▶ Establishing Logical Consequences

Establish logical consequences for certain behaviors.

1. Discuss your expectations regarding neatness, and outline steps to help the student organize his or her classwork.
2. Present and rehearse a list of rules regarding the organization of schoolwork.
3. Establish logical consequences for breaking those rules
   (e.g., do not allow students to go to recess until their desks are clean).
4. Explain cause-and-effect relationships, and discuss ways to avoid negative consequences.

Level of Motivation	Behavior Style			
	Self-Assertive	Socially Interactive	Analytic	Accommodating
1. Self-Absorbed				
2. Approval Oriented	■	■		
3. Interpersonal Loyalty				
4. Others Oriented				

▶ Positive Peer-Group Reinforcement

Provide incentives for peers to motivate students to behave appropriately.

1. Discuss specific organizational expectations (e.g., maintaining a list of homework assignments).
2. Set a realistic goal for the class, as well as a list of possible rewards.
3. Monitor progress closely, and enthusiastically acknowledge the students' improvement.
4. Give individual assistance to those having difficulty achieving the goal.
5. Reward the class as a group when the goal is met.

Reinforcement of Limits *(continued)*

Level of Motivation	Behavior Style			
	Self-Assertive	Socially Interactive	Analytic	Accommodating
1. Self-Absorbed	■	■	■	■
2. Approval Oriented		■		
3. Interpersonal Loyalty				
4. Others Oriented				

▶ Charting Progress

Use charts to monitor misbehavior and check the student's progress.

1. Discuss the specific problem with the student.
2. Explain the purpose of the chart and how it will be used.
3. Establish goals and rewards for improvement.
4. Monitor the student's behavior.

Control

Level of Motivation	Behavior Style			
	Self-Assertive	Socially Interactive	Analytic	Accommodating
1. Self-Absorbed	■	■	■	■
2. Approval Oriented				
3. Interpersonal Loyalty				
4. Others Oriented				

▶ Requiring a Plan for Improvement

Separate the student from the rest of the class, and have him or her prepare a plan for improved behavior. Do not allow the student to return to the classroom until he or she presents an acceptable plan.

1. Designate a readily available relocation area within the classroom.

2. Have the student complete a written plan that addresses the following questions: What did I do? Why is it a problem? What rule did I break? How do I plan to improve my behavior?

3. Discuss the plan, and encourage the student to think about its practical application.

4. Refer to the plan often, and enforce the student's adherence to it.

5. If the misbehavior continues, have the student complete another plan.

▶ Deducting Points for Misbehavior

Deduct points (or tokens) or withhold privileges the student has earned.
(Deduction of points should occur in conjunction with a token reinforcement system.)

1. Define and discuss various types of disorganized behavior.

2. Inform the student that although he or she will earn points for appropriate behavior, a specified number of points will be deducted for disorganized behavior. When dealing with a group behavior problem, announce and post the terms of this rule.

3. Deduct points exactly as you have stipulated when disorganized behavior occurs.

4. If this strategy is not effective, consider increasing the frequency with which points are awarded and/or increasing the desirability of the rewards for which points can be redeemed (e.g., rather than 10 minutes of free reading time, substitute an opportunity to play an enjoyable computer game that is normally restricted).

5. If disorganized behavior persists, increase the number of points deducted for each subsequent offense (e.g., 10 points for the first time, 25 points for the second time, etc.).

DISTRACTING OTHERS

Diverting other students' attention from their assigned tasks

Prevention

Level of Motivation	Behavior Style			
	Self-Assertive	Socially Interactive	Analytic	Accommodating
1. Self-Absorbed		■	■	■
2. Approval Oriented			■	■
3. Interpersonal Loyalty			■	■
4. Others Oriented				

▶ ## Increasing Physical Proximity

Spend more time near the student throughout the class period.

1. Circulate throughout the classroom, especially while lecturing.
2. While continuing to lecture, walk toward the student who is distracting others.
3. Sit near the student or otherwise maintain close proximity.
4. Get students around the misbehaving student to focus on the discussion by asking them questions, or ask the misbehaving student a question to refocus his or her attention on the appropriate activity.

Level of Motivation	Behavior Style			
	Self-Assertive	Socially Interactive	Analytic	Accommodating
1. Self-Absorbed				
2. Approval Oriented				
3. Interpersonal Loyalty			■	■
4. Others Oriented		■	■	■

▶ ## Sharing Authority and Decision Making

Give peers some authority to stop a student's misbehavior.

1. Initiate a class discussion or meeting about behavior that distracts others.
   Allow students to express their feelings and concerns. Keep the discussion general.
2. Discuss the need for a cooperative effort to help stop distracting behavior.
3. Designate a nonverbal signal to be used by student neighbors each time a student exhibits distracting behavior.
4. Reinforce cooperative behavior by both the misbehaving student and the student helper.

Limit Setting

Level of Motivation	Behavior Style			
	Self-Assertive	Socially Interactive	Analytic	Accommodating
1. Self-Absorbed				
2. Approval Oriented			■	■
3. Interpersonal Loyalty	■	■	■	■
4. Others Oriented				

▶ Using Affirmative Statements

Verbally acknowledge and emphasize the student's strengths and achievements.

1. Design activities to take advantage of the student's skills and abilities.
2. Emphasize and encourage the student's success at those activities.
3. Verbally acknowledge and praise each instance of improved behavior.

▶ Disguising Directives

Disguise verbal directives to get the student to behave and to avoid confrontation.

1. Give the class as a whole a hint that those who are misbehaving are sure to notice (e.g., "We all need to be careful not to bother our neighbors").
2. Ask the student a question if he or she does not respond to the hint (e.g., "Have you begun your algebra assignment yet?").
3. Try to avoid inviting a confrontation.

▶ Probing for Motives

Ask yourself questions to determine the goal behind the student's misbehavior.

1. Ask the following questions immediately after the student's misbehavior:
   - Do I feel annoyed? Attention-getting may be or is likely the goal.
   - Do I feel beaten or intimidated? Power may be or is likely the goal.
   - Do I feel wronged or hurt? Revenge may be or is likely the goal.
   - Do I feel incapable of reaching this student? Helplessness may be or is likely the goal.
2. Respond to the appropriate motive as follows:
   - *Attention-getting.* Deprive the student of attention.
   - *Power.* Do not allow open conflict. State the rules and consequences, and then move on.
   - *Revenge.* Determine the reason for the student's hurt.
   - *Helplessness.* Provide opportunities for the student to succeed.

Depending on the student's behavior, more intrusive strategies may be necessary.

Reinforcement of Limits

Level of Motivation	Behavior Style			
	Self-Assertive	Socially Interactive	Analytic	Accommodating
1. Self-Absorbed		■	■	■
2. Approval Oriented	■	■		
3. Interpersonal Loyalty				
4. Others Oriented				

▶ Stopping and Redirecting
Stop the student's inappropriate behavior, and redirect his or her attention to the task at hand.
1. Ask the student to stop the distracting behavior (e.g., say, "Stop talking to Mary").
2. Tell the student what he or she should be doing (e.g., say, "Begin your reading assignment").
3. Shortly thereafter, check to see if the student is continuing to obey your request.

▶ Asking "What" Questions
Ask "what" questions until the student acknowledges his or her misbehavior; do not accept excuses.
1. Ask a "what" question.
2. Get the student to describe his or her misbehavior without making excuses.
3. Ask a "how" question (e.g., "How did distracting others help you?").
4. Ask another "what" question (e.g., "What is a better way to handle this?").
5. Agree on a plan that includes rewards and consequences for continued misbehavior.

Level of Motivation	Behavior Style			
	Self-Assertive	Socially Interactive	Analytic	Accommodating
1. Self-Absorbed		■		■
2. Approval Oriented	■	■	■	
3. Interpersonal Loyalty				
4. Others Oriented				

▶ Token Rewards
Over a period of time, reward students who demonstrate appropriate behavior with tokens that can be redeemed for a prize.
1. Review the problem with the student, and explain the token rewards system.
2. Compile a checklist of prizes, privileges, and so on.
3. Determine how many tokens will be required to redeem a prize.
4. Establish a verbal or written contract.
5. Gradually move from continuous to intermittent rewards as the student is increasingly able to sustain correct behavior at each level.

Control

Level of Motivation	Behavior Style			
	Self-Assertive	Socially Interactive	Analytic	Accommodating
1. Self-Absorbed	■			
2. Approval Oriented				
3. Interpersonal Loyalty				
4. Others Oriented				

▶ Relocation Within the Classroom

Move the misbehaving student to a less problematic location within the classroom.

1. Determine whether the student's distance from the teacher contributes to frequent misbehavior.
2. Move the student closer to the teacher without breaking up the intended lesson plan.
3. Leave the student in the new location if possible.
   Discuss the possibility that other strategies may be necessary if misbehavior persists.

▶ Time Out

Move the student to a nonstimulating environment so that he or she can cool down and regain the ability to think rationally.

1. Designate a readily available relocation area away from distractions.
2. Determine the length of time the student will be required to stay in that area.
3. Discuss with the class the consequences of distracting others, and let students know that work missed while isolated will have to be made up.
4. Follow through exactly as promised. Increase the length of time out if the misbehavior continues.

▶ Requiring a Plan for Improvement

Separate the student from the rest of the class, and have him or her prepare a plan for improved behavior. Do not allow the student to return to the classroom until he or she presents an acceptable plan.

1. Designate a readily available relocation area away from distractions.
2. Have the student submit a written plan that addresses the following questions: What did I do? Why is it a problem? What rule did I break? How do I plan to avoid this behavior?
3. Discuss the plan, and encourage the student to rethink his or her behavior.
4. Enforce the student's adherence to the plan.

▶ Deducting Points for Misbehavior

Deduct points (or tokens) or withhold privileges the student has earned.
(Deduction of points should occur in conjunction with a token reinforcement system.)

1. Describe and discuss the types of behavior that distract others.
2. Inform the student that although he or she will earn points for appropriate behavior, a specified number of points will be deducted for distracting others. When dealing with a group behavior problem, announce and post the terms of this rule.
3. Deduct points exactly as you have stipulated when the offense occurs.
4. If this strategy is not effective, consider increasing the frequency with which points are awarded and/or increasing the desirability of the rewards for which points can be redeemed (e.g., rather than 10 minutes of free reading time, substitute an opportunity to play a game with a friend).
5. If distracting behavior persists, increase the number of points deducted for each subsequent offense (e.g., 10 points for the first time, 25 points for the second time, etc.).

Control *(continued)*

▶ Having a Parent in the Classroom

Bring one of the student's parents into the classroom to observe the student's behavior there.

Note. Before using this strategy, you may want to try one or more of the following three less intrusive strategies: Alerting Parents to Concerns, Exchanging Information With Parents, and Suggesting Parental Intervention Strategies (see under *Prevention, Limit Setting,* and *Reinforcement of Limits,* respectively, in chapter 3).

1. Ask one or both parents to attend school during the time that the student's distracting behavior usually occurs.
2. Notify the student that his or her parent(s) will be coming to class to observe.
3. Afterward, talk about what went on and discuss ways to remedy the situation. Include the student if appropriate.
4. Continue this strategy or devise a less intrusive approach.

EXCUSE MAKING

Continual requests that allowances be made to avoid obligations,
assignments, responsibility, or accountability

Prevention

Level of Motivation	Behavior Style			
	Self-Assertive	Socially Interactive	Analytic	Accommodating
1. Self-Absorbed				
2. Approval Oriented				
3. Interpersonal Loyalty			■	■
4. Others Oriented		■	■	■

▶ Asking Adult Questions

Use adult-oriented questions to appeal to the student's rational abilities.

1. Assume the student is operating in the rational, adult mode.

2. Ask a question that appeals to the student as an adult (e.g., "What can we do to eliminate this problem?" or "What can you do to prevent this from occurring again?").

3. Avoid condemnatory questions or comments (e.g., "Why do you always make excuses?").

4. Continue discussion with the student until there is a tangible and acceptable plan for avoiding the need for excuses.

Limit Setting

Level of Motivation	Behavior Style			
	Self-Assertive	Socially Interactive	Analytic	Accommodating
1. Self-Absorbed				
2. Approval Oriented			■	■
3. Interpersonal Loyalty	■	■	■	■
4. Others Oriented				

▶ **Announcing/Rehearsing the Rules**

Establish rules regarding behavior in the classroom in order to define boundaries, expectations, and the consequences for misbehavior. Review them regularly.

1. Formulate five to seven rules for classroom behavior. Be sure to include a rule against excuse making.
2. Make the consequences for breaking those rules clear.
3. Post the rules.
4. Repeat the rules and consequences daily until the students have learned them.
5. Add or change rules as necessary.
6. Enforce the rules consistently.

▶ **Exchanging Information With Parents**

Work with the student's parents to gather information that might help resolve the problem.

   Note. Before using this strategy, you may want to try the less intrusive Alerting Parents to Concerns strategy (see under *Prevention* in chapter 3).

1. Determine the severity of the problem. Remind the parents of any earlier discussions regarding this problem.
2. Ask nonthreatening questions. Begin by simply discussing the student's behavior. As the parents become more open, probe for the underlying reasons for the student's behavior.
3. Avoid leading the parents to a solution.
4. Take notes. Remember, your goal is to gather information.
5. Agree to share information regarding any changes in the student's behavior.
6. In closing the conversation, reaffirm your support for their child's education and your willingness to communicate with them.
7. Thank them for their time and cooperation.

Reinforcement of Limits

Level of Motivation	Behavior Style			
	Self-Assertive	Socially Interactive	Analytic	Accommodating
1. Self-Absorbed		■	■	■
2. Approval Oriented	■	■		
3. Interpersonal Loyalty				
4. Others Oriented				

▶ Asking "What" Questions

Ask "what" questions until the student acknowledges his or her misbehavior; do not accept excuses.

1. Ask a "what" question.
2. Ask the student to describe his or her misbehavior without making excuses for it.
3. Ask a "how" question (e.g., "How did making excuses help you?").
4. Ask another "what" question (e.g., "What is a better way to handle this?").
5. Establish a plan for improvement that includes consequences for continued misbehavior.

▶ Using Written Contracts

Have the student agree, in writing, to follow a plan for improved behavior.

1. Choose an appropriate strategy or combination of strategies
   (e.g., Setting Achievable Goals, Token Rewards, or Charting Progress).
2. Discuss the strategy and agree on the details.
3. Write down the agreement, and have the student sign it along with you.
4. Reward the student only when all of the conditions of the contract have been met.

▶ Suggesting Parental Intervention Strategies

Enlist the parents' help in correcting the student's behavior.

   Note. Before using this strategy, you may want to try the less intrusive Alerting Parents to Concerns and/or Exchanging Information With Parents strategies (see under *Prevention* and *Limit Setting,* respectively, in chapter 3).

1. Think of ways that the parents could reduce the student's excuse making.
2. Call the parents and remind them of the facts concerning the ongoing problem, but this time, suggest some solutions.
3. Work out an agreement with the parents regarding the plan they will use, how they will monitor their success, and how you will be kept informed of their progress.

Control

Level of Motivation	Behavior Style			
	Self-Assertive	Socially Interactive	Analytic	Accommodating
1. Self-Absorbed	■			
2. Approval Oriented				
3. Interpersonal Loyalty				
4. Others Oriented				

▶ Requiring a Plan for Improvement

Separate the student from the rest of the class, and have him or her prepare a plan for improved behavior. Do not allow the student to return to the classroom until he or she presents an acceptable plan.

1. Tell the student that excuse making will result in the use of this strategy.
2. Designate a relocation area.
3. Have the student submit a written plan that addresses the following questions: What did I do? Why is it a problem? What rule did I break? How do I plan to avoid this problem?

▶ Deducting Points for Misbehavior

Deduct points (or tokens) or withhold privileges the student has earned.
(Deduction of points should occur in conjunction with a token reinforcement system.)

1. Choose the number of points that will be deducted for making excuses.
2. Inform the student that although he or she will earn points for appropriate behavior, the number of points you have chosen will be deducted when he or she makes excuses. When dealing with a group behavior problem, announce and post the terms of this rule.
3. Deduct points exactly as you have stipulated when excuse making occurs.
4. If this strategy is not effective, consider increasing the frequency with which points are awarded and/or increasing the desirability of the rewards for which points can be redeemed (e.g., rather than 10 minutes of free reading time, substitute an opportunity to play an enjoyable computer game that is normally restricted).
5. Increase the number of points deducted for each subsequent occurrence of excuse making (e.g., 10 points for the first time, 25 points for the second time, etc.).

FIGHTING

Physical conflict intended to inflict harm on another

Reinforcement of Limits

Level of Motivation	Behavior Style			
	Self-Assertive	Socially Interactive	Analytic	Accommodating
1. Self-Absorbed	■	■	■	■
2. Approval Oriented		■		
3. Interpersonal Loyalty				
4. Others Oriented				

▶ Asking "What" Questions

Ask "what" questions until the student acknowledges his or her misbehavior; do not accept excuses.

1. After the student who was fighting has calmed down, ask a "what" question (e.g., "What were you doing?").
2. Continue to ask "what" questions until the student verbalizes his or her behavior without trying to justify it.
3. Ask a "how" question (e.g., "How did this help you solve the problem?").
4. Ask another "what" question (e.g., "What should you do the next time this situation occurs?").
5. Establish an agreement with the student as to how he or she will behave in the future. Have the student rehearse that response.

Level of Motivation	Behavior Style			
	Self-Assertive	Socially Interactive	Analytic	Accommodating
1. Self-Absorbed		■	■	■
2. Approval Oriented	■	■		
3. Interpersonal Loyalty				
4. Others Oriented				

▶ Suggesting Parental Intervention Strategies

Enlist the parents' help in correcting the student's behavior.

Note. Before using this strategy, you may want to try the less intrusive Alerting Parents to Concerns and/or Exchanging Information With Parents strategies (see under *Prevention* and *Limit Setting,* respectively, in chapter 3).

1. Contact the parents, and review the facts concerning the problem.
2. Describe the student's behavior as objectively as possible. Refrain from making any judgments regarding his or her character.
3. Discuss with the parents any possible solutions they may have, and also suggest your own. Write them down.
4. Elicit an agreement from the parents regarding what measures they will take at home and how you will keep each other informed of the student's progress.

Control

Level of Motivation	Behavior Style			
	Self-Assertive	Socially Interactive	Analytic	Accommodating
1. Self-Absorbed	■	■	■	■
2. Approval Oriented	■	■	■	■
3. Interpersonal Loyalty	■	■	■	■
4. Others Oriented	■	■	■	■

▶ Coordinating Outside Intervention

Coordinate help or support from an outside source
(e.g., a mental health or family service agency, the legal system, etc.).

1. Keep a record of all instances of fighting and "near fighting" behavior that you observe.
2. Share this record with parents and/or school officials.
3. If all the necessary parties agree, contact outside agencies and establish a cooperative plan with appropriate monitoring and follow-up. (Be sure to go through appropriate school officials as directed by your school's policies.)

▶ Requiring a Plan for Improvement

Separate the student from the rest of the class, and have him or her prepare a plan for improved behavior. Do not allow the student to return to the classroom until he or she presents an acceptable plan.

1. Designate a relocation area away from stimulating objects or students.
2. Have the student complete a written plan that addresses the following questions: What did I do? Why is it a problem? What rule did I break? How do I plan to avoid this problem?
3. Discuss the plan with the student, and work on problem areas together.
4. Have the student sign the plan. Rewrite the plan if the student does not adhere to it.
5. Continue this process until a workable plan is devised.

▶ Detention

Keep the student after school for a specified period of time.

1. Make it clear that detention will be used as a method of discipline.
2. Use the detention time to develop a relationship with the student.
3. Work to improve the student's attitude toward school and his or her fellow students.
4. Work out a plan with the student to identify problem areas and take steps toward improvement. Help the student find alternatives to fighting.
5. End the detention on a positive note if possible.
6. Increase detention time for subsequent offenses.

GUM CHEWING

Chewing gum or eating without permission

Prevention

Level of Motivation	Behavior Style			
	Self-Assertive	Socially Interactive	Analytic	Accommodating
1. Self-Absorbed				
2. Approval Oriented				
3. Interpersonal Loyalty			■	■
4. Others Oriented		■	■	■

▶ Sharing Authority and Decision Making

Give peers some authority to help stop a student's misbehavior.

1. Review the class rule that students are not to chew gum or eat in class.

2. Review the reasons for that rule (e.g., such behavior is distracting, messy, unsanitary, etc.).

3. Discuss the need for a cooperative effort to help stop gum chewing in class.

4. Develop a plan whereby students remind each other to put gum and food in the trash can on their way into the classroom. Make reminder posters to put near the trash can.
Guide students to make a rule that students who chew gum or eat in the classroom must do cleanup.

5. Praise those students who remember to throw away gum or food before class.

Limit Setting

Level of Motivation	Behavior Style			
	Self-Assertive	Socially Interactive	Analytic	Accommodating
1. Self-Absorbed				
2. Approval Oriented			■	■
3. Interpersonal Loyalty	■	■	■	■
4. Others Oriented	■	■	■	■

▶ Disguising Directives

Disguise verbal directives to get the student to behave and to avoid confrontation.

1. Give the class as a whole a hint that those who are misbehaving are sure to notice (e.g., "Let's be sure we are all obeying the rule about gum chewing").

2. Give a disguised verbal directive to the student who does not respond to the hint (e.g., "Do you need to throw something in the waste basket?").

3. Try to avoid using a facial expression that might unintentionally invite a confrontation.

Level of Motivation	Behavior Style			
	Self-Assertive	Socially Interactive	Analytic	Accommodating
1. Self-Absorbed				
2. Approval Oriented			■	■
3. Interpersonal Loyalty	■	■		
4. Others Oriented	■	■	■	■

▶ Direct Commands

Make specific demands, spoken with authority, concerning the student's behavior.

1. Make a direct, positive command (e.g., "We do not allow gum chewing in class. Please discard yours.").

2. Anticipate situations where a command must be given, and practice your tone and posture. Choose your words based on the response you anticipate from the student in question.

3. Analyze the command's effect. Did the student stop chewing the gum?

Limit Setting *(continued)*

	Behavior Style			
Level of Motivation	Self-Assertive	Socially Interactive	Analytic	Accommodating
1. Self-Absorbed		■	■	■
2. Approval Oriented	■	■		
3. Interpersonal Loyalty				
4. Others Oriented				

▶ ## Exchanging Information With Parents

Work with the student's parents to gather information that might help resolve the problem.

Note. Before using this strategy, you may want to try the less intrusive Alerting Parents to Concerns strategy (see under *Prevention* in chapter 3).

1. Determine the severity of the problem, and decide how to approach the parents.
2. Describe the student's gum chewing as objectively as possible.
3. Discuss with the parents any possible solutions they may have, and also suggest your own. Avoid leading the parents to a solution.
4. Take notes. Remember, your goal is to gather information that might be helpful in solving the problem.
5. In closing the conversation, reaffirm your support for their child's education and your willingness to communicate with them.
6. Thank them for their time and cooperation.

Reinforcement of Limits

Level of Motivation	Behavior Style			
	Self-Assertive	Socially Interactive	Analytic	Accommodating
1. Self-Absorbed		■	■	■
2. Approval Oriented	■	■		
3. Interpersonal Loyalty				
4. Others Oriented				

▶ **Positive Peer-Group Reinforcement**

Provide incentives for peers to motivate students to behave appropriately.

1. Determine the overall maturity level of the class, and their ability to respond positively.
2. Set an obtainable goal for the class (e.g., say, "If I don't see anyone chewing gum in this class today, the entire class will receive a 'no homework' pass for tomorrow night").
3. Monitor the situation carefully, and ask students to encourage each other.
4. Reward accomplishment of the goal.

Control

Level of Motivation	Behavior Style			
	Self-Assertive	Socially Interactive	Analytic	Accommodating
1. Self-Absorbed	■			
2. Approval Oriented				
3. Interpersonal Loyalty				
4. Others Oriented				

▶ Deducting Points for Misbehavior

Deduct points (or tokens) or withhold privileges the student has earned.
(Deduction of points should occur in conjunction with a token reinforcement system.)

1. Choose the number of points a student can earn for each day that he or she does not chew gum or eat in class, and the number of points that will be deducted for gum chewing.

2. Inform the student of these rules for earning or losing points.
   When dealing with a group behavior problem, announce and post these rules.

3. Deduct points exactly as you have stipulated when gum chewing occurs.

4. If this strategy is not effective, consider increasing the frequency with which points are awarded and/or increasing the desirability of the rewards for which points can be redeemed (e.g., rather than 10 minutes of free reading time, substitute an opportunity to play an enjoyable computer game that is normally restricted).

5. If the misbehavior persists, increase the number of points or tokens deducted for each subsequent offense (e.g., 10 points for the first time, 25 points for the second time, etc.).

HALLWAY PROBLEMS

Misbehavior in the hallway

Prevention

Level of Motivation	Behavior Style			
	Self-Assertive	Socially Interactive	Analytic	Accommodating
1. Self-Absorbed				
2. Approval Oriented				
3. Interpersonal Loyalty			■	■
4. Others Oriented		■	■	■

▶ Sharing Authority and Decision Making

Give peers some authority to help stop a student's misbehavior.

1. Review the school rule that students are to behave in the hallway.
2. Discuss with the students the need for a cooperative effort to help stop the misbehavior.
3. Through discussion, generate a list of behaviors that are a problem in the hallway.
   Decide what should be punished, and make a list of suggested consequences for those behaviors.
   Avoid voting, but get consensus where possible.
4. Retain veto power, but use it only when absolutely necessary.
5. Develop a system for monitoring the students' progress and enforcing the rule.

Reinforcement of Limits

Level of Motivation	Behavior Style			
	Self-Assertive	Socially Interactive	Analytic	Accommodating
1. Self-Absorbed		■	■	■
2. Approval Oriented	■	■	■	■
3. Interpersonal Loyalty	■	■	■	■
4. Others Oriented				

▶ Stopping and Redirecting

Stop the student's inappropriate behavior, and redirect his or her attention to the task.

1. Tell the student to stop the misbehavior (e.g., say, "Stop jumping up and down in line").
2. Redirect the student to the appropriate behavior (e.g., say, "Walk in line calmly and quietly").
3. Ask the student a question shortly thereafter to see if he or she has obeyed
   (e.g., say, "Are you walking calmly and quietly?").

▶ Asking "What" Questions

Ask "what" questions until the student acknowledges his or her misbehavior; do not accept excuses.

1. Ask a "what" question that addresses the misbehavior
   (e.g., "What rule are you breaking in the hallway right now?").
2. Continue asking "what" questions until the student answers without making excuses.
3. Ask a "how" question (e.g., "How does this behavior help you get to music class?").
4. Ask another "what" question to elicit a solution (e.g., "What is a better way to walk in the hall?").
5. Make suggestions if the student does not respond.
6. Obtain a verbal agreement from the student regarding the need for improved behavior.

Reinforcement of Limits *(continued)*

Level of Motivation	Behavior Style			
	Self-Assertive	Socially Interactive	Analytic	Accommodating
1. Self-Absorbed				
2. Approval Oriented	■	■	■	■
3. Interpersonal Loyalty	■	■		■
4. Others Oriented				

▶ **Positive Peer-Group Reinforcement**

Provide incentives for peers to motivate students to behave appropriately.

1. Determine the overall maturity level of the class.
2. Set a realistic goal for the class (e.g., "If everyone can walk to music class and keep their hands to themselves, the class can have five extra minutes of recess").
3. Monitor progress closely.
4. If the goal is not reached, discuss with the class how they could have been successful.

Level of Motivation	Behavior Style			
	Self-Assertive	Socially Interactive	Analytic	Accommodating
1. Self-Absorbed		■	■	■
2. Approval Oriented	■	■		
3. Interpersonal Loyalty				
4. Others Oriented				

▶ **Using Written Contracts**

Have the student agree, in writing, to follow a plan for improved behavior.

1. Discuss with the student the most appropriate way to behave in the hallway.
2. Establish a systematic plan for improvement, and agree on details such as which rewards would be worth working for, the frequency of rewards, and the conditions that must be met in order to receive rewards.
3. Sign a written agreement with the student. Hold the student to that agreement. Revise the plan as necessary.

Control

Level of Motivation	Behavior Style			
	Self-Assertive	Socially Interactive	Analytic	Accommodating
1. Self-Absorbed	■			
2. Approval Oriented				
3. Interpersonal Loyalty				
4. Others Oriented				

▶ Exclusion From Fun Activities

Exclude the student from an activity he or she enjoys.

1. Determine which activity the student enjoys most.
2. Warn the student that the next time misbehavior occurs in the hallway the favored activity will be forfeited.
3. If the student misbehaves again, follow through exactly as promised.
4. Allow the student to observe the activity from a distance.
5. For each subsequent time the student misbehaves in the hallway, increase the time away from the activity.

▶ Time Out for a Specified Period or Activity

Establish rules in advance for the use of specified periods of time out in response to angry outbursts.

1. Identify the types of hallway behavior that will result in time out.
2. Designate a relocation area free from distracting objects or people.
3. Discuss with the class the use of time out and the consequences for continued misbehavior (e.g., forfeited hallway privileges, different locker times, etc.).
4. Carry out the time-out procedure exactly as promised.

▶ Requiring a Plan for Improvement

Separate the student from the rest of the class, and have him or her prepare a plan for improved behavior. Do not allow the student to return to the classroom until he or she presents an acceptable plan.

1. Decide which hallway behavior merits this response.
2. Designate a relocation area free from any stimulation.
3. Have the student complete a written plan that addresses the following questions: What did I do in the hallway? Why is it a problem? What rule did I break? How do I plan to avoid misbehavior in the hallway?
4. Have the student sign the plan, and enforce his or her adherence to it.
5. Rewrite the plan if the behavior does not change.

▶ Detention

Keep the student after school for a specified period of time.

1. Make it clear that detention will be used as a method of discipline for hallway misbehavior.
2. Use detention time to develop a relationship with the student.
3. Ask questions to reveal the student's needs and frustrations.
4. Work out a plan with the student to improve hallway behavior.
5. End detention on a positive note if possible.

HYGIENE PROBLEMS

Lack of attention to personal cleanliness—for example, bad odor,
dirty or messy hair, or dirty or messy clothes

Prevention

Level of Motivation	Behavior Style			
	Self-Assertive	Socially Interactive	Analytic	Accommodating
1. Self-Absorbed				■
2. Approval Oriented		■	■	■
3. Interpersonal Loyalty	■	■	■	■
4. Others Oriented	■			■

▶ Identifying Idealized Characters

Encourage the student to imitate the positive behavior of an idealized character.

1. Talk with students about desirable appearance and cleanliness characteristics.
2. Ask students to name the characters they admire, and review with students the positive characteristics of those individuals.
3. Point out traits that represent character qualities students are expected to exhibit.
4. Reward students for improved appearance and cleanliness.

Level of Motivation	Behavior Style			
	Self-Assertive	Socially Interactive	Analytic	Accommodating
1. Self-Absorbed				
2. Approval Oriented				
3. Interpersonal Loyalty			■	■
4. Others Oriented	■		■	■

▶ Probing for Values

Listen for and encourage the student to express closely held values.

1. Listen to the student during situations where he or she seems to be revealing values.
2. If the student does not express positive values concerning appearance, neatness, or cleanliness, ask nonthreatening questions about such issues during the discussion.
3. Look for consistency and repetition to make sure the student's values are not just the mood of the moment.
4. Set hygiene goals directly related to the student's values, and acknowledge and praise progress toward better hygiene.

Limit Setting

Level of Motivation	Behavior Style			
	Self-Assertive	Socially Interactive	Analytic	Accommodating
1. Self-Absorbed				
2. Approval Oriented			■	■
3. Interpersonal Loyalty	■	■	■	■
4. Others Oriented	■	■	■	■

▶ Disguising Directives

Disguise verbal directives to get the student to behave and to avoid confrontation.

1. Have several classes on good hygiene.
2. Give a hint about poor hygiene to the whole class.
3. Give a hint to the specific individual about his or her poor hygiene (e.g., "Do you check every day to make sure your clothes are fresh smelling and your body and hair are clean?").

▶ Modeling Expected Behavior

Demonstrate by example the behavior you want the student to exhibit.

1. Determine whether the student understands the concept of good hygiene.
2. Model correct behavior by coming to school dressed neatly and cleanly. Discuss with the class procedures for maintaining good hygiene.
3. Provide other examples of good hygiene for students to emulate.

▶ Exchanging Information With Parents

Work with the student's parents to gather information that might help resolve the problem.

Note. Before using this strategy, you may want to try the less intrusive Alerting Parents to Concerns strategy (see under *Prevention* in chapter 3).

1. Determine the severity of the problem. Decide which information you should share with the parents and which information is irrelevant.
2. Prepare for the phone call by writing down questions and deciding which aspects of the problem will be presented.
3. Do not lead the parents to a solution.
4. Write down any useful information you receive.
5. In closing the conversation, reaffirm your support for their child's education and your willingness to communicate with them.
6. Thank them for their time and cooperation.

Reinforcement of Limits

Level of Motivation	Behavior Style			
	Self-Assertive	Socially Interactive	Analytic	Accommodating
1. Self-Absorbed		■	■	■
2. Approval Oriented	■	■		
3. Interpersonal Loyalty				
4. Others Oriented				

▶ Token Rewards

Over a period of time, reward students who demonstrate appropriate behavior
with tokens that can be redeemed for a prize.

1. Develop a list of rewards the students can earn (e.g., special jobs, extra recess time, etc.).
2. Decide how many tokens it will take to earn the reward.
3. Define the behavior required to earn tokens
   (e.g., coming to school with face and hands clean, clean clothes, or combed hair).
4. As soon as the goal is reached, allow the student to turn in his or her tokens for the reward.

▶ Tangible Reinforcement

Give students tangible, immediately satisfying rewards for appropriate behavior.

1. Develop a list of tangible rewards appropriate for the student (e.g., chewing gum or stickers).
2. Clearly define the behavior to be rewarded
   (e.g., coming to school with face and hands clean and hair combed).
3. Decide how often to give reinforcement.
4. Switch to token rewards as soon as behavior is under control.

▶ Suggesting Parental Intervention Strategies

Enlist the parents' help in correcting the student's behavior.

   Note. Before using this strategy, you may want to try the less intrusive Alerting Parents to
Concerns and/or Exchanging Information With Parents strategies (see under *Prevention* and
Limit Setting, respectively, in chapter 3).

1. Think of ways the parents could help the student (e.g., get the student up earlier to give him or her more time to get ready, or check the student's appearance before he or she walks out the door).
2. Call the parents and suggest some solutions.
3. Come to an agreement with the parents as to what they will do.
4. Monitor the student's progress.

Control

Level of Motivation	Behavior Style			
	Self-Assertive	Socially Interactive	Analytic	Accommodating
1. Self-Absorbed	■			
2. Approval Oriented				
3. Interpersonal Loyalty				
4. Others Oriented				

▶ Exclusion From Fun Activities

Exclude the student from an activity he or she enjoys.

1. Warn the student that coming to school dirty or wearing dirty clothes will cause him or her to miss going on a field trip.

2. If the student's hygiene is unacceptable on the day of the field trip, make arrangements for him or her to stay with the principal or another teacher.

3. Allow the student to hear reports about the field trip.

Level of Motivation	Behavior Style			
	Self-Assertive	Socially Interactive	Analytic	Accommodating
1. Self-Absorbed	■	■	■	■
2. Approval Oriented	■	■	■	■
3. Interpersonal Loyalty	■	■	■	■
4. Others Oriented	■	■	■	■

▶ Coordinating Outside Intervention

Coordinate help or support from an outside source
(e.g., a mental health or family service agency, the legal system, etc.).

1. Determine whether the problem is one you can handle or one that needs help from the parents or an outside agency (e.g., a counselor or social worker who can check on the student's home life).

2. Keep an accurate record of the personal hygiene problems you observe.

3. Share this record with parents and/or school officials.

4. Meet with the parents to discuss the problem and possible interventions, including assistance and support from outside agencies.

5. Contact agencies and establish a cooperative plan with appropriate monitoring and follow-up. (Be sure to go through appropriate school officials as directed by your school's policies.)

Control *(continued)*

Level of Motivation	Behavior Style			
	Self-Assertive	Socially Interactive	Analytic	Accommodating
1. Self-Absorbed	■			
2. Approval Oriented				
3. Interpersonal Loyalty				
4. Others Oriented				

▶ Requiring a Plan for Improvement

Separate the student from the rest of the class, and have him or her prepare a plan for improved behavior. Do not allow the student to return to the classroom until he or she presents an acceptable plan.

1. Establish that poor hygiene will be treated with this strategy.
2. Designate a nonstimulating, readily available relocation area for the student to go to.
3. Have the student complete a written plan that addresses the following questions: What did I do? Why is it a problem? What rule did I break? How do I plan to avoid this problem?
4. Discuss the student's plan, and encourage him or her to cooperate.
5. Enforce the student's adherence to the plan. Refer to it often.
6. Have the student write another plan if the first plan fails.

HYPERACTIVITY

Excessive activity, short attention span, or inability to concentrate or remain still

Prevention

Level of Motivation	Behavior Style			
	Self-Assertive	Socially Interactive	Analytic	Accommodating
1. Self-Absorbed			■	■
2. Approval Oriented		■	■	■
3. Interpersonal Loyalty			■	■
4. Others Oriented	■	■	■	■

▶ **Nonverbal Communication**

Use eye contact, body movements, or hand signals to gain the student's attention.

1. Establish signals to alert the student that he or she is either doing well or needs to refocus.

2. Use positive gestures to acknowledge efforts to be calm and concentrate (e.g., smile, nod approval, or give a thumbs-up).

3. Acknowledge off-task behavior and inappropriate movement with a negative gesture such as a frown, a stare, raised eyebrows, or shaking your head. Use these as reminders to correct behavior.

4. Develop special signals with the student who is hyperactive to indicate when he or she should quietly move to a designated place for a change of activity.

Limit Setting

Level of Motivation	Behavior Style			
	Self-Assertive	Socially Interactive	Analytic	Accommodating
1. Self-Absorbed				
2. Approval Oriented			■	■
3. Interpersonal Loyalty		■	■	■
4. Others Oriented				

▶ Student Self-Monitoring

Have the student monitor his or her own behavior using charts or other means to record progress.

1. Record and chart the frequency of behavior that you have defined as hyperactive.
2. Discuss your observation with the student and make sure that he or she understands the problem.
3. Set step-by-step goals for the student to work toward improvement.
4. Reward the student for successful attainment of goals.
5. Teach the student how to record and chart his or her own behavior (e.g., have the student put a check on a chart each time he or she remains seated, on task, and quiet for 5 minutes).
6. Assess with the student how accurate and successful the self-monitoring has been.

Reinforcement of Limits

Level of Motivation	Behavior Style			
	Self-Assertive	Socially Interactive	Analytic	Accommodating
1. Self-Absorbed		■	■	■
2. Approval Oriented	■	■	■	■
3. Interpersonal Loyalty	■	■	■	■
4. Others Oriented				

▶ Charting Progress

Use charts to monitor misbehavior and check the student's progress.

1. Determine what triggers the excessive activity or loss of attention.
2. Break the excessive activity into its smallest parts.
3. Work with the student to develop step-by-step goals for change.
4. Chart progress toward goals on a daily basis, for each activity of the school day if possible.
5. Establish rewards for goal attainment.

▶ Suggesting Parental Intervention Strategies

Enlist the parents' help in correcting the student's behavior.

Note. Before using this strategy, you may want to try the less intrusive Alerting Parents to Concerns and/or Exchanging Information With Parents strategies (see under *Prevention* and *Limit Setting,* respectively, in chapter 3).

1. Contact the parents, and review the facts concerning the problem.
2. Describe the student's behavior as objectively as possible.
   Refrain from making any judgments regarding his or her character.
3. Discuss with the parents any possible solutions they may have, and also suggest your own. Write them down.
4. Elicit an agreement from the parents regarding what measures they will take at home and how you will keep each other informed of the student's progress.

Control

Level of Motivation	Behavior Style			
	Self-Assertive	Socially Interactive	Analytic	Accommodating
1. Self-Absorbed	■			
2. Approval Oriented				
3. Interpersonal Loyalty				
4. Others Oriented				

▶ Isolation Within the Classroom

Temporarily move the student to an isolated area of the classroom where he or she can continue to work.

1. Establish ahead of time with the class that hyperactivity will result in the use of this strategy.
2. Designate a relocation area free from any distracting objects or persons.
3. When hyperactivity occurs again, follow through exactly as promised.
4. Increase the time away from the class for each subsequent occurrence of hyperactivity.

Level of Motivation	Behavior Style			
	Self-Assertive	Socially Interactive	Analytic	Accommodating
1. Self-Absorbed		■	■	■
2. Approval Oriented	■	■	■	■
3. Interpersonal Loyalty				
4. Others Oriented				

▶ Removing Stimuli

Remove any object that acts as a stimulus for misbehavior.

1. Determine who or what causes the student to become overly active.
2. Determine whether the stimulus can be removed without hindering the student's learning process.
3. Remove the stimulus.
4. Monitor the student's behavior to determine the effectiveness of the stimulus removal. Did the behavior stop?

Control *(continued)*

Level of Motivation	Behavior Style			
	Self-Assertive	Socially Interactive	Analytic	Accommodating
1. Self-Absorbed	■			
2. Approval Oriented				
3. Interpersonal Loyalty				
4. Others Oriented				

▶ Time Out for a Specified Period or Activity

Establish rules in advance for the use of specified periods of time out in response to angry outbursts.

1. Determine the type of disruption that will result in time out.
2. Designate a relocation area free from stimulating objects or people.
3. Discuss the reasons for time out with the class and the consequences for continued misbehavior.
4. Carry out the time out procedure exactly as promised.
5. Increase the length of time out for each subsequent disruption.

▶ Deducting Points for Misbehavior

Deduct points (or tokens) or withhold privileges the student has earned.
(Deduction of points should occur in conjunction with a token reinforcement system.)

1. Describe and discuss the behaviors that you have categorized as hyperactive.
2. Inform the student that although he or she will earn points for appropriate behavior, a specified number of points will be deducted for hyperactive behavior.
3. Deduct points exactly as you have stipulated when the student exhibits hyperactive behavior.
4. If this strategy is not effective, consider increasing the frequency with which points are awarded and/or increasing the desirability of the rewards for which points can be redeemed (e.g., rather than 10 minutes of free reading time, substitute an opportunity to play an enjoyable computer game that is normally restricted).
5. If the problem persists, increase the number of points deducted for each instance of hyperactive behavior (e.g., 10 points for the first time, 25 points for the second time, etc.).

INABILITY TO SETTLE DOWN

Inability or unwillingness to refrain from excessive and inappropriate activity at the beginning or end of activities or during transitions between activities

Prevention

Level of Motivation	Behavior Style			
	Self-Assertive	Socially Interactive	Analytic	Accommodating
1. Self-Absorbed				
2. Approval Oriented				
3. Interpersonal Loyalty			■	■
4. Others Oriented	■	■	■	■

▶ **Ignoring Misbehavior**

Eliminate the student's payoff for inappropriate attention-getting behavior by refusing to acknowledge it.

1. Determine whether the student is attempting to get your attention by not settling down at the proper time.
2. Ignore the student who is not settling down, but expect an increase in the misbehavior at first.
3. Continue to ignore the misbehavior for a period of time, especially if this strategy seems to be working.

▶ **Increasing Physical Proximity**

Spend more time near the student throughout the class period.

1. Circulate throughout the classroom, especially during times when students have difficulty settling down.
2. Walk up and down the aisles near the student.
3. Remain near the student until he or she calms down.
4. Continue with the lesson, asking questions and focusing discussion toward the student.

▶ **Nonverbal Communication**

Use eye contact, body movements, or hand signals to gain the student's attention.

1. Physically acknowledge positive behavior with a smile, nod, or other gesture.
2. Physically acknowledge excessive or inappropriate behavior with negative gestures, such as raising your eyebrows, frowning, or rolling your eyes.
3. Use more positive nonverbal communication than negative.
4. Use specific nonverbal communication consistently.

Limit Setting

Level of Motivation	Behavior Style			
	Self-Assertive	Socially Interactive	Analytic	Accommodating
1. Self-Absorbed				
2. Approval Oriented			■	■
3. Interpersonal Loyalty	■	■		
4. Others Oriented				

▶ Disguising Directives

Disguise verbal directives to get the student to behave and to avoid confrontation.

1. Hint to the entire class that they need to settle down more quickly.
2. Give a disguised verbal directive to the misbehaving student
   (e.g., "Would you like to start working on your spelling now?").
3. Watch the student's facial expression to insure that the statement was not taken negatively.

▶ Direct Commands

Make specific demands, spoken with authority, concerning the student's behavior.

1. Try some other strategies first, if possible.
2. Think of a positive way to tell the student to settle down.
3. Anticipate situations where a command must be given and practice the tone of voice
   and posture you will use.
4. Analyze the effect of your command.

▶ Student Self-Monitoring

Have the student monitor his or her own behavior using charts or other means to record progress.

1. Chart the student's behavior—that is, make a note each time he or she does not settle down.
2. Discuss your observations with the student, and make sure he or she understands the problem.
3. Set step-by-step goals for the student to correct his or her behavior.
4. Establish a reward for the successful attainment of a goal.
5. Teach the student how to chart his or her own behavior
   (e.g., have the student put a check on a chart each time he or she is seated before the bell rings).
6. Assess with the student how accurate and successful the self-monitoring has been.

Reinforcement of Limits

Level of Motivation	Behavior Style			
	Self-Assertive	Socially Interactive	Analytic	Accommodating
1. Self-Absorbed		■	■	■
2. Approval Oriented	■	■		
3. Interpersonal Loyalty				
4. Others Oriented				

▶ Stopping and Redirecting
Stop the student's inappropriate behavior, and redirect his or her attention to the task at hand.
1. Determine what causes the student's inability to settle down
   (e.g., the student sitting behind him or her).
2. Ask the student to settle down in his or her seat.
3. Tell the student to begin working on the appropriate subject.
4. Check within a very short time to see if the student has obeyed.

▶ Asking "What" Questions
Ask "what" questions until the student acknowledges his or her misbehavior; do not accept excuses.
1. Ask the student a "what" question (e.g., "What are you doing?").
2. Continue to ask "what" questions until the student answers for his or her misbehavior without excuse.
3. Ask a "how" question next (e.g., "How does not settling down help you to get your work done?").
4. Ask another "what" question (e.g., "What would be a better way to come into class tomorrow?").
5. Establish a verbal plan to change the student's behavior.
6. Remind the student of the plan if he or she is unable to settle down occasionally thereafter.

Level of Motivation	Behavior Style			
	Self-Assertive	Socially Interactive	Analytic	Accommodating
1. Self-Absorbed				
2. Approval Oriented	■	■	■	■
3. Interpersonal Loyalty	■	■		
4. Others Oriented				

▶ Positive Peer-Group Reinforcement
Provide incentives for peers to motivate students to behave appropriately.
1. Determine the overall maturity level of the class and their ability to respond positively.
2. Set a realistic goal for the class (e.g., say, "Yesterday, it took 10 minutes for the class to get ready for math. I will time you today to see if you can settle down within 8 minutes.").
3. Demonstrate how the class can decrease the amount of time taken to settle down.
4. Encourage teamwork to achieve the goal, and reward accomplishment of the goal.
5. Be sure that one student does not become the scapegoat if the class does not meet the goal.

Control

Level of Motivation	Behavior Style			
	Self-Assertive	Socially Interactive	Analytic	Accommodating
1. Self-Absorbed	■	■	■	■
2. Approval Oriented	■	■	■	■
3. Interpersonal Loyalty				
4. Others Oriented				

▶ **Removing Stimuli**

Remove any object that acts as a stimulus for misbehavior.

1. Determine whether a particular stimulus is keeping the student from settling down.

2. Remove the stimulus without disrupting the class or lesson plan if possible.

3. Replace the stimulus after a time to see if the student is able to remain settled even when exposed to the temptation provided by the stimulus.

Control *(continued)*

Level of Motivation	Behavior Style			
	Self-Assertive	Socially Interactive	Analytic	Accommodating
1. Self-Absorbed	■			
2. Approval Oriented				
3. Interpersonal Loyalty				
4. Others Oriented				

▶ Time Out for a Specified Period or Activity

Establish rules in advance for the use of specified periods of time out in response to angry outbursts.

1. Designate a readily available relocation area for time out.
2. Increase the length of time the student is removed from the classroom for each subsequent outburst throughout the day.
3. Discuss the use of this strategy with the class and what will happen if the system fails.
4. Follow through exactly as promised.
5. Be sure the student does not return to the class until his or her work has been completed and appropriate behavior is displayed.

▶ Requiring a Plan for Improvement

Separate the student from the rest of the class, and have him or her prepare a plan for improved behavior. Do not allow the student to return to the classroom until he or she presents an acceptable plan.

1. Designate a nonstimulating, readily available, isolated relocation area.
2. Have the student complete a written plan that addresses the following questions: What did I do? Why is it a problem? What rule did I break? How do I plan to avoid this problem?
3. Discuss the plan with the student. Work through any problem areas together.
4. Hold the student to the plan, and refer to it often. Inform the student that the plan will be rewritten if it is not followed consistently.

▶ Having a Parent in the Classroom

Bring one of the student's parents into the classroom to observe the student's behavior there.

Note. Before using this strategy, you may want to try one or more of the following three less intrusive strategies: Alerting Parents to Concerns, Exchanging Information With Parents, and Suggesting Parental Intervention Strategies (see under *Prevention, Limit Setting,* and *Reinforcement of Limits,* respectively, in chapter 3).

1. Ask one or both parents to attend a typical class for at least one hour.
2. Notify the student that his or her parent(s) will be coming to class to observe.
3. Have the parent(s) sit near the back of the room.
4. Make time after the class to talk with the parent(s) about what went on and to discuss ways to remedy the situation.

LACK OF MOTIVATION

Little or no interest in learning or completing assignments

Prevention

Level of Motivation	Behavior Style			
	Self-Assertive	Socially Interactive	Analytic	Accommodating
1. Self-Absorbed				
2. Approval Oriented				
3. Interpersonal Loyalty			■	■
4. Others Oriented		■	■	■

▶ **Probing for Values**

Listen for and encourage the student to express closely held values.

1. Watch for situations in which the student reveals his or her values.
   When possible, encourage continued conversation.

2. Try to identify subjects that interest the student. In a one-on-one situation, bring up those subjects and probe for additional insights into the student's values. Encourage the student to share his or her ideas, feelings, and experiences.

3. Look for consistency and repetition to make sure that the values expressed are not simply the student's mood of the moment.

4. Link assignments to revealed values, and try to help the student understand the connection.
   Do not coerce the student based on values he or she has revealed.

5. Commend the student's revealed values, and acknowledge his or her increased motivation.

Limit Setting

Level of Motivation	Behavior Style			
	Self-Assertive	Socially Interactive	Analytic	Accommodating
1. Self-Absorbed				
2. Approval Oriented			■	■
3. Interpersonal Loyalty	■	■	■	■
4. Others Oriented	■	■	■	■

▶ Using Affirmative Statements

Verbally acknowledge and emphasize the student's strengths and achievements.

1. Discover the student's areas of interest and ability.
2. Provide opportunities for the student to be involved in those activities.
3. Acknowledge the student's strengths with positive statements, encouragement, and praise.

▶ Appealing to Values

Confront the student about his or her misbehavior and compare it to the positive values he or she holds.

1. Observe the student and record the values he or she demonstrates when behaving appropriately.
2. When the student misbehaves, compare his or her typical, proper behavior to the rule-breaking behavior.
3. Let the student think about the situation and identify the values abandoned while misbehaving. If privacy seems necessary, have the student write out his or her thoughts.
4. Make sure that the student understands what behavior is expected and believes in the values needed to behave appropriately.

Level of Motivation	Behavior Style			
	Self-Assertive	Socially Interactive	Analytic	Accommodating
1. Self-Absorbed				
2. Approval Oriented			■	■
3. Interpersonal Loyalty	■	■	■	■
4. Others Oriented				

▶ Student Self-Monitoring

Have the student monitor his or her own behavior using charts or other means to record progress.

1. Identify the subjects or activities the student seems least motivated to participate in or complete.
2. Define an overall goal for the student and the small steps necessary to complete the assignment or participate successfully in an activity.
3. Have the student make a chart to be marked as he or she completes each step toward the objective or goal.
4. Establish rewards for the completion of each step and attainment of the final goal.

Reinforcement of Limits

Level of Motivation	Behavior Style			
	Self-Assertive	Socially Interactive	Analytic	Accommodating
1. Self-Absorbed		■	■	■
2. Approval Oriented	■	■		
3. Interpersonal Loyalty				
4. Others Oriented				

▶ Establishing Logical Consequences

Establish logical consequences for certain behaviors.

1. Make a list of rules regarding work assignments.
2. Design logical consequences for late or incomplete assignments.
3. Make sure the consequences for not doing assignments are clearly understood (e.g., "If your spelling work for today is not complete, you will receive a zero in the grade book").
4. Follow through exactly as promised if the assignment is not completed.

▶ Positive Peer-Group Reinforcement

Provide incentives for peers to motivate students to behave appropriately.

1. Determine the overall maturity level of the class.
2. Set an obtainable goal for the class, with meaningful consequences for misbehavior (e.g., if the entire class turns in their math assignment on time, give everyone a night with no math homework).
3. Monitor class behavior closely as they work toward their goal (e.g., say, "I see that everyone in the third row has turned in their math; they must not want math homework").
4. If misbehavior occurs, put a check on the board. A specified number of checks should result in a predetermined consequence. Do not allow any student to become a scapegoat if the class fails to reach its goal.
5. Reward accomplishment of the goal.

▶ Using Written Contracts

Have the student agree, in writing, to follow a plan for improved behavior.

1. Try to determine the reason for the student's lack of motivation.
2. Discuss with the student what rewards would be worth working for. Write down every suggestion the student volunteers.
3. Choose one or two reasonable suggestions that you can agree to fulfill.
4. Write down exactly what completed assignments will result in a reward.
5. Both the teacher and the student should sign the contract.
6. Hold the student to the conditions of the contract. Rewrite the contract if necessary.

▶ Suggesting Parental Intervention Strategies

Enlist the parents' help in correcting the student's behavior.

Note. Before using this strategy, you may want to try the less intrusive Alerting Parents to Concerns and/or Exchanging Information With Parents strategies (see under *Prevention* and *Limit Setting,* respectively, in chapter 3).

1. Contact the parents, and review the facts concerning the problem.
2. Describe the student's behavior as objectively as possible. Refrain from making any judgments regarding his or her character.
3. Discuss with the parents any possible solutions they may have, and also suggest your own. Write them down.
4. Elicit an agreement from the parents regarding what measures they will take at home and how you will keep each other informed of the student's progress.

Control

Level of Motivation	Behavior Style			
	Self-Assertive	Socially Interactive	Analytic	Accommodating
1. Self-Absorbed	■			
2. Approval Oriented				
3. Interpersonal Loyalty				
4. Others Oriented				

▶ Requiring a Plan for Improvement

Separate the student from the rest of the class, and have him or her prepare a plan for improved behavior. Do not allow the student to return to the classroom until he or she presents an acceptable plan.

1. Designate an isolated relocation area.
2. Have the student complete a written plan that addresses the following questions: What did I do? Why is it a problem? What rule did I break? How do I plan to avoid this problem?
3. Discuss the plan with the student, and rewrite any problem areas together.
4. Remind the student of the plan if the misbehavior occurs again.
5. Have the student rewrite the plan if the misbehavior continues.

▶ Deducting Points for Misbehavior

Deduct points (or tokens) or withhold privileges the student has earned.
(Deduction of points should occur in conjunction with a token reinforcement system.)

1. Define and discuss appropriate and inappropriate work habits.
2. Choose the number of points that will be deducted for unacceptable work habits.
3. Inform the student that although he or she will earn points for appropriate behavior, a specified number of points will be deducted for inappropriate work habits. When dealing with a group behavior problem, announce and post the terms of this rule.
4. Deduct points exactly as you have stipulated when the student demonstrates insufficient motivation.
5. If this strategy is not effective, consider increasing the frequency with which points are awarded and/or increasing the desirability of the rewards for which points can be redeemed (e.g., rather than 10 minutes of free reading time, substitute an opportunity to play an enjoyable computer game that is normally restricted).
6. If the problem persists, increase the number of points deducted for each subsequent offense (e.g., 10 points for the first time, 25 points for the second time, etc.).

LATE ASSIGNMENTS

Inability or unwillingness to complete assignments within the allotted time frame

Prevention

Level of Motivation	Behavior Style			
	Self-Assertive	Socially Interactive	Analytic	Accommodating
1. Self-Absorbed				
2. Approval Oriented				
3. Interpersonal Loyalty			■	■
4. Others Oriented		■	■	■

▶ Checking for Understanding

To avoid misbehavior caused by frustration, have the student repeat instructions to make sure that he or she clearly understands what is expected.

1. Explain directions or present information in a number of ways
   (e.g., orally, in writing, or using diagrams, outlines, or flow charts).

2. Emphasize due dates and why they are important.

3. Give instructions that parallel the actual task as closely as possible, and ask the student to repeat or demonstrate those instructions.

4. Ask the student about the assignment.

Limit Setting

Level of Motivation	Behavior Style			
	Self-Assertive	Socially Interactive	Analytic	Accommodating
1. Self-Absorbed				
2. Approval Oriented			■	■
3. Interpersonal Loyalty	■	■	■	■
4. Others Oriented	■	■	■	■

▶ **Disguising Directives**

Disguise verbal directives to get the student to behave and to avoid confrontation.

1. Frequently remind the class about due dates and the importance of submitting assignments on time.

2. Give a disguised verbal directive to the target student (e.g., "How is your paper progressing?" or "I will need your help to get ready for the next assignment").

3. Watch the student's facial expression to see if he or she picked up the indirect statement.

4. If the student does not respond to indirect statements, you may need to move to direct intervention.

Reinforcement of Limits

Level of Motivation	Behavior Style			
	Self-Assertive	Socially Interactive	Analytic	Accommodating
1. Self-Absorbed		■	■	■
2. Approval Oriented	■	■		
3. Interpersonal Loyalty				
4. Others Oriented				

▶ Establishing Logical Consequences

Establish logical consequences for certain behaviors.

1. Make a rule regarding turning in assignments on time, and post it in a conspicuous location.
2. Have the students rehearse the rule until they know and understand the required deadlines and expectations.
3. Establish logical consequences for turning in late assignments, and follow through immediately when misbehavior occurs.
4. Make a clear connection between the misbehavior and its consequences (e.g., say, "Because you turned in your assignment late, you will have to do the next assignment during recess to make sure it is done on time").

▶ Setting Achievable Goals

Establish achievable goals to improve behavior step-by-step.

1. As a first step toward a major long-term goal to improve behavior, set a reasonable short-term goal (e.g., the student must bring his or her homework in at least three times a week).
2. Use rewards to encourage the student to reach the goal.
3. Switch to a more challenging goal once the initial goal has been accomplished.
4. When the long-term goal has been achieved, gradually discontinue the rewards.

▶ Charting Progress

Use charts to monitor misbehavior and check the student's progress.

1. Divide the assignment into small segments.
2. Talk to the student about the assignment, and set a schedule for the completion of each segment.
3. Write the schedule on a chart so that progress can be monitored.
4. When the student meets the deadline for a segment, put a mark on the chart indicating completion.
5. If the entire assignment is turned in on time, praise the student and repeat the process for the next assignment.

Control

Level of Motivation	Behavior Style			
	Self-Assertive	Socially Interactive	Analytic	Accommodating
1. Self-Absorbed	■			
2. Approval Oriented				
3. Interpersonal Loyalty				
4. Others Oriented				

▶ Exclusion From Fun Activities

Exclude the student from an activity he or she enjoys.

1. Determine which activity or privilege the student would most hate to forfeit.
2. Warn the student that you will deny the activity to all students whose assignments are late.
3. Follow through exactly as promised.
4. Allow the student to observe the activity from a distance while he or she completes the late assignment.

▶ Requiring a Plan for Improvement

Separate the student from the rest of the class, and have him or her prepare a plan for improved behavior. Do not allow the student to return to the classroom until he or she presents an acceptable plan.

1. Designate an isolated relocation area.
2. Have the student complete a written plan that addresses the following questions: What did I do? Why is turning in assignments late a problem? What rule did I break? How do I plan to get assignments turned in on time?
3. Discuss the plan with the student and rewrite any problem areas together.
4. Have the student sign and date the plan. Rewrite the plan if the student does not adhere to it.

▶ Deducting Points for Misbehavior

Deduct points (or tokens) or withhold privileges the student has earned.
(Deduction of points should occur in conjunction with a token reinforcement system.)

1. Choose the number of points that will be deducted for late completion of assignments.
2. Inform the student that although he or she will earn points for appropriate behavior, the number of points you have chosen will be deducted when assignments are handed in late. When dealing with a group behavior problem, announce and post the terms of this rule.
3. Deduct points exactly as you have stipulated the next time an assignment is turned in late.
4. If this strategy is not effective, consider increasing the frequency with which points are awarded and/or increasing the desirability of the rewards for which points can be redeemed (e.g., rather than 10 minutes of free reading time, substitute an opportunity to play a game with a friend).
5. If the problem persists, increase the number of points deducted for each late submission of an assignment within a given period of time (e.g., 10 points for the first late assignment that week, 25 points for the second, etc.).

▶ Detention

Keep the student after school for a specified period of time.

1. If, after trying other strategies, the student continues to turn assignments in late, try detention as a method of discipline.
2. During detention, the student should be held responsible for completing late assignments.
3. Counsel the student, and attempt to make him or her see the importance of turning assignments in on time.
4. End the detention on a positive note. Compliment the student for completing the assignment.
5. You may want to pair this strategy with Requiring a Plan for Improvement (see under *Control* in chapter 3).

LEAVING SEAT WITHOUT PERMISSION

Impulsively or inappropriately leaving seat without permission

Prevention

Level of Motivation	Behavior Style			
	Self-Assertive	Socially Interactive	Analytic	Accommodating
1. Self-Absorbed				
2. Approval Oriented				
3. Interpersonal Loyalty			■	■
4. Others Oriented	■	■	■	■

▶ Increasing Physical Proximity

Spend more time near the student throughout the class period.

1. Circulate throughout the classroom, especially during lectures.

2. Walk up and down the aisles near the misbehaving student without stopping the lecture.

3. Sit on an empty desk or chair near the student during times when he or she often gets up without permission.

4. Acknowledge the student's efforts to remain seated and on task.

Limit Setting

Level of Motivation	Behavior Style			
	Self-Assertive	Socially Interactive	Analytic	Accommodating
1. Self-Absorbed				
2. Approval Oriented			■	■
3. Interpersonal Loyalty	■	■	■	■
4. Others Oriented	■	■	■	■

▶ Announcing/Rehearsing the Rules

Establish rules regarding behavior in the classroom in order to define boundaries, expectations, and the consequences for misbehavior. Review them regularly.

1. Announce the rule regarding getting up without permission.
2. Make the consequences for not following the rule very clear.
3. Post the rule in a conspicuous place in the front of the classroom.
4. Repeat the rule and the consequences for breaking it at the beginning of each day until the students are able to recite and follow it automatically.
5. Repeat the consequences occasionally.
6. When you suspect that a student is about to get up without permission, ask him or her to recite the rule.
7. Enforce the rule consistently, following through with consequences for each infraction.
8. Explain the reason for the rule, if necessary.

▶ Disguising Directives

Disguise verbal directives to get the student to behave and to avoid confrontation.

1. Give a hint to the class as a whole.
2. Give a disguised verbal directive to the target student if he or she does not respond to the hint (e.g., say, "Is there some reason why you are out of your seat?").
3. Keep a calm facial expression to avoid a confrontation.
4. If there is a confrontation, use a more intrusive strategy.

Reinforcement of Limits

Level of Motivation	Behavior Style			
	Self-Assertive	Socially Interactive	Analytic	Accommodating
1. Self-Absorbed	■	■	■	■
2. Approval Oriented		■		
3. Interpersonal Loyalty				
4. Others Oriented				

▶ Stopping and Redirecting

Stop the student's inappropriate behavior, and redirect his or her attention to the task at hand.

1. Tell the student to get back in his or her seat.
2. Tell the student what he or she should be concentrating on.
3. Check shortly thereafter to make sure the student has obeyed.

▶ Asking "What" Questions

Ask "what" questions until the student acknowledges his or her misbehavior; do not accept excuses.

1. Ask a "what" question (e.g., "What are you doing?").
2. Continue to ask "what" questions until the student describes his or her behavior without making excuses.
3. Ask a "how" question (e.g., "How did this help you get your work done?").
4. Ask another "what" question (e.g., "What should you do next time?").
5. Make a verbal agreement with the student that includes specific consequences for misbehavior.

Control

Level of Motivation	Behavior Style			
	Self-Assertive	Socially Interactive	Analytic	Accommodating
1. Self-Absorbed	■			
2. Approval Oriented				
3. Interpersonal Loyalty				
4. Others Oriented				

▶ Relocation Within the Classroom

Move the misbehaving student to a less problematic location within the classroom.

1. Move the student closer to the teacher or to an area with fewer distractions.
2. Try to move the student with the least amount of disruption possible.
3. Leave the student in the new location if his or her behavior improves.
4. Discuss further consequences if the student continues to get out of his or her seat.

▶ Requiring a Plan for Improvement

Separate the student from the rest of the class, and have him or her prepare a plan for improved behavior. Do not allow the student to return to the classroom until he or she presents an acceptable plan.

1. Relocate the student to an area away from stimulating objects or people.
2. Have the student complete a written plan that addresses the following questions: What did I do? Why is it a problem? What rule did I break? How do I plan to avoid this problem?
3. Discuss the plan, and work through any problem areas together.
4. Enforce the student's adherence to the plan, and refer to it when he or she misbehaves.

▶ Deducting Points for Misbehavior

Deduct points (or tokens) or withhold privileges the student has earned.
(Deduction of points should occur in conjunction with a token reinforcement system.)

1. Choose the number of points that will be deducted for leaving one's seat without permission.
2. Inform the student that although he or she will earn points for appropriate behavior, the number of points you have chosen will be deducted when he or she gets up without permission. When dealing with a group behavior problem, announce and post the terms of this rule.
3. Deduct points exactly as you have stipulated if the misbehavior continues.
4. If this strategy is not effective, consider increasing the frequency with which points are awarded and/or increasing the desirability of the rewards for which points can be redeemed (e.g., rather than 10 minutes of free reading time, substitute an opportunity to play a game with a friend).
5. If the problem persists, increase the number of points deducted for each subsequent offense (e.g., 10 points for the first time, 25 points for the second time, etc.).

LOSING OR MISTREATING MATERIALS

Losing assigned materials, treating them carelessly, or not maintaining them in good condition

Prevention

Level of Motivation	Behavior Style			
	Self-Assertive	Socially Interactive	Analytic	Accommodating
1. Self-Absorbed				
2. Approval Oriented				
3. Interpersonal Loyalty			■	■
4. Others Oriented		■	■	■

▶ Introducing Role Models
Acknowledge positive behavior that the student should model.

1. Verbally acknowledge and praise a student who is careful and responsible with school materials or who treats such material with respect.
2. Monitor the target student closely to determine whether he or she tries to emulate the praised behavior.
3. Acknowledge and praise the student for following the modeled behavior.
4. Reward continued good behavior.

▶ Probing for Values
Listen for and encourage the student to express closely held values.

1. Watch for situations in which the student reveals his or her values. If convenient, encourage conversation at such times.
2. Listen for subjects that interest the student. Then, in a one-on-one situation, bring up those subjects and probe for his or her values.
3. Look for consistency and repetition to make sure the values expressed are not simply the student's mood of the moment.
4. Revealed values can give the teacher insight into how to construct an intervention plan that will focus on encouraging the student to behave in accordance with his or her values.
5. Be quick to reinforce desired behavior and give encouragement.

Limit Setting

Level of Motivation	Behavior Style			
	Self-Assertive	Socially Interactive	Analytic	Accommodating
1. Self-Absorbed				
2. Approval Oriented			■	■
3. Interpersonal Loyalty	■	■	■	■
4. Others Oriented	■	■	■	■

▶ Announcing/Rehearsing the Rules

Establish rules regarding behavior in the classroom in order to define boundaries, expectations, and the consequences for misbehavior. Review them regularly.

1. Formulate a list of five to seven rules. Make sure that a rule regarding the need to respect school materials is on the list.
2. Post the rules in a conspicuous place.
3. Repeat the rules at the beginning of each day until the students can follow and recite them automatically.
4. Have the student who is mistreating materials restate and write out the classroom rules in his or her own words.
5. Be sure there are clearly understood consequences for mistreatment of school materials, and follow through consistently when misbehavior occurs.

▶ Appealing to Values

Confront the student about his or her misbehavior, and compare it to the positive values he or she holds.

1. Observe the student, and record the times when he or she treats school materials properly.
2. When materials are mistreated, contrast that misbehavior with the student's typical positive behavior.
3. Allow the student to think about the situation and answer the following question: "What value did I demonstrate when treating school material properly?"
4. Have the student write down his or her answer.
5. Make sure the student understands the correct behavior and how it fits into his or her existing value system.

▶ Probing for Motives

Ask yourself questions to determine the goal behind the student's misbehavior.

1. Ask yourself the following questions immediately after the misbehavior:
   - Do I feel annoyed? Attention-getting may be or is likely the goal.
   - Do I feel beaten or intimidated? Power may be or is likely the goal.
   - Do I feel wronged or hurt? Revenge may be or is likely the goal.
   - Do I feel incapable of reaching this student? Helplessness may be or is likely the goal.
2. Respond to the appropriate motive as follows:
   - *Attention-getting.* Deprive the student of attention.
   - *Power.* Do not allow open conflict. State the rules and consequences, and then move on.
   - *Revenge.* Determine the reason for the student's hurt feelings.
   - *Helplessness.* Provide opportunities for the student to succeed.

Reinforcement of Limits

Level of Motivation	Behavior Style			
	Self-Assertive	Socially Interactive	Analytic	Accommodating
1. Self-Absorbed		■	■	■
2. Approval Oriented	■	■		
3. Interpersonal Loyalty				
4. Others Oriented				

▶ Establishing Logical Consequences
Establish logical consequences for certain behaviors.

1. Make a list of classroom rules. Be sure to include a rule regarding the need to take responsibility for school materials.
2. Establish logical consequences for losing or mistreating school materials (e.g., say, "If you lose your book, you will have to pay for it before you can participate in the class field trip").
3. Rehearse the rule regarding the expected treatment of school materials and the consequences for breaking that rule.
4. Make sure that the punishment and the rewards fit the behavior.

▶ Asking "What" Questions
Ask "what" questions until the student acknowledges his or her misbehavior; do not accept excuses.

1. Ask a "what" question that addresses the behavior (e.g., "What are you writing on that should not be written on?").
2. Continue asking "what" questions until the student verbalizes his or her misbehavior without making excuses.
3. Ask a "how" question next (e.g., "How did writing in your book help you review for the test?").
4. Ask another "what" question (e.g., "What should you be writing your notes on?").
5. Make a verbal plan that includes finding a lost item, repairing a damaged piece of property, or some similar consequence.
6. Restate the consequences if the problem continues to occur.

Reinforcement of Limits *(continued)*

Level of Motivation	Behavior Style			
	Self-Assertive	Socially Interactive	Analytic	Accommodating
1. Self-Absorbed				
2. Approval Oriented			■	■
3. Interpersonal Loyalty	■	■		
4. Others Oriented				

▶ **Positive Peer-Group Reinforcement**

Provide incentives for peers to motivate students to behave appropriately.

1. Determine the overall maturity level of the students who are misbehaving to see if peer-group reinforcement will work.
2. Set a realistic goal for the class (e.g., "Books will be checked on Thursday. If each person's books are accounted for, the class will receive no homework.").
3. Demonstrate how the class should maintain their books and materials.
4. Reward accomplishment of the goal.

Level of Motivation	Behavior Style			
	Self-Assertive	Socially Interactive	Analytic	Accommodating
1. Self-Absorbed		■	■	■
2. Approval Oriented	■	■		
3. Interpersonal Loyalty				
4. Others Oriented				

▶ **Suggesting Parental Intervention Strategies**

Enlist the parents' help in correcting the student's behavior.

Note. Before using this strategy, you may want to try the less intrusive Alerting Parents to Concerns and/or Exchanging Information With Parents strategies (see under *Prevention* and *Limit Setting,* respectively, in chapter 3).

1. Contact the parents, and review the facts concerning the problem.
2. Describe the student's behavior as objectively as possible.
   Refrain from making any judgments regarding his or her character.
3. Discuss with the parents any possible solutions they may have, and also suggest your own. Write them down.
4. Elicit an agreement from the parents regarding what measures they will take at home and how you will keep each other informed of the student's progress.

Control

Level of Motivation	Behavior Style			
	Self-Assertive	Socially Interactive	Analytic	Accommodating
1. Self-Absorbed	■			
2. Approval Oriented				
3. Interpersonal Loyalty				
4. Others Oriented				

▶ Isolation Within the Classroom

Temporarily move the student to an isolated area of the classroom where he or she can continue to work.

1. Decide how often to allow the behavior to occur before implementing this strategy.
2. Designate an isolated, nonstimulating relocation area within the classroom.
3. Be sure the class understands which behaviors lead to this consequence.
4. Follow through exactly as promised when school materials are lost or mistreated.

▶ Requiring a Plan for Improvement

Separate the student from the rest of the class, and have him or her prepare a plan for improved behavior. Do not allow the student to return to the classroom until he or she presents an acceptable plan.

1. Establish that persistent writing on desks or in books will be treated in this manner.
2. Designate an isolated, nonstimulating relocation area.
3. Have the student submit a written plan that addresses the following questions: What did I do? Why is losing or mistreating school materials a problem? What rule did I break? How do I plan to avoid this problem?
4. Discuss the plan with the student. Rewrite any problem areas together.
5. Hold the student to the plan, and refer to it often.
6. Have the student rewrite the plan if the misbehavior continues.

▶ Detention

Keep the student after school for a specified period of time.

1. Make it clear that detention will be used as a method of discipline for the mistreatment of school materials. Let students know the type of behavior that will result in detention.
2. Use detention time to develop a relationship with the student.
3. Have the student use some of the detention time to repair the mistreated materials or do service work around the school.
4. Work out a plan with the student to stop the mistreatment of materials (e.g., have the student erase the marks in a large stack of books that other students have written in).
5. End the detention on a positive note if possible.
6. Increase detention time for subsequent occurrences of writing on desks or chairs.

LYING

Answering untruthfully, or creating untrue scenarios regarding behavior or activities

Prevention

Level of Motivation	Behavior Style			
	Self-Assertive	Socially Interactive	Analytic	Accommodating
1. Self-Absorbed				
2. Approval Oriented		■	■	■
3. Interpersonal Loyalty	■	■	■	■
4. Others Oriented	■	■	■	■

▶ Identifying Idealized Characters

Encourage the student to imitate the positive behavior of an idealized character.

1. Talk with the students about which characters (potential role models) they consider to be most important.

2. Ask the students to reveal the things they admire most about those characters.
   Bring up the topics of truthfulness and honesty if they don't come up without prompting.

3. Discuss the ways that the idealized character exhibits the honesty you would like the students to emulate and how the students might develop similar traits.

4. Point out significant examples of lying that would be inconsistent with the character's honesty.

5. Reward efforts to correct misbehavior.

Limit Setting

Level of Motivation	Behavior Style			
	Self-Assertive	Socially Interactive	Analytic	Accommodating
1. Self-Absorbed				
2. Approval Oriented			■	■
3. Interpersonal Loyalty	■	■	■	■
4. Others Oriented	■	■	■	■

▶ Appealing to Values

Confront the student about his or her misbehavior, and compare it to the positive values he or she holds.

1. Observe the student's values in relation to lying.
2. Contrast the student's typical behavior with his or her dishonest behavior (e.g., say, "You usually tell the truth, which makes me believe that you think honesty is important").
3. Ask the student to think about the situation carefully and to explain why they seem to have abandoned their values.
4. If privacy is necessary, ask the student to provide a written explanation.
5. Make sure the student understands the correct behavior and has the values necessary to demonstrate that behavior.

▶ Reflecting Verbal Responses

Verbally reflect the essence of a student's argument in order to clarify his or her true feelings.

1. Listen carefully to the student, and attempt to determine his or her hidden message.
2. Repeat that message to the student (e.g., say, "So you dislike having homework because it's hard to do sometimes?").
3. Continue to repeat such messages until no further clarification is forthcoming.
4. Ask the student for suggestions about how to resolve the situation.
5. If this strategy is unsuccessful, consider moving to a more intrusive Control strategy.

▶ Probing for Motives

Ask yourself questions to determine the goal behind the student's misbehavior.

1. Ask yourself the following questions immediately after lying occurs:
   - Do I feel annoyed? Attention-getting may be or is likely the goal.
   - Do I feel beaten or intimidated? Power may be or is likely the goal.
   - Do I feel wronged or hurt? Revenge may be or is likely the goal.
   - Do I feel incapable of reaching this student? Helplessness may be or is likely the goal.
2. Respond to the appropriate motive as follows:
   - *Attention-getting.* Deprive the student of attention.
   - *Power.* Do not allow open conflict. State the rules and consequences, and then move on.
   - *Revenge.* Determine the reason for the student's hurt feelings.
   - *Helplessness.* Provide opportunities for the student to succeed.

Reinforcement of Limits

Level of Motivation	Behavior Style			
	Self-Assertive	Socially Interactive	Analytic	Accommodating
1. Self-Absorbed		■	■	■
2. Approval Oriented	■	■		
3. Interpersonal Loyalty				
4. Others Oriented				

▶ **Establishing Logical Consequences**

Establish logical consequences for certain behaviors.

1. Make a list of classroom rules. Be sure to include a rule requiring honesty.

2. Have the students rehearse the rule regarding honesty.

3. Establish logical consequences for untruthful answers (e.g., say, "If you continue to not be truthful about why your homework is not complete, you will receive a zero for your homework").

4. Make sure that the student accepts responsibility for his or her misbehavior and understands the connection between lying and its consequences.

▶ **Charting Progress**

Use charts to monitor misbehavior and check the student's progress.

1. Identify and define the misbehavior (e.g., tell the student that you don't believe the truth was told concerning his or her whereabouts after recess).

2. Discuss with the student why lying is a problem and why it must be corrected.

3. Set a goal, or a series of steps toward a goal, to correct the misbehavior.

4. Write each goal on a chart as it is being worked on so that the student's progress can be monitored (i.e., each time the student reaches a goal, place a check mark on the chart).

▶ **Using Written Contracts**

Have the student agree, in writing, to follow a plan for improved behavior.

1. Choose the most appropriate reinforcement technique for the student (tokens, privileges, etc.).

2. Discuss with the student the strategy to be used and the use of a written contract to enforce adherence to that strategy.

3. Agree on the exact details of the contract, such as the frequency of rewards, conditions for receiving rewards, and so on.

4. Sign the contract, and have the student sign it. Hold the student to the contract. Revise it when necessary.

Control

Level of Motivation	Behavior Style			
	Self-Assertive	Socially Interactive	Analytic	Accommodating
1. Self-Absorbed	■	■	■	■
2. Approval Oriented	■	■		
3. Interpersonal Loyalty				
4. Others Oriented				

▶ Exclusion From Fun Activities

Exclude the student from an activity he or she enjoys.

1. Determine which school activity the student enjoys most.
2. Inform the student that lying will cause him or her to be excluded from that activity.
3. Follow through exactly as promised if the student is found lying again.
4. Allow the student to observe the activity from a distance.

▶ Coordinating Outside Intervention

Coordinate help or support from an outside source
(e.g., a mental health or family service agency, the legal system, etc.).

1. Have a private discussion with the student regarding the consequences of lying—that is, how it hurts the student and others.
2. Keep an accurate record of the student's pattern of lying.
3. If you feel that you are unable or unqualified to handle the behavior, contact the parents and inform them of the situation. If the problem seems to require the help of outside agencies, attempt to get agreement from the parents and have appropriate school officials make contact.
4. Work directly with the parents, administrators, or agency personnel to resolve the problem and eliminate the behavior.

Control *(continued)*

Level of Motivation	Behavior Style			
	Self-Assertive	Socially Interactive	Analytic	Accommodating
1. Self-Absorbed	■			
2. Approval Oriented				
3. Interpersonal Loyalty				
4. Others Oriented				

▶ Requiring a Plan for Improvement

Separate the student from the rest of the class, and have him or her prepare a plan for improved behavior. Do not allow the student to return to the classroom until he or she presents an acceptable plan.

1. Designate an isolated, nonstimulating relocation area.
2. Have the relocated student complete a written plan that addresses the following questions: What did I do? Why is lying a problem? What rule did I break? How do I plan to avoid lying?
3. Discuss the plan with the student. Work through any problem areas together.
4. Hold the student to the plan, and refer to it often.
5. Have the student rewrite the plan if it does not work.

▶ Detention

Keep the student after school for a specified period of time.

1. Make it clear that detention will be used as a method of discipline in response to lying.
2. Use the detention time to develop a relationship.
   Ask the student questions to determine the reasons behind his or her lying.
3. Work out a plan with the student to help correct the behavior.
4. End detention on a positive note if possible.
5. Increase detention time for each subsequent instance of lying.

▶ Having a Parent in the Classroom

Bring one of the student's parents into the classroom to observe the student's behavior there.

   Note. Before using this strategy, you may want to try one or more of the following three less intrusive strategies: Alerting Parents to Concerns, Exchanging Information With Parents, and Suggesting Parental Intervention Strategies (see under *Prevention, Limit Setting,* and *Reinforcement of Limits,* respectively, in chapter 3).

1. Notify the student that you are going to ask one of his or her parents to attend class, and have him or her agree to this strategy.
2. Call one or both parents, and ask them to attend school during the time that the student's lying usually occurs.
3. Set aside time afterward to talk about what went on and to discuss ways to remedy the situation.

NAME CALLING

Intentionally insulting another person by calling him or her names
or making derogatory references to his or her family, friends, or belongings

Prevention

Level of Motivation	Behavior Style			
	Self-Assertive	Socially Interactive	Analytic	Accommodating
1. Self-Absorbed				
2. Approval Oriented				
3. Interpersonal Loyalty			■	■
4. Others Oriented	■	■	■	■

▶ Using Humor to Relieve Stress

Use humor to lighten a stressful situation.

1. When the student begins to show frustration with others or begins name calling, intervene with adult-level humor that he or she understands.

2. Do not use childish, sarcastic, or cutting humor.

3. Use humor to focus on what is truly funny about the situation or to redirect the conversation. Get students to relax and evaluate their behavior before they become too involved in name calling.

Limit Setting

Level of Motivation	Behavior Style			
	Self-Assertive	Socially Interactive	Analytic	Accommodating
1. Self-Absorbed				
2. Approval Oriented			■	■
3. Interpersonal Loyalty	■	■	■	■
4. Others Oriented	■	■	■	■

► **Describing Misbehavior as It Occurs**

Describe to the student what he or she has just done, is doing, or is about to do.

1. Describe to the student what he or she has just done (e.g., say, "Right now, you are calling Sharon a dummy. She is lowering her head and she is very quiet.").

2. Wait to see if the student understands why this behavior is wrong.

3. Allow the student to suggest solutions to the situation.

4. Describe how name calling affects others (e.g., say, "When you call Sharon names, it hurts her feelings and makes her sad").

Level of Motivation	Behavior Style			
	Self-Assertive	Socially Interactive	Analytic	Accommodating
1. Self-Absorbed				
2. Approval Oriented			■	■
3. Interpersonal Loyalty		■	■	■
4. Others Oriented	■	■	■	■

► **Appealing to Values**

Confront the student about his or her misbehavior, and compare it to the positive values he or she holds.

1. Observe and record the student's positive values in other areas of classroom behavior.

2. When name calling occurs, remind the student of his or her positive behavior in other situations (e.g., say, "You are usually respectful when working with others").

3. Without leading the student, allow him or her to think about the situation and why ordinarily positive values were abandoned.

4. Rehearse more appropriate responses to frustration with others.

Limit Setting *(continued)*

Level of Motivation	Behavior Style			
	Self-Assertive	Socially Interactive	Analytic	Accommodating
1. Self-Absorbed				
2. Approval Oriented			■	■
3. Interpersonal Loyalty	■	■	■	■
4. Others Oriented	■	■	■	■

▶ Probing for Motives

Ask yourself questions to determine the goal behind the student's misbehavior.

1. Ask the following questions immediately after the student's misbehavior:
    *   Do I feel annoyed? Attention-getting may be or is likely the goal.
    *   Do I feel beaten or intimidated? Power may be or is likely the goal.
    *   Do I feel wronged or hurt? Revenge may be or is likely the goal.
    *   Do I feel incapable of reaching this student? Helplessness may be or is likely the goal.

2. Respond to the appropriate motive as follows:
    *   *Attention-getting.* Deprive the student of attention.
    *   *Power.* Do not allow open conflict. State the rules and consequences, and then move on.
    *   *Revenge.* Determine the reason for the student's hurt feelings.
    *   *Helplessness.* Provide opportunities for the student to succeed.

Reinforcement of Limits

Level of Motivation	Behavior Style			
	Self-Assertive	Socially Interactive	Analytic	Accommodating
1. Self-Absorbed		■	■	■
2. Approval Oriented	■	■		
3. Interpersonal Loyalty				
4. Others Oriented				

▶ Asking "What" Questions

Ask "what" questions until the student acknowledges his or her misbehavior; do not accept excuses.

1. When the student calls another student a name, ask a "what" question (e.g., "What did you just do?").
2. Continue to ask "what" questions until the student verbalizes his or her misbehavior without making excuses.
3. Ask a "how" question next (e.g., "How does being called that name make Tom feel?").
4. Ask another "what" question (e.g., "What would be a better way to speak to someone the next time you are angry?").
5. Obtain a verbal agreement to stop the name calling.

Level of Motivation	Behavior Style			
	Self-Assertive	Socially Interactive	Analytic	Accommodating
1. Self-Absorbed				
2. Approval Oriented	■	■	■	■
3. Interpersonal Loyalty	■	■		
4. Others Oriented				

▶ Positive Peer-Group Reinforcement

Provide incentives for peers to motivate students to behave appropriately.

1. Determine the overall maturity level of the class and the student's ability to respond positively.
2. Set a realistic goal for the class (e.g., if they stop name calling, their recess will be increased by 5 minutes).
3. Closely monitor progress toward the goal before school, at recess, and after school.
4. Based on the students' interests, determine a reward for meeting the goal.
5. Demonstrate how students should respond to name calling (e.g., ignore it, laugh it off, walk away, etc.).
6. Reward attainment of the goal.

Reinforcement of Limits *(continued)*

Level of Motivation	Behavior Style			
	Self-Assertive	Socially Interactive	Analytic	Accommodating
1. Self-Absorbed		■	■	■
2. Approval Oriented	■	■		
3. Interpersonal Loyalty				
4. Others Oriented				

▶ Charting Progress

Use charts to monitor misbehavior and check the student's progress.

1. Divide the misbehavior into its smallest components
   (e.g., the setting in which it occurs, the person to whom it is directed, etc.).
2. Discuss with the student why name calling is a problem.
3. Work with the student to set goals to correct the misbehavior
   (e.g., decrease the number of occurrences of name calling for one week).
4. Record each instance in which the student consciously avoids name calling.
5. Reward attainment of goals.

Control

Level of Motivation	Behavior Style			
	Self-Assertive	Socially Interactive	Analytic	Accommodating
1. Self-Absorbed		■	■	■
2. Approval Oriented	■	■	■	■
3. Interpersonal Loyalty	■			
4. Others Oriented				

▶ Relocation Within the Classroom

Move the misbehaving student to a less problematic location within the classroom.

1. Identify the object or person that is causing the student to engage in name calling.
2. Move the student to a place in the classroom away from that distraction.
3. Try to move the student without interrupting the lesson.
4. Leave the student in the new location for a specified time or until you see evidence of changed behavior.
5. If the misbehavior resumes after the student returns to his or her original location, develop a plan that includes specific requirements for return to the normal seating plan.

Control *(continued)*

Level of Motivation	Behavior Style			
	Self-Assertive	Socially Interactive	Analytic	Accommodating
1. Self-Absorbed	■			
2. Approval Oriented				
3. Interpersonal Loyalty				
4. Others Oriented				

▶ Exclusion From Fun Activities

Exclude the student from an activity he or she enjoys.

1. Determine which activity the student would most hate to be excluded from.
2. Tell the student that name calling will result in exclusion from that activity.
3. Follow through exactly as promised the next time name calling occurs.
4. Allow the excluded student to observe the activity from a distance.
5. Increase the time away from the activity for each subsequent time name calling occurs.

▶ Time Out

Move the student to a nonstimulating environment so that he or she can cool down and regain the ability to think rationally.

1. Determine at what point time out will be used for name calling (e.g., the third occurrence).
2. Designate a nonstimulating relocation area for the time out.
3. Allow the student back into the classroom only when he or she has cooled off, as evidenced by the completion of a simple assignment or activity.
4. Discuss the problem that caused the name calling.
5. Increase the length of time spent in time out for each subsequent name-calling incident.
6. During recess, after school, or at home under his or her parents' supervision, have the student make up the work missed during time out.

▶ Time Out for a Specified Period or Activity

Establish rules in advance for the use of specified periods of time out in response to angry outbursts.

1. Tell the class that time out for a specified period of time will be used in response to name calling.
2. Designate a nonstimulating relocation area that is readily available when name calling occurs.
3. Increase the number of minutes in time out for each subsequent occurrence of name calling throughout the day.

OBSCENE GESTURES

Physical actions that communicate an offensive message

Limit Setting

Level of Motivation	Behavior Style			
	Self-Assertive	Socially Interactive	Analytic	Accommodating
1. Self-Absorbed				
2. Approval Oriented			■	■
3. Interpersonal Loyalty	■	■	■	■
4. Others Oriented				

▶ Direct Commands

Make specific demands, spoken with authority, concerning the student's behavior.

1. Think of a way to state the command positively.
2. Practice what you will say, how you will say it, and the correct body language to use.
3. Use a statement such as "Put your hand down" or "Use your fingers for something more constructive."
4. Check for the effect of the command.

▶ Appealing to Values

Confront the student about his or her misbehavior, and compare it to the positive values he or she holds.

1. Observe and record the student's reactions in various situations.
2. Contrast his or her gesturing behavior with proper behavior and the values he or she once demonstrated.
3. Let the student determine why obscene gesturing does not match his or her values.
4. Obtain a verbal agreement from the student to return to the positive values he or she has shown in other areas.

▶ Probing for Motives

Ask yourself questions to determine the goal behind the student's misbehavior.

1. Ask yourself the following questions immediately after the student makes an obscene gesture:
   - Do I feel annoyed? Attention-getting may be or is likely the goal.
   - Do I feel beaten or intimidated? Power may be or is likely the goal.
   - Do I feel wronged or hurt? Revenge may be or is likely the goal.
   - Do I feel incapable of reaching this student? Helplessness may be or is likely the goal.
2. Respond to the appropriate motive as follows:
   - *Attention-getting.* Deprive the student of attention.
   - *Power.* Do not allow open conflict. State the rules and consequences, and then move on.
   - *Revenge.* Determine the reason for the student's hurt feelings.
   - *Helplessness.* Provide opportunities for the student to succeed.

Reinforcement of Limits

Level of Motivation	Behavior Style			
	Self-Assertive	Socially Interactive	Analytic	Accommodating
1. Self-Absorbed		■	■	
2. Approval Oriented	■	■		
3. Interpersonal Loyalty				
4. Others Oriented				

▶ ## Establishing Logical Consequences

Establish logical consequences for certain behaviors.

1. Make a list of classroom rules that includes a rule forbidding obscene gestures, and make sure the students know these rules.
2. Rehearse the rules and the consequences for breaking them until each student fully understands.
3. Upon misbehavior, explain the connection between the behavior and its consequences (e.g., say, "Because using obscene gestures shows an inability to communicate successfully, you will stay after school to learn more about proper communication").
4. Administer the consequences consistently.

▶ ## Asking "What" Questions

Ask "what" questions until the student acknowledges his or her misbehavior; do not accept excuses.

1. Ask a "what" question that zeroes in on the problem.
2. Continue to ask "what" questions until the student describes the problem without making excuses.
3. Ask a "how" question (e.g., "How did making an obscene gesture help solve the problem?").
4. Ask another "what" question (e.g., "What can you do next time instead?"). Be ready to make suggestions if the student is having difficulty finding good solutions.
5. Obtain a verbal agreement from the student regarding the consequences for continued misbehavior.

Control

Level of Motivation	Behavior Style			
	Self-Assertive	Socially Interactive	Analytic	Accommodating
1. Self-Absorbed	■	■	■	■
2. Approval Oriented	■	■	■	■
3. Interpersonal Loyalty				
4. Others Oriented				

▶ **Relocation Within the Classroom**

Move the misbehaving student to a less problematic location within the classroom.

1. Determine who or what is contributing to the student's misbehavior.
2. Without disrupting the lesson plan, move the student closer to you in the classroom or to an isolated place away from the distracting person or activity.
3. Leave the student in the new location for a specified period of time or until the student exhibits a changed attitude or improved behavior.

Level of Motivation	Behavior Style			
	Self-Assertive	Socially Interactive	Analytic	Accommodating
1. Self-Absorbed	■			
2. Approval Oriented				
3. Interpersonal Loyalty				
4. Others Oriented				

▶ **Requiring a Plan for Improvement**

Separate the student from the rest of the class, and have him or her prepare a plan for improved behavior. Do not allow the student to return to the classroom until he or she presents an acceptable plan.

1. Designate a separate, nonstimulating relocation area.
2. Have the student submit a written plan that addresses the following questions: What did I do? Why are obscene gestures a problem? What rule did I break? How do I plan to avoid this problem?
3. Discuss the plan with the student. Work through any problem areas together.
4. Have the student date and sign the plan.
5. Hold the student to the plan. Rewrite the plan if the student continues to misbehave.

▶ **Detention**

Keep the student after school for a specified period of time.

1. Make it clear that detention will be used as a discipline method, and specify how long it will last. Tell the student that he or she will be in the room with the teacher to ensure that they will have each other's undivided attention.
2. Use detention time to try to get to know the student better.
3. Work on weak academic areas in order to improve the student's performance and, hopefully, his or her attitude about school.
4. Provide instruction in proper communication skills.
5. End the time positively, if possible.
6. Increase detention time for each subsequent offense.

OVERSENSITIVITY

Taking unwarranted offense from harmless or meaningless remarks, glances, or the perceived attitudes of others

Prevention

Level of Motivation	Behavior Style			
	Self-Assertive	Socially Interactive	Analytic	Accommodating
1. Self-Absorbed		■	■	■
2. Approval Oriented			■	■
3. Interpersonal Loyalty			■	■
4. Others Oriented				

▶ Increasing Physical Proximity
Spend more time near the student throughout the class period.
1. Circulate throughout the classroom, especially while lecturing.
2. Walk up and down the aisles near the student while lecturing.
3. Sit on an empty desk near the student, or otherwise stay in close proximity to him or her.
4. Ask the student questions or focus discussion near him or her.

▶ Nonverbal Communication
Use eye contact, body movements, or hand signals to gain the student's attention.
1. Acknowledge positive behavior by smiling, nodding, or otherwise gesturing approval.
2. Acknowledge negative behavior by raising your eyebrows, frowning, rolling your eyes, or shaking your head.
3. Try to use mostly positive cues.

▶ Using Humor to Relieve Stress
Use humor to lighten a stressful situation.
1. Do not use humor that could be perceived as cutting or sarcastic.
2. Use humor with a student who (a) is consistently overserious or negative, (b) has lost his or her sense of security and is ready to panic, (c) is on the verge of misbehavior, or (d) is becoming frustrated with an academic topic.
3. Use adult-level humor that the student will understand.

Limit Setting

Level of Motivation	Behavior Style			
	Self-Assertive	Socially Interactive	Analytic	Accommodating
1. Self-Absorbed				
2. Approval Oriented		■		
3. Interpersonal Loyalty				
4. Others Oriented			■	■

▶ Announcing/Rehearsing the Rules

Establish rules regarding behavior in the classroom in order to define boundaries, expectations, and the consequences for misbehavior. Review them regularly.

1. Decide on five to seven rules for classroom behavior, and review them often with the students. Be sure to include a rule that addresses oversensitivity (e.g., "Talk—with permission—to someone if you are insulted").
2. Make the consequences for breaking the rules very clear.
3. Post the rules so that the class can see them.
4. Rehearse strategies for conflict resolution and mediation.
5. Repeat the rules at the beginning of each day until the students can recite and follow them automatically.
6. When a rule is broken, carry out the consequences as promised.

▶ Using Affirmative Statements

Verbally acknowledge and emphasize the student's strengths and achievements.

1. Find the student's areas of interest and ability.
2. Design activities to assert those strengths.
3. Emphasize improvement, not perfection.
4. Criticize the student's misbehavior, not his or her character.

▶ Disguising Directives

Disguise verbal directives to get the student to behave and to avoid confrontation.

1. Give the class as a whole a hint about the problem.
2. Give a disguised verbal directive to the oversensitive student if he or she misses the hint (e.g., say, "Do you think you would do better on your test tomorrow if you listened to the review now?").
3. Monitor the student's behavior to determine whether the strategy is effective.

Reinforcement of Limits

Level of Motivation	Behavior Style			
	Self-Assertive	Socially Interactive	Analytic	Accommodating
1. Self-Absorbed				
2. Approval Oriented		■	■	■
3. Interpersonal Loyalty	■	■	■	■
4. Others Oriented				

▶ Asking "What" Questions

Ask "what" questions until the student acknowledges his or her misbehavior; do not accept excuses.

1. Ask a "what" question (e.g., "What did you do?").
2. Ask the student to verbalize his or her concern.
3. Ask a "how" question (e.g., "How did this reaction help you?").
4. Ask another "what" question (e.g., "What is a better way to handle this type of situation?").
5. Agree on a plan that includes consequences for continued oversensitivity.

Control

Level of Motivation	Behavior Style			
	Self-Assertive	Socially Interactive	Analytic	Accommodating
1. Self-Absorbed		■	■	■
2. Approval Oriented		■	■	■
3. Interpersonal Loyalty				
4. Others Oriented				

▶ Time Out

Move the student to a nonstimulating environment so that he or she can cool down and regain the ability to think rationally.

1. Determine at what point time out will be used to help the student regain composure.
2. Designate a nonstimulating, readily available relocation area for the time out.
3. Allow the relocated student back in the classroom when he or she regains self-control.
4. Discuss the problem with the student. Help the oversensitive student decide how to maintain self-control the next time a similar situation occurs, and to view others' behavior in a rational way.

PHYSICAL AGGRESSION

Aggressive physical behavior such as pushing, shoving, hitting, or tripping

Prevention

Level of Motivation	Behavior Style			
	Self-Assertive	Socially Interactive	Analytic	Accommodating
1. Self-Absorbed				
2. Approval Oriented				
3. Interpersonal Loyalty			■	■
4. Others Oriented	■	■	■	■

▶ Alerting Parents to Concerns

Contact parents to express your concern about the student's attitude or behavior.

1. Assess the severity of the problem to determine how to approach the parents.
   Is it a problem that can be easily solved, or does it concern the law?

2. If the problem is serious, be frank. If it is not serious, avoid alarming the parents.

3. Describe the incidents of physical aggression as objectively as possible.
   Do not make any statement regarding the student's character.

4. Write down any information the parents provide that might be helpful in solving or understanding the student's problem.

5. Avoid leading the parents to a solution, but be open to discussing possible solutions if they choose to do so.

6. In closing the conversation, reaffirm your support for their child's education and your willingness to communicate with them.

7. Thank them for their time and cooperation.

Reinforcement of Limits

Level of Motivation	Behavior Style			
	Self-Assertive	Socially Interactive	Analytic	Accommodating
1. Self-Absorbed		■	■	■
2. Approval Oriented	■	■	■	■
3. Interpersonal Loyalty	■	■	■	■
4. Others Oriented				

▶ Stopping and Redirecting
Stop the student's inappropriate behavior, and redirect his or her attention to the task at hand.
1. Tell the student to stop his or her misbehavior (e.g., say, "Stop pushing").
2. Redirect the student to the appropriate behavior
   (e.g., say, "Pick up your pencil and begin your math assignment").
3. Ask the student a question shortly thereafter to monitor his or her behavior
   (e.g., "Are you working on your math?").

▶ Asking "What" Questions
Ask "what" questions until the student acknowledges his or her misbehavior; do not accept excuses.
1. Ask the student a "what" question about his or her behavior (e.g., "What are you doing?").
2. Continue asking "what" questions until the student answers without making excuses.
3. Ask a "how" question (e.g., "How does hitting your classmate get your pencil back?").
4. Ask another "what" question (e.g., "What would be a better way to handle this situation next time?").
5. Offer suggestions if the student has no solutions.
6. Obtain a verbal agreement from the student to change the behavior.

▶ Positive Peer-Group Reinforcement
Provide incentives for peers to motivate students to behave appropriately.
1. Determine the overall maturity level of the class.
2. Set an obtainable goal for the class (e.g., say, "If there is no physical aggression of any kind today, the class will get a special treat this afternoon").
3. Closely monitor the students' progress toward the goal.
4. Describe ways for the students to refrain from hitting others
   (e.g., talking to the teacher, or trying to calm down when angry).
5. Reward attainment of the goal.

Reinforcement of Limits *(continued)*

Level of Motivation	Behavior Style			
	Self-Assertive	Socially Interactive	Analytic	Accommodating
1. Self-Absorbed		■	■	■
2. Approval Oriented	■	■		
3. Interpersonal Loyalty				
4. Others Oriented				

▶ Using Written Contracts

Have the student agree, in writing, to follow a plan for improved behavior.

1. Choose the most appropriate strategy for improving the student's behavior.
2. Discuss with the student the strategy to be used and the need for a written agreement.
3. Agree on the exact details of the contract, such as the frequency of rewards, conditions for receiving rewards, and the consequences of continued misbehavior.
4. Sign a written agreement with the student. Hold the student to the agreement and rewrite it if necessary.
5. Get the signature of the principal or a parent if that will strengthen the plan.

Control

Level of Motivation	Behavior Style			
	Self-Assertive	Socially Interactive	Analytic	Accommodating
1. Self-Absorbed	■			
2. Approval Oriented				
3. Interpersonal Loyalty				
4. Others Oriented				

▶ Isolation Within the Classroom

Temporarily move the student to an isolated area of the classroom where he or she can continue to work.

1. Establish ahead of time that physical aggression will result in a student's removal to a separate area of the classroom.
2. Designate a relocation area that is free from any stimulating objects or persons.
3. When the behavior occurs again, follow through exactly as promised.
4. Increase the time away from the class for each subsequent occurrence of the behavior.
5. If this strategy proves ineffective, try another strategy, or combine this with Requiring a Plan for Improvement.

▶ Exclusion From Fun Activities

Exclude the student from an activity he or she enjoys.

1. Determine which school activity is most favored by the student.
2. Warn the student that the next time physical aggression occurs, he or she will be removed from that activity.
3. When the behavior occurs again, follow through exactly as promised.
4. Allow the student to view the activity from a distance.
5. Increase the amount of time away from the activity for each subsequent occurrence of the misbehavior.

▶ Requiring a Plan for Improvement

Separate the student from the rest of the class, and have him or her prepare a plan for improved behavior. Do not allow the student to return to the classroom until he or she presents an acceptable plan.

1. Designate a relocation area away from stimulating objects or students.
2. Have the student complete a written plan that addresses the following questions: What did I do? Why is physical aggression a problem? What rule did I break? How do I plan to avoid this problem?
3. Discuss problem areas with the student until an agreement is reached.
4. Have the student sign the plan. Rewrite the plan if the student does not adhere to it.
5. Continue this process until a workable plan is devised.

PROFANITY

Foul, profane, or inappropriate language

Prevention

Level of Motivation	Behavior Style			
	Self-Assertive	Socially Interactive	Analytic	Accommodating
1. Self-Absorbed				
2. Approval Oriented				
3. Interpersonal Loyalty			■	■
4. Others Oriented		■	■	■

▶ Asking Adult Questions

Use adult-oriented questions to appeal to the student's rational abilities.

1. Assume that the student is rational even though he or she has used bad language.

2. Ask questions that appeal to the student's rational mode (e.g., "What are we going to do about the way you sometimes talk?" or "How should you respond when something makes you feel like saying bad words?").

3. Avoid questions or comments that condemn the student (e.g., "Why do you use such bad language?" or "Stop using profanity. You are embarrassing us!").

4. Affirm the student's efforts to stop using bad language, even if he or she is not totally successful right away.

Limit Setting

Level of Motivation	Behavior Style			
	Self-Assertive	Socially Interactive	Analytic	Accommodating
1. Self-Absorbed				
2. Approval Oriented			■	■
3. Interpersonal Loyalty	■	■	■	■
4. Others Oriented				

▶ Announcing/Rehearsing the Rules

Establish rules regarding behavior in the classroom in order to define boundaries, expectations, and the consequences for misbehavior. Review them regularly.

1. Formulate five to seven rules necessary for a good classroom atmosphere.
2. Make the consequences for violating the rules logical and clear.
3. Post the rules in a conspicuous place at the front of the classroom.
4. Repeat the rules at the beginning of each day until the students are able to recite and follow them automatically.
5. If bad language is a significant problem, comment positively when there has been an extended period of time with no bad language.
6. Add or alter the rules as experience dictates.
7. Follow through with consequences as promised.

Level of Motivation	Behavior Style			
	Self-Assertive	Socially Interactive	Analytic	Accommodating
1. Self-Absorbed				
2. Approval Oriented			■	■
3. Interpersonal Loyalty	■	■		
4. Others Oriented		■	■	■

▶ Direct Commands

Make specific demands, spoken with authority, concerning the student's behavior.

1. State your demand in a positive manner (e.g., "I want you to use correct language").
2. Tailor the command to the age and maturity level of the student.
3. Anticipate situations where the command must be given, and practice the correct posture and tone of voice.
4. Analyze the effect of your command. Did the bad language stop afterward?

Limit Setting *(continued)*

Level of Motivation	Behavior Style			
	Self-Assertive	Socially Interactive	Analytic	Accommodating
1. Self-Absorbed				
2. Approval Oriented			■	■
3. Interpersonal Loyalty	■	■		
4. Others Oriented	■	■	■	■

▶ Probing for Motives

Ask yourself questions to determine the goal behind the student's misbehavior.

1. Ask yourself the following questions immediately after the student uses bad language:
   - Do I feel annoyed? Attention-getting may be or is likely the goal.
   - Do I feel beaten or intimidated? Power may be or is likely the goal.
   - Do I feel wronged or hurt? Revenge may be or is likely the goal.
   - Do I feel incapable of reaching this student? Helplessness may be or is likely the goal.
2. Respond to the appropriate motive as follows:
   - *Attention-getting.* Deprive the student of attention.
   - *Power.* Do not allow open conflict. State the rules and consequences, and then move on.
   - *Revenge.* Determine the reason for the student's hurt feelings.
   - *Helplessness.* Provide opportunities for the student to succeed.
3. Once you have determined the student's goal, you may want to use some alternative strategies to increase the effectiveness of your intervention.

Reinforcement of Limits

Level of Motivation	Behavior Style			
	Self-Assertive	Socially Interactive	Analytic	Accommodating
1. Self-Absorbed		■	■	■
2. Approval Oriented	■	■		
3. Interpersonal Loyalty				
4. Others Oriented				

▶ Asking "What" Questions

Ask "what" questions until the student acknowledges his or her misbehavior; do not accept excuses.

1. Ask a "what" question that addresses the student's bad language (e.g., "What sort of language was that?").
2. Continue asking "what" questions until the student describes his or her behavior without making excuses.
3. Ask a "how" question (e.g., "How did profanity help you complete your math assignment?").
4. Follow up with another "what" question (e.g., "What would be a better way to respond next time?").
5. Obtain a verbal commitment from the student to stop the profanity.

▶ Positive Peer-Group Reinforcement

Provide incentives for peers to motivate students to behave appropriately.

1. Determine the overall maturity level of the class and their ability to respond positively.
2. Discuss the problem of profanity, and set an obtainable goal for the class.
3. Establish a measurement system that will allow the students to know exactly how well they are doing.
4. Reward accomplishment of the goal.

Level of Motivation	Behavior Style			
	Self-Assertive	Socially Interactive	Analytic	Accommodating
1. Self-Absorbed	■			
2. Approval Oriented				
3. Interpersonal Loyalty				
4. Others Oriented				

▶ Using Written Contracts

Have the student agree, in writing, to follow a plan for improved behavior.

1. Choose the most appropriate type of reward for the student (e.g., tokens to be redeemed for candy, nights without homework, public praise, leadership positions, etc.).
2. Develop a written contract to be used with the student. Obtain an agreement from the student regarding the exact steps to be taken to eliminate his or her profanity. Sign the contract, and have the student sign it.
3. Reward the student only when all of the conditions of the contract have been met.

Control

Level of Motivation	Behavior Style			
	Self-Assertive	Socially Interactive	Analytic	Accommodating
1. Self-Absorbed	■			
2. Approval Oriented				
3. Interpersonal Loyalty				
4. Others Oriented				

▶ Isolation Within the Classroom

Temporarily move the student to an isolated area of the classroom where he or she can continue to work.

1. Decide at what point this strategy will be implemented.
2. Designate an isolated, nonstimulating relocation area within the classroom.
3. Be sure the class understands which behavior will lead to this consequence.
4. Follow through exactly as promised when profanity occurs.

▶ Requiring a Plan for Improvement

Separate the student from the rest of the class, and have him or her prepare a plan for improved behavior. Do not allow the student to return to the classroom until he or she presents an acceptable plan.

1. Designate a readily available relocation area away from others.
2. Have the student complete a written plan that addresses the following questions: What did I do? Why is it a problem? What rule did I break? How do I plan to avoid this behavior in the future?
3. Do not allow the student to return to the classroom until he or she has completed an acceptable plan for improvement. Have the parents or principal sign the plan if appropriate.
4. Hold the student to the plan. Have the student rewrite the plan if it does not work.
5. Isolate the student only as long as it takes to complete an acceptable plan. Isolation should not be used as punishment in this case, but rather as an effort to have the student approach the problem in a logical, rational manner.

▶ Detention

Keep the student after school for a specified period of time.

1. Be sure to make it clear to students that detention will be used as a method of discipline in response to profanity.
2. Use detention time to develop a relationship with the student.
3. Help the student understand that there are alternatives to the use of profanity.
4. Work out a plan that helps the student see the problem clearly and establish goals for improvement.
5. End the detention on a positive note if at all possible.

PROPERTY DESTRUCTION

Any activity that results in damage to or destruction of property

Reinforcement of Limits

Level of Motivation	Behavior Style			
	Self-Assertive	Socially Interactive	Analytic	Accommodating
1. Self-Absorbed	■	■	■	■
2. Approval Oriented	■	■	■	■
3. Interpersonal Loyalty				
4. Others Oriented				

▶ Establishing Logical Consequences

Establish logical consequences for certain behaviors.

1. Make a list of classroom rules. Be sure that destruction of school property is prohibited by one of the rules.
2. Rehearse the rules, and the consequences for breaking them, with the students until they fully understand.
3. Follow through exactly as promised when destruction of property occurs.

Level of Motivation	Behavior Style			
	Self-Assertive	Socially Interactive	Analytic	Accommodating
1. Self-Absorbed				
2. Approval Oriented				
3. Interpersonal Loyalty	■	■	■	■
4. Others Oriented	■	■	■	■

▶ Asking "What" Questions

Ask "what" questions until the student acknowledges his or her misbehavior; do not accept excuses.

1. When the student destroys property, ask, "What are you doing?"
2. Get the student to describe his or her misbehavior without making excuses.
3. Ask a "how" question (e.g., "How does destroying property help you earn the respect of others?").
4. Ask another "what" question (e.g., "What should you be doing?").
5. Obtain a verbal commitment from the student to change the behavior.

Reinforcement of Limits *(continued)*

Level of Motivation	Behavior Style			
	Self-Assertive	Socially Interactive	Analytic	Accommodating
1. Self-Absorbed	■	■	■	■
2. Approval Oriented	■	■	■	■
3. Interpersonal Loyalty				
4. Others Oriented				

▶ ## Using Written Contracts

Have the student agree, in writing, to follow a plan for improved behavior.

1. Choose a reinforcement technique.
2. Explain to the student the system to be used, and agree on the details.
3. Allow the student to suggest consequences and rewards.
4. Reward the student only when all of the conditions of the contract have been met.

Level of Motivation	Behavior Style			
	Self-Assertive	Socially Interactive	Analytic	Accommodating
1. Self-Absorbed		■	■	■
2. Approval Oriented	■	■		
3. Interpersonal Loyalty				
4. Others Oriented				

▶ ## Suggesting Parental Intervention Strategies

Enlist the parents' help in correcting the student's behavior.

Note. Before using this strategy, you may want to try the less intrusive Alerting Parents to Concerns and/or Exchanging Information With Parents strategies (see under *Prevention* and *Limit Setting,* respectively, in chapter 3).

1. Contact the parents, and review the facts concerning the problem.
2. Describe the student's behavior as objectively as possible.
   Refrain from making any judgments regarding his or her character.
3. Discuss with the parents any possible solutions they may have, and also suggest your own. Write them down.
4. Elicit an agreement from the parents regarding what measures they will take at home and how you will keep each other informed of the student's progress.

Control

Level of Motivation	Behavior Style			
	Self-Assertive	Socially Interactive	Analytic	Accommodating
1. Self-Absorbed	■	■	■	■
2. Approval Oriented	■	■	■	■
3. Interpersonal Loyalty				
4. Others Oriented				

▶ Requiring a Plan for Improvement

Separate the student from the rest of the class, and have him or her prepare a plan for improved behavior. Do not allow the student to return to the classroom until he or she presents an acceptable plan.

1. Designate an isolated relocation area.
2. Have the student complete a written plan that addresses the following questions: What did I do? Why is it a problem? What rule did I break? How do I plan to avoid this problem?
3. Discuss the plan with the student. Work out problem areas and reach an agreement.
4. Include consequences for not following the plan (e.g., paying for repair of damaged property).
5. Hold the student to the plan, and refer to it often. Use provisions in the plan to justify further discipline if necessary. Develop a new plan if the first one is ineffective.

▶ Deducting Points for Misbehavior

Deduct points (or tokens) or withhold privileges the student has earned.
(Deduction of points should occur in conjunction with a token reinforcement system.)

1. Choose the number of points that will be deducted for damaging property. In this case, points can also be equivalent to the money that the student would have to pay to repair or replace the damaged property. Points could be returned once the money has been paid.
2. Warn the student that although he or she will earn points for appropriate behavior, the number of points you have chosen will be deducted when he or she damages any property. When dealing with a group behavior problem, announce and post the terms of this rule.
3. Deduct points exactly as you have stipulated when property damage occurs.
4. If the problem persists, increase the number of points deducted for each subsequent offense (e.g., 10 points for the first time, 25 points for the second time, etc.).

▶ Detention

Keep the student after school for a specified period of time.

1. Make it clear that detention will be used in response to property destruction.
2. Use the detention time to develop a relationship with the student. Probe for the causes of his or her misbehavior. Ask questions that address the student's frustration, and provide individual tutoring where needed.
3. Work out a plan to help the student see why destruction of property is a problem.
4. Have the student clean up or repair damaged property.
5. End detention on a positive note if at all possible.

SHYNESS

Fear or reluctance to communicate with or relate to others

Prevention

Level of Motivation	Behavior Style			
	Self-Assertive	Socially Interactive	Analytic	Accommodating
1. Self-Absorbed				
2. Approval Oriented				
3. Interpersonal Loyalty			■	■
4. Others Oriented		■	■	■

▶ Checking for Understanding

To avoid misbehavior caused by frustration, have the student repeat instructions to make sure that he or she clearly understands what is expected.

1. Explain directions or present information in a number of ways (e.g., orally, in writing, or using diagrams, outlines, or flow charts).
2. Give instructions that parallel the actual task as closely as possible.
3. Ask the student to repeat or explain your instructions.
4. Monitor the student's performance to see if he or she understood.

▶ Probing for Values

Listen for and encourage the student to express closely held values.

1. Watch for situations in which the student seems to be revealing his or her values. When possible, encourage continued conversation at such times.
2. Identify specific areas of interest to the student.
3. One by one, bring up those topics, and encourage the student to share his or her ideas, feelings, and experiences.
4. Encourage conversation one step at a time. For example, ask for a short response first, then gradually move toward the sharing of ideas.

▶ Alerting Parents to Concerns

Contact parents to express your concern about the student's attitude or behavior.

1. Determine whether the student's shyness is severe enough to warrant the parents' concern.
2. Decide ahead of time which specific observations you will share with the parents, to avoid misunderstandings.
3. Avoid leading the parents to a solution. Simply bring your concern to their attention.
4. Write down any information the parents provide that might be helpful in solving the student's problem.
5. In closing the conversation, reaffirm your support for their child's education and welfare, as well as your willingness to communicate with them.
6. Thank them for their time and cooperation.

Limit Setting

Level of Motivation	Behavior Style			
	Self-Assertive	Socially Interactive	Analytic	Accommodating
1. Self-Absorbed				
2. Approval Oriented			■	■
3. Interpersonal Loyalty		■		
4. Others Oriented				

▶ Using Affirmative Statements
Verbally acknowledge and emphasize the student's strengths and achievements.
1. Find the student's areas of interest and ability.
2. Design activities that use those interests and abilities.
3. Emphasize improvement, not perfection.
4. Criticize the student's action, not the student's worth.
5. Match the student with other students who are willing to help him or her.
6. Avoid placing the student in a competitive situation with other students.

▶ Appealing to Values
Confront the student about his or her misbehavior, and compare it to the positive values he or she holds.
1. Observe and record the student's values.
2. Note the circumstances or events that seem to cause the student's shyness.
3. Ask, very gently and discreetly, if those factors bother or upset the student.
4. Appeal to the student's values as you confront the factors that seem to encourage his or her wall of silence.

▶ Reflecting Verbal Responses
Verbally reflect the essence of a student's argument in order to clarify his or her true feelings.
1. Listen to the student, and try to determine his or her hidden message.
2. Repeat that message.
3. Do not try to guess what the student intends to say. Reflect only what is actually said.
4. Continue to repeat the student's message until no further clarification is forthcoming.

Reinforcement of Limits

Level of Motivation	Behavior Style			
	Self-Assertive	Socially Interactive	Analytic	Accommodating
1. Self-Absorbed		■	■	■
2. Approval Oriented	■	■		
3. Interpersonal Loyalty	■			
4. Others Oriented	■			

▶ Asking "What" Questions

Ask "what" questions to help the student become more comfortable in the current activity.

1. Ask a "what" question that addresses either an area of interest to the student or an activity in which he or she is involved (e.g., "What color are you going to use for the bicycle in your painting? Tell me about your picture.").
2. Make notes concerning any interests or abilities that may be revealed.
3. Continue to ask "what" questions to encourage the student to engage in lengthier and more personal conversations.

▶ Tangible Reinforcement

Give students tangible, immediately satisfying rewards for appropriate behavior.

1. Talk privately with the student.
2. Compliment his or her recent responses in class.
3. Set up a system to reward the student's efforts to overcome shyness (as indicated by increased participation in class, etc.).
4. One appropriate reward might be 10 minutes alone with the teacher. During this time, the student would be encouraged to share personal experiences, thus taking a step toward becoming more involved with other people.

▶ Charting Progress

Use charts to monitor misbehavior and check the student's progress.

1. Discuss with the student his or her fear of responding in class, or other manifestations of shyness.
2. Share any similar problems that you may have overcome.
3. Set a goal—or a series of steps toward a goal—to alleviate the problem.
4. Write the goal on a chart, and mark that chart whenever the student overcomes shyness and responds—whether verbally or by other means.
5. Emphasize the confidentiality of the chart.

SPITTING

Forcefully ejecting saliva from the mouth

Limit Setting

Level of Motivation	Behavior Style			
	Self-Assertive	Socially Interactive	Analytic	Accommodating
1. Self-Absorbed	■	■	■	■
2. Approval Oriented	■	■	■	■
3. Interpersonal Loyalty	■	■	■	■
4. Others Oriented				

▶ Probing for Motives

Ask yourself questions to determine the goal behind the student's misbehavior.

1. Ask yourself the following questions immediately after spitting occurs:
   - Do I feel annoyed? Attention-getting may be or is likely the goal.
   - Do I feel beaten or intimidated? Power may be or is likely the goal.
   - Do I feel wronged or hurt? Revenge may be or is likely the goal.
   - Do I feel incapable of reaching this student? Helplessness may be or is likely the goal.

2. Respond to the appropriate motive as follows:
   - *Attention-getting.* Deprive the student of attention.
   - *Power.* Do not allow open conflict. State the rules and consequences, and then move on.
   - *Revenge.* Determine the reason for the student's hurt feelings.
   - *Helplessness.* Provide opportunities for the student to succeed.

Reinforcement of Limits

Level of Motivation	Behavior Style			
	Self-Assertive	Socially Interactive	Analytic	Accommodating
1. Self-Absorbed		■	■	■
2. Approval Oriented	■	■	■	■
3. Interpersonal Loyalty	■	■	■	■
4. Others Oriented				

▶ Establishing Logical Consequences

Establish logical consequences for certain behaviors.

1. Make a rule regarding spitting and its consequences.

2. Rehearse the rule, and the consequences for breaking it, until students fully understand.

3. Follow through with the consequences as promised, making sure that the student can see the connection between his or her misbehavior and its consequences.

Control

Level of Motivation	Behavior Style			
	Self-Assertive	Socially Interactive	Analytic	Accommodating
1. Self-Absorbed	■			
2. Approval Oriented				
3. Interpersonal Loyalty				
4. Others Oriented				

▶ Exclusion From Fun Activities

Exclude the student from an activity he or she enjoys.

1. Determine which activity the student most likes to participate in.
2. Warn the student that spitting will cause him or her to either be removed from that activity (if spitting occurs during the activity) or be denied participation in the activity in the future.
3. Follow through exactly as promised.
4. Allow the student to observe the activity from a distance or hear about it from other students.
5. Establish specific conditions for the student's future participation.

▶ Requiring a Plan for Improvement

Separate the student from the rest of the class, and have him or her prepare a plan for improved behavior. Do not allow the student to return to the classroom until he or she presents an acceptable plan.

1. Designate a separate relocation area away from any stimulating objects or people.
2. Have the student complete a written plan that addresses the following questions: What did I do? Why is it a problem? What rule did I break? How do I plan to avoid this problem?
3. Discuss the plan, and have the student rethink any problem areas.
4. Have the student date and sign the plan.
5. Hold the student to the plan. Rewrite the plan if the student continues to misbehave in this way.

▶ Detention

Keep the student after school for a specified period of time.

1. Make sure that the students know that detention will be used as a form of discipline in response to spitting.
2. Specify the amount of time to be spent in detention beforehand.
3. Use the detention time to build a relationship with the student. Try to discover the student's underlying motives or problems.
4. Work on any weak academic skills that may be causing the student's bad attitude toward learning.
5. Help the student work out a plan to change the inappropriate behavior.
6. If spitting continues, increase detention time.

STEALING

Taking property without the owner's permission

Limit Setting

Level of Motivation	Behavior Style			
	Self-Assertive	Socially Interactive	Analytic	Accommodating
1. Self-Absorbed				
2. Approval Oriented			■	■
3. Interpersonal Loyalty	■	■	■	■
4. Others Oriented	■	■	■	■

▶ Appealing to Values

Confront the student about his or her misbehavior, and compare it to the positive values he or she holds.

1. Use this strategy only if the student has been generally honest in the past and has not stolen before.
2. Reveal to the student that you have proof of his or her stealing.
3. Remind the student of his or her honest behavior in the past and the values he or she has expressed concerning honesty.
4. Encourage the student to think about the situation relative to his or her value system. Ask why the good behavior has been abandoned.
5. Assure the student that he or she possesses the values necessary to behave properly.

Reinforcement of Limits

Level of Motivation	Behavior Style			
	Self-Assertive	Socially Interactive	Analytic	Accommodating
1. Self-Absorbed	■	■	■	■
2. Approval Oriented	■	■	■	■
3. Interpersonal Loyalty	■	■	■	■
4. Others Oriented				

▶ Establishing Logical Consequences

Establish logical consequences for certain behaviors.

1. Establish a list of classroom rules. Make sure that a rule prohibiting stealing is included on the list.
2. Rehearse the rules with the class. Explain the consequences for stealing
   (e.g., say, "Anything stolen from another person must be either returned or paid for in full").
3. Follow through exactly as promised the next time stealing occurs.

Level of Motivation	Behavior Style			
	Self-Assertive	Socially Interactive	Analytic	Accommodating
1. Self-Absorbed				
2. Approval Oriented			■	■
3. Interpersonal Loyalty	■	■	■	■
4. Others Oriented				

▶ Positive Peer-Group Reinforcement

Provide incentives for peers to motivate students to behave appropriately. (When there has been a problem with one or more students in the class, which seems to be habitual, is known to the entire class, and is acknowledged by the guilty student or students, this strategy can be very effective.)

1. Determine the overall maturity level of the class.
2. Set a goal for the class of no stealing during a specified period of time.
3. Decide on a reward for the class if the goal is met (e.g., a party or free time).
4. Change strategies if stealing continues.

Reinforcement of Limits *(continued)*

Level of Motivation	Behavior Style			
	Self-Assertive	Socially Interactive	Analytic	Accommodating
1. Self-Absorbed		■	■	■
2. Approval Oriented	■	■		
3. Interpersonal Loyalty				
4. Others Oriented				

▶ **Suggesting Parental Intervention Strategies**
Enlist the parents' help in correcting the student's behavior.

Note. Before using this strategy, you may want to try the less intrusive Alerting Parents to Concerns and/or Exchanging Information With Parents strategies (see under *Prevention* and *Limit Setting,* respectively, in chapter 3).

1. Think of ways that the parents could help the student solve the problem of stealing (e.g., by talking with their child or establishing negative consequences).
2. Contact the parents, inform them of the problem, and recommend some solutions—things they can do.
3. Get the parents to agree to a plan, and spell out what each person's role is to be.
4. Agree to meet again to discuss the student's progress.
5. Adjust the plan as needed.

Control

Level of Motivation	Behavior Style			
	Self-Assertive	Socially Interactive	Analytic	Accommodating
1. Self-Absorbed	■	■	■	■
2. Approval Oriented	■	■	■	■
3. Interpersonal Loyalty	■	■	■	■
4. Others Oriented				

▶ Coordinating Outside Intervention

Coordinate help or support from an outside source
(e.g., a mental health or family service agency, the legal system, etc.).

1. Maintain an accurate record of the student's behavior problem and of the success of each of the various intervention strategies you have used.
2. Insure that you have utilized all appropriate school services (e.g., counselors, social workers, school psychologists, etc.), and that they are in agreement that outside help is needed.
3. Contact the student's parents and inform them that the problem has reached a level that requires assistance from outside groups or agencies.
4. Contact appropriate agencies and arrange for a meeting with parents, school personnel, and agency representatives.
5. Explain the nature and severity of the problem to all present at the meeting. Work together as a group to devise an appropriate plan that spells out precisely what each party will do.

▶ Requiring a Plan for Improvement

Separate the student from the rest of the class, and have him or her prepare a plan for improved behavior. Do not allow the student to return to the classroom until he or she presents an acceptable plan.

1. Designate a separate relocation area for the student, away from any stimulating objects or people.
2. Have the student complete a written plan that addresses the following questions: What did I do? Why is it a problem? What rule did I break? How do I plan to avoid this problem?
3. Discuss the plan, and have the student rethink any problem areas.
4. Have the student date and sign the plan.
5. Enforce the student's adherence to the plan. Rewrite the plan if he or she continues to steal.

SUSPECTED DRUG USE

Behavioral or physical indications that the student may be taking drugs—for example, sudden or steady decline in achievement on tests, classwork, or projects; missed classes; a decline in personal hygiene; or constantly bloodshot eyes

Limit Setting

Level of Motivation	Behavior Style			
	Self-Assertive	Socially Interactive	Analytic	Accommodating
1. Self-Absorbed				
2. Approval Oriented			■	■
3. Interpersonal Loyalty	■	■	■	■
4. Others Oriented	■	■	■	■

▶ **Appealing to Values**

Confront the student about his or her misbehavior, and compare it to the positive values he or she holds.

1. Note changes in behavior, such as missed homework assignments, excuse making, broken promises, a passive attitude, lack of motivation, and drug jokes.

2. Listen carefully to discussions in which the student expresses personal values, and create a list of behaviors that the student values.

3. Reveal to the student the changes in behavior that you have noticed.

4. Encourage the student to think about the situation relative to his or her value system, and ask why the good behaviors have been abandoned.

5. Allow the student to write out his or her answer if necessary.

6. Assure the student that he or she possesses the values necessary to behave correctly.

▶ **Reflecting Verbal Responses**

Verbally reflect the essence of a student's argument in order to clarify his or her true feelings.

1. Note changes in behavior, such as missed homework assignments, excuse making, broken promises, a passive attitude, lack of motivation, and drug jokes.

2. Listen to the student and try to determine his or her encoded message.

3. Repeat that message.

4. Continue to repeat such messages until no further clarification is forthcoming.

5. Reflect only what is actually said; avoid guessing about the student's underlying meaning.

▶ **Exchanging Information With Parents**

Work with the student's parents to gather information that might help resolve the problem.

   Note. Before using this strategy, you may want to try the less intrusive Alerting Parents to Concerns strategy (see under *Prevention* in chapter 3).

1. Note changes in behavior, such as missed homework assignments, excuse making, broken promises, a passive attitude, lack of motivation, and drug jokes.

2. Prepare a thorough list of questions prior to the visit. Do not accuse the parents.

3. Describe your observations of the student's behavior, and remind the parents of his or her earlier problems and the discipline methods that have already been tried.

4. Avoid leading the parents to a solution.

5. Write down any information communicated by the parents that might be helpful in solving the student's problem.

6. Arrange a system whereby you and the parents agree to contact each other if there are any changes in the student's behavior.

7. In closing the conversation, reaffirm your support for their child's education and welfare, as well as your willingness to work with them.

8. Thank them for their time and cooperation.

Reinforcement of Limits

Level of Motivation	Behavior Style			
	Self-Assertive	Socially Interactive	Analytic	Accommodating
1. Self-Absorbed	■			
2. Approval Oriented				
3. Interpersonal Loyalty				
4. Others Oriented				

► Token Rewards

Over a period of time, reward students who demonstrate appropriate behavior with tokens that can be redeemed for a prize.

1. Note changes in behavior, such as missed homework assignments, excuse making, broken promises, a passive attitude, lack of motivation, and drug jokes.
2. Develop a checklist of prizes or privileges that the student can earn.
3. Determine how many tokens will be needed to redeem a prize.
4. Reward the student for the kinds of appropriate behavior that can be readily ascertained and that are usually incompatible with continued drug use: completed homework, improved daily grades, demonstrated initiative in areas that were previously problematic (e.g., volunteering in class).
5. Establish a verbal or written agreement regarding prohibited behavior.
6. As behavior improves, reduce the frequency of rewards.
7. If this strategy does not work, retain records for future assessment.

Reinforcement of Limits *(continued)*

Level of Motivation	Behavior Style			
	Self-Assertive	Socially Interactive	Analytic	Accommodating
1. Self-Absorbed		■	■	■
2. Approval Oriented	■	■		
3. Interpersonal Loyalty				
4. Others Oriented				

▶ Using Written Contracts

Have the student agree, in writing, to follow a plan for improved behavior.

Note. This strategy is most effective with a student in the early, experimental stages of drug use.

1. Note changes in behavior, such as missed homework assignments, excuse making, broken promises, a passive attitude, lack of motivation, and drug jokes.

2. Choose an appropriate intervention strategy for the student (e.g., Token Rewards, Charting Progress, or Setting Achievable Goals).

3. Discuss with the student the strategy to be used, and agree on the details.

4. Implement the strategy as follows:

   • Give immediate rewards for improved behavior (e.g., homework completed on time).

   • Give rewards for accomplishment of small steps toward correct behavior.

   • Give rewards frequently.

5. Evaluate the student's progress regularly, and be prepared to try more intrusive measures quickly if there is no change in his or her behavior within a reasonable length of time.

▶ Suggesting Parental Intervention Strategies

Enlist the parents' help in correcting the student's behavior.

Note. Before using this strategy, you may want to try the less intrusive Alerting Parents to Concerns and/or Exchanging Information With Parents strategies (see under *Prevention* and *Limit Setting,* respectively, in chapter 3).

1. Note changes in behavior, such as missed homework assignments, excuse making, broken promises, a passive attitude, lack of motivation, and drug jokes.

2. Think of ways that the parents could help the student (e.g., by spending more time together or setting curfew limits).

3. Call the parents and remind them of the facts concerning the problem, but this time, make suggestions.

4. Come to an agreement with the parents as to what they will do.

5. Monitor their progress on that agreement, as well as the student's behavior.

Control

Level of Motivation	Behavior Style			
	Self-Assertive	Socially Interactive	Analytic	Accommodating
1. Self-Absorbed	■	■	■	■
2. Approval Oriented		■		
3. Interpersonal Loyalty				
4. Others Oriented				

▶ Coordinating Outside Intervention

Coordinate help or support from an outside source
(e.g., a mental health or family service agency, the legal system, etc.).

1. Note changes in behavior, such as missed homework assignments, excuse making, broken promises, a passive attitude, lack of motivation, and drug jokes.

2. Keep accurate records of the student's behavior and of your prior contact with his or her parents.

3. Meet with the parents to discuss the need for outside intervention.

4. If the parents are in agreement, work with your principal and/or pupil service team to involve the appropriate agency or personnel.

5. Cooperate fully with programs designed to assist the student.

Control *(continued)*

Level of Motivation	Behavior Style			
	Self-Assertive	Socially Interactive	Analytic	Accommodating
1. Self-Absorbed	■			
2. Approval Oriented				
3. Interpersonal Loyalty				
4. Others Oriented				

▶ Requiring a Plan for Improvement

Separate the student from the rest of the class, and have him or her prepare a plan for improved behavior. Do not allow the student to return to the classroom until he or she presents an acceptable plan.

1. Note changes in behavior, such as missed homework assignments, excuse making, broken promises, a passive attitude, lack of motivation, and drug jokes.
2. Relocate the student to an area away from distracting objects or people.
3. Do not isolate the student completely.
4. Have the student submit a written plan that addresses the following questions: What did I do? Why is it a problem? What rule did I break? How do I plan to avoid this problem?

▶ Detention

Have the student remain after school or come to school on Saturday for a specified period of time.

1. Note changes in behavior, such as missed homework assignments, excuse making, broken promises, a passive attitude, lack of motivation, and drug jokes.
2. Try to spend detention time in close proximity to the student.
3. Use the detention time to develop a relationship.
4. Discuss classroom problems, and try to encourage the student to develop a positive attitude about school, life, and him- or herself.
5. Help the student work out a plan to see his or her problems and how to deal with them.
6. End the detention on a positive note if possible.

▶ Having a Parent in the Classroom

Bring one of the student's parents into the classroom to observe the student's behavior there.

   Note. Before using this strategy, you may want to try one or more of the following three less intrusive strategies: Alerting Parents to Concerns, Exchanging Information With Parents, and Suggesting Parental Intervention Strategies (see under *Prevention, Limit Setting,* and *Reinforcement of Limits,* respectively, in chapter 3).

1. Call one or both of the student's parents, and ask them to attend class during the time the student's misbehavior is most noticeable.
2. Notify the student that his or her parent(s) will be coming to class to observe.
3. Afterward, talk about what went on and discuss ways to remedy the situation.
   If the parents are at a loss for ideas, the teacher may need to structure the discussion.
4. Continue with this strategy or devise a less intrusive plan if you think that having the parent(s) in class was a powerful signal to the student.

TALKING

Verbal communication at a time when it is not permitted,
or excessive communication that infringes on the rights of others

Prevention

Level of Motivation	Behavior Style			
	Self-Assertive	Socially Interactive	Analytic	Accommodating
1. Self-Absorbed				
2. Approval Oriented				
3. Interpersonal Loyalty			■	■
4. Others Oriented		■	■	■

▶ Increasing Physical Proximity

Spend more time near the student throughout the class period.

1. Circulate throughout the classroom, especially while lecturing.
2. Walk up and down the aisles near the student who is talking, or stand near the student.
3. Sit down at a desk near the student for short periods of time.
4. Ask the student questions, or focus discussion near him or her.

Limit Setting

Level of Motivation	Behavior Style			
	Self-Assertive	Socially Interactive	Analytic	Accommodating
1. Self-Absorbed				
2. Approval Oriented			■	■
3. Interpersonal Loyalty	■	■	■	■
4. Others Oriented	■	■	■	■

▶ **Announcing/Rehearsing the Rules**

Establish rules regarding behavior in the classroom in order to define boundaries, expectations, and the consequences for misbehavior. Review them regularly.

1. Establish five to seven rules necessary for a good classroom atmosphere. Be sure to include a rule regarding talking.
2. Stress the consequences for disobeying the rules.
3. Post the rules in a conspicuous place.
4. Repeat the rules every day until the students can recite and follow them automatically.
5. Add or change rules that are burdensome, unnecessary, or unworkable.
6. Be consistent in carrying out the consequences for each infraction.

▶ **Probing for Motives**

Ask yourself questions to determine the goal behind the student's misbehavior.

1. Ask yourself the following questions immediately after the student's misbehavior:
   - Do I feel annoyed? Attention-getting may be or is likely the goal.
   - Do I feel beaten or intimidated? Power may be or is likely the goal.
   - Do I feel wronged or hurt? Revenge may be or is likely the goal.
   - Do I feel incapable of reaching this student? Helplessness may be or is likely the goal.
2. Respond to the appropriate motive as follows:
   - *Attention-getting.* Deprive the student of attention.
   - *Power.* Do not allow open conflict. State the rules and consequences, and then move on.
   - *Revenge.* Determine the reason for the student's hurt feelings.
   - *Helplessness.* Provide opportunities for the student to succeed.

Reinforcement of Limits

Level of Motivation	Behavior Style			
	Self-Assertive	Socially Interactive	Analytic	Accommodating
1. Self-Absorbed		■	■	■
2. Approval Oriented	■	■		
3. Interpersonal Loyalty				
4. Others Oriented				

▶ **Stopping and Redirecting**
Stop the student's inappropriate behavior, and redirect his or her attention to the task at hand.

1. Identify the causes for the student's talking.
2. Tell the student to stop talking.
3. Tell the student to concentrate on the appropriate task.
4. Check to see if the student continues to work.

Level of Motivation	Behavior Style			
	Self-Assertive	Socially Interactive	Analytic	Accommodating
1. Self-Absorbed				
2. Approval Oriented			■	■
3. Interpersonal Loyalty	■	■	■	■
4. Others Oriented	■	■	■	■

▶ **Establishing Logical Consequences**
Establish logical consequences for certain behaviors.

1. Announce a rule regarding talking, and establish logical consequences
   (e.g., if two students continue to talk with one another, move them to another part of the classroom to continue their discussion with the understanding that all time missed in class must be made up afterward, including the time required for the teacher's intervention).
2. Rehearse the rule and the consequences for breaking it until students fully understand.
3. Follow through with the consequences for talking without permission, and make sure the students can see the connection between talking in class and the ensuing consequences.

Reinforcement of Limits *(continued)*

Level of Motivation	Behavior Style			
	Self-Assertive	Socially Interactive	Analytic	Accommodating
1. Self-Absorbed		■	■	■
2. Approval Oriented	■	■		
3. Interpersonal Loyalty				
4. Others Oriented				

▶ Asking "What" Questions

Ask "what" questions until the student acknowledges his or her misbehavior; do not accept excuses.

1. Ask the student a "what" question when talking occurs (e.g., "What are you doing?").

2. Continue to ask "what" questions until the student describes his or her behavior without making excuses.

3. Ask a "how" question (e.g., "How does talking while I give instructions help you complete the assignment correctly?").

4. Ask another "what" question (e.g., "What would be a better way to behave?").
Help the student find solutions.

5. Establish a plan for improvement that includes consequences for continued misbehavior.

Control

Level of Motivation	Behavior Style			
	Self-Assertive	Socially Interactive	Analytic	Accommodating
1. Self-Absorbed	■	■	■	■
2. Approval Oriented	■	■	■	■
3. Interpersonal Loyalty		■	■	■
4. Others Oriented				

▶ Isolation Within the Classroom

Temporarily move the student to an isolated area of the classroom where he or she can continue to work.

1. Establish ahead of time that talking at inappropriate times will result in temporary isolation.
2. Choose a relocation area that is free from any stimulating objects or persons.
3. When talking occurs again, follow through exactly as promised.
4. Increase the time away from the class for each subsequent occurrence of the behavior.

Talking Back

Verbally responding to a teacher in a manner that is a direct challenge
to the teacher's authority or an inappropriate response to a direction or question

Limit Setting

	Behavior Style			
Level of Motivation	Self-Assertive	Socially Interactive	Analytic	Accommodating
1. Self-Absorbed				
2. Approval Oriented			■	■
3. Interpersonal Loyalty	■	■	■	■
4. Others Oriented	■	■	■	■

▶ Probing for Motives

Ask yourself questions to determine the goal behind the student's misbehavior.

1. Ask yourself the following questions immediately after the student talks back:
    * Do I feel annoyed? Attention-getting may be or is likely the goal.
    * Do I feel beaten or intimidated? Power may be or is likely the goal.
    * Do I feel wronged or hurt? Revenge may be or is likely the goal.
    * Do I feel incapable of reaching this student? Helplessness may be or is likely the goal.

2. Respond to the appropriate motive as follows:
    * *Attention-getting.* Deprive the student of attention.
    * *Power.* Do not allow open conflict. State the rules and consequences, and then move on.
    * *Revenge.* Determine the reason for the student's hurt feelings.
    * *Helplessness.* Provide opportunities for the student to succeed.

Reinforcement of Limits

Level of Motivation	Behavior Style			
	Self-Assertive	Socially Interactive	Analytic	Accommodating
1. Self-Absorbed		■	■	■
2. Approval Oriented	■	■	■	■
3. Interpersonal Loyalty	■	■	■	■
4. Others Oriented				

▶ Establishing Logical Consequences
Establish logical consequences for certain behaviors.
1. Present a list of classroom rules, and be sure to include a rule concerning talking back.
2. Rehearse the rules and the consequences for breaking them until each student fully understands.
3. When talking back occurs, choose the appropriate logical consequence, and explain the connection to the student.

▶ Asking "What" Questions
Ask "what" questions until the student acknowledges his or her misbehavior; do not accept excuses.
1. Ask a "what" question that zeroes in on the problem.
2. Continue to ask "what" questions until the student verbalizes the problem without making excuses.
3. Ask a "how" question (e.g., "How did talking back help solve the problem?").
4. Ask another "what" question (e.g., "What could you do next time, instead of talking back?").
5. Offer suggestions if the student has difficulty finding good solutions.
6. Obtain a verbal agreement from the student that includes consequences for continued misbehavior.

▶ Charting Progress
Use charts to monitor misbehavior and check the student's progress.
1. Identify and analyze the circumstances that precede the student's talking back.
2. Discuss the misbehavior with the student, and make sure he or she understands the problem.
3. Set a goal to correct the behavior. Divide it into workable steps, and aim for mastery of one step at a time.
4. Chart the student's progress toward the goal.
5. Establish a reward for completion of the goal, if appropriate.

Control

Level of Motivation	Behavior Style			
	Self-Assertive	Socially Interactive	Analytic	Accommodating
1. Self-Absorbed	■			
2. Approval Oriented				
3. Interpersonal Loyalty				
4. Others Oriented				

▶ Requiring a Plan for Improvement

Separate the student from the rest of the class, and have him or her prepare a plan for improved behavior. Do not allow the student to return to the classroom until he or she presents an acceptable plan.

1. Designate a separate relocation area, away from any stimulating objects or people.
2. Have the student complete a written plan that addresses the following questions: What did I do? Why is it a problem? What rule did I break? How do I plan to avoid this problem?
3. Discuss the plan, and have the student rethink problem areas.
4. Have the student date and sign the plan.
5. Hold the student to the plan. Have him or her rewrite it if the misbehavior continues.

▶ Deducting Points for Misbehavior

Deduct points (or tokens) or withhold privileges the student has earned.
(Deduction of points should occur in conjunction with a token reinforcement system.)

1. Choose the number of points that will be deducted for talking back.
2. Inform the student that although he or she will earn points for appropriate behavior, the number of points you have chosen will be deducted when he or she talks back. When dealing with a group behavior problem, announce and post the terms of this rule.
3. Initially, a nonverbal cue (e.g., one hand held up with the palm facing the student as a signal to "stop") could be given as a warning if the student begins to talk back.
4. After the warning, deduct points exactly as you have stipulated if the misbehavior continues.
5. If this strategy is not effective, consider increasing the frequency with which points are awarded and/or increasing the desirability of the rewards for which points can be redeemed (e.g., rather than 10 minutes of free reading time, substitute an opportunity to play an enjoyable computer game that is normally restricted).
6. If the problem persists, increase the number of points deducted for each subsequent offense (e.g., 10 points for the first time, 25 points for the second time, etc.).

▶ Detention

Keep the student after school for a specified period of time.
Note. Use this strategy only after you have tried other strategies.

1. Make it clear that detention will be used in response to talking back. Tell the student that he or she will remain in the room with the teacher, so that the teacher can have his or her undivided attention.
2. Use detention time to build a relationship with the student.
3. Work with the student to improve his or her negative attitude and areas of academic weakness.
4. End the detention time positively, if possible.
5. Increase the length of detention for subsequent misbehavior.

Control *(continued)*

▶ **Having a Parent in the Classroom**

Bring one of the student's parents into the classroom to observe the student's behavior there.

Note. Before using this strategy, you may want to try one or more of the following three less intrusive strategies: Alerting Parents to Concerns, Exchanging Information With Parents, and Suggesting Parental Intervention Strategies (see under *Prevention, Limit Setting,* and *Reinforcement of Limits,* respectively, in chapter 3).

1. Ask one or both of the student's parents to attend class for one hour during a time when the student's talking back is most likely to occur.

2. Let the student know that his or her parent(s) will be coming to class to observe. Do not surprise the student.

3. Have the parent(s) sit at the rear of the classroom and observe—without participating in classroom activities.

4. Schedule time to talk with the parent(s) after the visit to discuss the student's behavior and how it compares with his or her normal behavior during that time period. Include the student if appropriate.

5. Work with the parent(s) to develop a cooperative plan to help the student maintain appropriate behavior.

TANTRUMS

Acting out frustration or uncontrolled anger—for example,
kicking, screaming, biting, verbal outbursts, or holding one's breath

Prevention

Level of Motivation	Behavior Style			
	Self-Assertive	Socially Interactive	Analytic	Accommodating
1. Self-Absorbed				
2. Approval Oriented				
3. Interpersonal Loyalty			■	■
4. Others Oriented		■	■	■

▶ Asking Adult Questions

Use adult-oriented questions to appeal to the student's rational abilities.

1. After the tantrum is over, assume that the student is operating in the adult mode.

2. Ask a question that meets the needs of the adult mode (e.g., "What can you do to solve this problem?").

3. Revert to the parent mode only if adult-to-adult communication is not working.

4. Never revert to the child mode. Avoid condemnatory questions or comments
   (e.g., "Why do you have tantrums like a baby?").

Limit Setting

Level of Motivation	Behavior Style			
	Self-Assertive	Socially Interactive	Analytic	Accommodating
1. Self-Absorbed				
2. Approval Oriented				
3. Interpersonal Loyalty				
4. Others Oriented			■	■

▶ Disguising Directives

Disguise verbal directives to get the student to behave and to avoid confrontation.

1. Give the class as a whole a hint about the problem of reacting to frustration with tantrums.

2. Give a disguised verbal directive to the target student (e.g., "Would you like to start working on your assignment now?" or "Would you like to ask a question about the assignment?").

3. Focus on the activity or task, and avoid direct confrontation.

Reinforcement of Limits

Level of Motivation	Behavior Style			
	Self-Assertive	Socially Interactive	Analytic	Accommodating
1. Self-Absorbed		■	■	■
2. Approval Oriented	■	■	■	■
3. Interpersonal Loyalty	■	■	■	■
4. Others Oriented				

▶ Asking "What" Questions

Ask "what" questions until the student acknowledges his or her misbehavior; do not accept excuses.

1. Ask a "what" question that addresses the student's misbehavior
   (e.g., "What are you doing with your arms right now?" or "What are you kicking?").
2. Continue asking "what" questions until the student describes his or her misbehavior without making excuses.
3. Ask a "how" question (e.g., "How did this outburst help you?").
4. Ask another "what" question (e.g., "What would be a better way to show me how you feel?").
5. Devise a verbal plan for improvement that is agreeable to both the student and the teacher. The plan should include consequences for continued misbehavior.

▶ Suggesting Parental Intervention Strategies

Enlist the parents' help in correcting the student's behavior.

Note. Before using this strategy, you may want to try the less intrusive Alerting Parents to Concerns and/or Exchanging Information With Parents strategies (see under *Prevention* and *Limit Setting,* respectively, in chapter 3).

1. Meet with the student's parents to discuss the circumstances surrounding his or her tantrums and the frequency of the behavior. Do the tantrums occur at home as well as at school? If so, how are the parents handling the problem at home?
2. If appropriate, use the same or a similar approach to the problem at home and at school. Reach an agreement with the parents and the student as to what the consequences for continued misbehavior will be, and establish some type of reward for consistent appropriate behavior.
3. Arrange weekly communication between yourself and the parents to discuss the student's progress.

Control

Level of Motivation	Behavior Style			
	Self-Assertive	Socially Interactive	Analytic	Accommodating
1. Self-Absorbed	■			
2. Approval Oriented				
3. Interpersonal Loyalty				
4. Others Oriented				

▶ Relocation Within the Classroom

Move the misbehaving student to a less problematic location within the classroom.

1. Make sure the other students have tasks they can work on independently while you respond to the tantrum.
2. As quickly as possible, move the unruly student to a semiprivate area of the classroom.
3. Try to reassure and calm the student by holding his or her shoulder or by just sitting with him or her.
4. Leave the student in the new location until he or she has regained control and calmed down.
5. Follow up with a suitable longer-term strategy that is appropriate to the student and the situation.

Level of Motivation	Behavior Style			
	Self-Assertive	Socially Interactive	Analytic	Accommodating
1. Self-Absorbed		■	■	■
2. Approval Oriented	■	■	■	■
3. Interpersonal Loyalty				
4. Others Oriented				

▶ Exclusion From Fun Activities

Exclude the student from an activity he or she enjoys.

1. Determine which activity the student enjoys most. Warn the student that any disruptions during that time will result in his or her removal from the activity.
2. The next time the activity is disrupted by a tantrum, promptly remove the student, thereby demonstrating that such inappropriate behavior will not be tolerated in the classroom environment.
3. Allow the student to observe the activity from a distance as long as he or she does not become disruptive.
4. Speak to the student in private after the tantrum is over, and invite him or her to rejoin the group.

Control *(continued)*

Level of Motivation	Behavior Style			
	Self-Assertive	Socially Interactive	Analytic	Accommodating
1. Self-Absorbed	■			
2. Approval Oriented				
3. Interpersonal Loyalty				
4. Others Oriented				

▶ **Time Out**

Move the student to a nonstimulating environment outside the classroom so that he or she can cool down and regain the ability to think rationally.

1. Determine whether the student has lost control of his or her behavior.
2. Designate a specific relocation area where the student can go to regain control.
3. Bring the student back into the classroom only after he or she has cooled off, as evidenced by the completion of an assignment or task.
4. Seek a solution to the problem that caused the tantrum.
5. Increase the duration of time out for each subsequent incident.
6. Be sure the student makes up missed work. Such work should be done at recess, during lunch, after school, or at home.

▶ **Requiring a Plan for Improvement**

Separate the student from the rest of the class, and have him or her prepare a plan for improved behavior. Do not allow the student to return to the classroom until he or she presents an acceptable plan.

1. Designate a separate relocation area, away from any stimulating objects or people.
2. Have the student complete a written plan that addresses the following questions: What did I do? Why is it a problem? What rule did I break? How do I plan to avoid this problem?
3. Discuss the plan, and have the student rethink any problem areas.
4. Have the student date and sign the plan, and refer to it often. If the tantrums occur again, have the student rewrite the plan.

▶ **Having a Parent in the Classroom**

Bring one of the student's parents into the classroom to observe the student's behavior there.

Note. Before using this strategy, you may want to try one or more of the following three less intrusive strategies: Alerting Parents to Concerns, Exchanging Information With Parents, and Suggesting Parental Intervention Strategies (see under *Prevention, Limit Setting,* and *Reinforcement of Limits,* respectively, in chapter 3).

1. Ask one or both parents to attend a typical class period for at least one hour.
2. Notify the student that his or her parent(s) will be coming to class. It should not be a surprise.
3. Have the parent(s) sit near the back of the room to observe the class without becoming involved in classroom activities.
4. Schedule some time afterward to talk about what occurred compared to what usually happens, and to discuss ways to remedy the situation. Include the student if appropriate.
5. Agree on a plan, and continue to work with the parents until the tantrums cease or a better plan can be developed.

TARDINESS

Regularly arriving late for class, school, or school events

Prevention

Level of Motivation	Behavior Style			
	Self-Assertive	Socially Interactive	Analytic	Accommodating
1. Self-Absorbed				
2. Approval Oriented				
3. Interpersonal Loyalty			■	■
4. Others Oriented		■	■	■

► Sharing Authority and Decision Making

Give peers some authority to help stop a student's misbehavior.

1. Review the class or school rule that students are to arrive at class on time.
2. Discuss with the students the need for a cooperative effort to help stop tardiness.
3. Discuss the problems caused by tardiness (interruptions in class, missed lessons, etc.) and possible solutions (punishment, rewards for consistently being on time, etc.).
4. Develop a plan. Seek consensus when possible, but avoid taking a vote.
5. Give certain students—maybe even the worst offenders—tasks to help implement the plan.

Limit Setting

Level of Motivation	Behavior Style			
	Self-Assertive	Socially Interactive	Analytic	Accommodating
1. Self-Absorbed				
2. Approval Oriented			■	■
3. Interpersonal Loyalty	■	■	■	■
4. Others Oriented	■	■	■	■

▶ **Describing Misbehavior as It Occurs**

Describe to the student what he or she has just done, is doing, or is about to do.

1. Describe to the student exactly what is happening, without accusations (e.g., say, "This is the second time you have been late this week").
2. Wait for a sign that the student understands why the behavior is wrong.
3. Allow the student to offer a potential solution to the problem.
4. Describe the effects of his or her tardiness on others and the possible consequences for continued misbehavior.

▶ **Appealing to Values**

Confront the student about his or her misbehavior, and compare it to the positive values he or she holds.

1. Observe the student, and note the values he or she seems to have, especially those related to punctuality.
2. Explain to the student the importance of punctuality.
   Contrast the behavior you expect with the tardiness the student is exhibiting.
3. Encourage the student to consider how and why he or she has abandoned otherwise positive values in this case.
4. After class, ask the student to explain his or her values and how they will be demonstrated by being on time for class.

▶ **Probing for Motives**

Ask yourself questions to determine the goal behind the student's misbehavior.

1. When the student is tardy, ask yourself the following questions:
   * Do I feel annoyed? Attention-getting may be or is likely the goal.
   * Do I feel beaten or intimidated? Power may be or is likely the goal.
   * Do I feel wronged or hurt? Revenge may be or is likely the goal.
   * Do I feel incapable of reaching this student? Helplessness may be or is likely the goal.
2. Respond to the appropriate motive as follows:
   * *Attention-getting.* Deprive the student of attention.
   * *Power.* Do not allow open conflict. State the rules and consequences, and then move on.
   * *Revenge.* Determine the reason for the student's hurt feelings.
   * *Helplessness.* Provide opportunities for the student to succeed.

Reinforcement of Limits

Level of Motivation	Behavior Style			
	Self-Assertive	Socially Interactive	Analytic	Accommodating
1. Self-Absorbed		■	■	■
2. Approval Oriented	■	■		
3. Interpersonal Loyalty				
4. Others Oriented				

▶ Establishing Logical Consequences
Establish logical consequences for certain behaviors.

1. Inform students that you expect them to be punctual for class. Establish specific rules regarding tardiness. Rehearse the rules until they are easily recalled and clearly understood.
2. Choose consequences that have a logical connection to tardiness (e.g., say, "For every minute you are late, you will spend a minute at lunch or after school making up missed work").
3. Clearly state and occasionally rehearse the consequences for infractions, so that students know what will happen if they break the rule.
4. When a student is late, calmly but firmly restate the penalty for tardiness. Be sure that the student understands the connection between his or her behavior and its consequences. Be consistent with both expectations and enforcement so that the consequences are seen as a logical extension of tardiness.

▶ Asking "What" Questions
Ask "what" questions until the student acknowledges his or her misbehavior; do not accept excuses.

1. Ask "what" questions that directly address the tardiness, until the student describes his or her misbehavior without making excuses.
2. Ask a "how" question to focus on the negative result of the action, as well as the potential benefit of changed behavior.
3. Come to an agreement on how the student will avoid being late in the future. Hold the student to that agreement.

▶ Charting Progress
Use charts to monitor misbehavior and check the student's progress.

1. Observe and discuss with the student the frequency of his or her tardiness.
2. Decide on a mutually agreeable plan to increase punctuality, and set rewards for attainment of specific goals.
3. Write the goals on a chart so that the student's progress can be monitored.
4. Reward achievement of goals as promised.

Control

Level of Motivation	Behavior Style			
	Self-Assertive	Socially Interactive	Analytic	Accommodating
1. Self-Absorbed	■	■	■	■
2. Approval Oriented	■	■	■	■
3. Interpersonal Loyalty	■	■	■	■
4. Others Oriented	■	■	■	■

▶ ## Coordinating Outside Intervention

Coordinate help or support from an outside source
(e.g., a mental health or family service agency, the legal system, etc.).

1. Keep accurate, detailed records of the student's tardiness. Is there a pattern?
   Is tardiness more likely to occur on certain days or for certain activities?

2. Determine whether you are able or qualified to handle the problem.

3. Contact the student's parents to discuss the problem and how they can help.
   Suggest contacting an outside agency for help.

4. Be sure you know your school's policies on agency contact and involvement. Contact the principal
   or appropriate agencies directly if the parents could be the problem. (Again, follow school policies.)

Control *(continued)*

Level of Motivation	Behavior Style			
	Self-Assertive	Socially Interactive	Analytic	Accommodating
1. Self-Absorbed	■			
2. Approval Oriented				
3. Interpersonal Loyalty				
4. Others Oriented				

▶ Requiring a Plan for Improvement

Separate the student from the rest of the class, and have him or her prepare a plan for improved behavior. Do not allow the student to return to the classroom until he or she presents an acceptable plan.

1. Designate a relocation area away from peers where the student can complete a plan. This area should be free of any stimulation—that is, it should be a boring, undesirable place to have to spend time.
2. Have the relocated student complete a written plan that addresses the following questions: What did I do? What rule did I break? Why is it a problem? How do I plan to avoid this problem?
3. Go over the plan with the student. Encourage the student to acknowledge the problem, and to realistically address future compliance with the rule.
4. Adhere tightly to the plan. If tardiness continues to be a problem, renegotiate the agreement with the student, and if necessary, rewrite the plan.

▶ Deducting Points for Misbehavior

Deduct points (or tokens) or withhold privileges the student has earned.
(Deduction of points should occur in conjunction with a token reinforcement system.)

1. Choose the number of points that will be deducted for tardiness.
2. Inform the student that although he or she will earn points for appropriate behavior, the number of points you have chosen will be deducted when he or she arrives late. When dealing with a group behavior problem, announce and post the terms of this rule.
3. Deduct points exactly as you have stipulated each time the student is tardy.
4. If this strategy is not effective, consider increasing the frequency with which points are awarded and/or increasing the desirability of the rewards for which points can be redeemed (e.g., rather than 10 minutes of free reading time, substitute an opportunity to play an enjoyable computer game that is normally restricted).
5. If the problem persists, increase the number of points deducted for each subsequent offense (e.g., 10 points for the first time, 25 points for the second time, etc.).

▶ Detention

Keep the student after school for a specified period of time.

1. Establish that the consequence for excessive tardiness will be detention.
2. When the student is tardy, immediately inform him or her of the impending detention. Notify the student's parents in accordance with school policy.
3. Utilize the detention time to establish communication—and hopefully, rapport—with the student. Probe for the cause of the misbehavior.
4. Address the possible results of tardiness. Get the student to at least admit that there is reason for concern.
5. Formulate a plan with the student to better manage his or her time.
6. End the detention on a positive note if possible.
7. Increase the length of the detention for each successive incident. Renegotiate plans when necessary to more accurately address the situation.

TATTLING

Continuously bringing the teacher stories about other students' misbehavior

Prevention

Level of Motivation	Behavior Style			
	Self-Assertive	Socially Interactive	Analytic	Accommodating
1. Self-Absorbed				
2. Approval Oriented				
3. Interpersonal Loyalty			■	■
4. Others Oriented	■	■	■	

▶ Checking for Understanding

To avoid misbehavior caused by frustration, have the student repeat instructions to make sure that he or she clearly understands what is expected.

1. Early in the school year, explain the difference between telling an adult about a student who may be doing something harmful and tattling to get someone else in trouble.
2. Explain the concept of tearing others down to build oneself up.
3. Describe appropriate reasons to report behavior, so that students will know what constitutes a legitimate cause for concern.

Level of Motivation	Behavior Style			
	Self-Assertive	Socially Interactive	Analytic	Accommodating
1. Self-Absorbed				
2. Approval Oriented				
3. Interpersonal Loyalty			■	■
4. Others Oriented	■	■	■	■

▶ Ignoring Misbehavior

Eliminate the student's payoff for inappropriate attention-getting behavior by refusing to acknowledge it.

1. Determine whether the student's tattling is being used as an attention-getting device.
2. Decide to endure the tattling for a short period of time.
3. When the student tattles, ignore him or her.
4. Expect increased tattling until the student realizes that it is a useless activity and stops the behavior.

▶ Identifying Idealized Characters

Encourage the student to imitate the positive behavior of an idealized character.

1. In conversations with the student, find out which characters he or she feels are most important.
2. Ask the student what he or she admires about that character.
   Later, find out as much about the character as possible to identify traits the student needs to emulate.
3. As tactfully as possible, compare the student's inappropriate behavior to the appropriate traits and behavior of the model character.
4. Acknowledge and praise emulation of the appropriate behaviors and characteristics, carefully pointing out any similarities to the idealized character.

Limit Setting

Level of Motivation	Behavior Style			
	Self-Assertive	Socially Interactive	Analytic	Accommodating
1. Self-Absorbed				
2. Approval Oriented			■	■
3. Interpersonal Loyalty		■		
4. Others Oriented				

▶ Direct Commands
Make specific demands, spoken with authority, concerning the student's behavior.
1. To assure a firm but friendly style, practice delivering the command beforehand.
2. State the demand to stop tattling.
3. Analyze the results. If the student does not stop, a more intrusive strategy may be called for.

▶ Reflecting Verbal Responses
Verbally reflect the essence of a student's argument in order to clarify his or her true feelings.
1. Listen carefully to the student, and attempt to determine his or her encoded message.
2. Repeat that message to the student
   (e.g., say, "When you tattle, at least someone is listening to you, right?").
3. Continue to repeat such messages until no further clarification is forthcoming.
4. Do not try to guess what the underlying problem may be—just reflect what is actually said.
5. If this strategy is unsuccessful, consider a more intrusive approach.

▶ Probing for Motives
Ask yourself questions to determine the goal behind the student's misbehavior.
1. Ask yourself the following questions immediately after tattling occurs:
   - Do I feel annoyed? Attention-getting may be or is likely the goal.
   - Do I feel beaten or intimidated? Power may be or is likely the goal.
   - Do I feel wronged or hurt? Revenge may be or is likely the goal.
   - Do I feel incapable of reaching this student? Helplessness may be or is likely the goal.
2. Respond to the appropriate motive as follows:
   - *Attention-getting.* Deprive the student of attention.
   - *Power.* Do not allow open conflict. State the rules and consequences, and then move on.
   - *Revenge.* Determine the reason for the student's hurt feelings.
   - *Helplessness.* Provide opportunities for the student to succeed.

Reinforcement of Limits

Level of Motivation	Behavior Style			
	Self-Assertive	Socially Interactive	Analytic	Accommodating
1. Self-Absorbed		■	■	■
2. Approval Oriented	■	■		
3. Interpersonal Loyalty				
4. Others Oriented				

▶ Stopping and Redirecting

Stop the student's inappropriate behavior, and redirect his or her attention to the task at hand.

1. When the student begins to tattle, tell him or her to stop it and to focus on the task at hand (e.g., say, "Stop tattling. Go back to your seat and do your spelling lesson!").
2. Check shortly thereafter to see if the student is on task.

▶ Asking "What" Questions

Ask "what" questions until the student acknowledges his or her misbehavior; do not accept excuses.

1. Ask "what" questions that directly address the misbehavior, until the student responds without making excuses.
2. Ask a "how" question that focuses on the negative results of tattling (e.g., "How did telling on your classmate help you do your schoolwork?").
3. Establish a plan for improved behavior that includes consequences for continued tattling.

▶ Charting Progress

Use charts to monitor misbehavior and check the student's progress.

1. Determine the student's motivation for tattling. Usually, it is a desire for attention.
2. Discuss tattling with the student, its effect on others, and why it is inappropriate. Be sure the student understands what the problem is.
3. Set goals, or a series of steps toward a goal, to end the tattling.
4. Make a chart. If possible, make photocopies of the chart to use over the next 3 to 4 weeks. It often takes at least 21 days to break a habit.
5. Set a specific goal (e.g., "No tattling for at least four out of five class periods, five days in a row").
6. Mark the chart for each period that tattling did not occur.
7. When one goal is met, set a more difficult goal. Let the student know that you are pleased with his or her progress.

Control

Level of Motivation	Behavior Style			
	Self-Assertive	Socially Interactive	Analytic	Accommodating
1. Self-Absorbed	■			
2. Approval Oriented				
3. Interpersonal Loyalty				
4. Others Oriented				

▶ Time Out for a Specified Period or Activity

Establish rules in advance for the use of specified periods of time out in response to angry outbursts.

1. Create or designate a relocation area away from peers to be used for time out. This area should be free of any and all stimulation—that is, a boring, undesirable place to have to spend time.
2. Explain clearly the difference between tattling (trying to get someone in trouble) and reporting (trying to avert trouble or prevent someone from getting hurt). Be sure that the student understands the difference.
3. When tattling occurs, implement the time out process in the designated area for a specified period of time that should increase with each offense. Discuss what will happen if this system fails.
4. Follow through consistently, as promised.

▶ Requiring a Plan for Improvement

Separate the student from the rest of the class, and have him or her prepare a plan for improved behavior. Do not allow the student to return to the classroom until he or she presents an acceptable plan.

1. Designate a relocation area where the student can complete a plan. This area should be away from peers, and free of any and all stimulation—in other words, a boring, undesirable place to have to spend time.
2. Have the student complete a written plan that addresses the following questions: What did I do? What rule did I break? Why is it a problem? How do I plan to avoid this problem?
3. Go over the plan with the student, and work through any problem areas.
4. Adhere tightly to the plan. If it fails, renegotiate the agreement with the student, and if necessary, rewrite the plan.

▶ Deducting Points for Misbehavior

Deduct points (or tokens) or withhold privileges the student has earned.
(Deduction of points should occur in conjunction with a token reinforcement system.)

1. Choose the number of points that will be deducted for tattling.
2. Inform the student that although he or she will earn points for appropriate behavior, the number of points you have chosen will be deducted when he or she tattles about classmates. When dealing with a group behavior problem, announce and post the terms of this rule.
3. Initially, a nonverbal signal could be given as a warning if the student begins to tattle (e.g., placing one finger against your lips as a signal to "hush").
4. After one warning, deduct points exactly as you have stipulated if the tattling continues.
5. If this strategy is not effective, consider increasing the frequency with which points are awarded and/or increasing the desirability of the rewards for which points can be redeemed (e.g., rather than 10 minutes of free reading time, substitute an opportunity to play a game with a friend).
6. If the problem persists, dispense with the warning and increase the number of points deducted for each subsequent offense (e.g., 10 points for the first time, 25 points for the second time, etc.).

TEASING

Excessively taunting other students, making fun of the physical or behavioral peculiarities of others, humiliating another student in front of others, and so on

Prevention

Level of Motivation	Behavior Style			
	Self-Assertive	Socially Interactive	Analytic	Accommodating
1. Self-Absorbed				
2. Approval Oriented		■	■	■
3. Interpersonal Loyalty	■	■	■	■
4. Others Oriented	■			

▶ Using a Businesslike Teaching Style
Maintain a serious, businesslike atmosphere in the classroom.
1. Design structured lesson plans that include opening statements, transitions, and closing statements.
2. Structure the entire school day, including group activities, to keep relationships businesslike.
3. Dress in a conservative, mature manner.
4. Structure behavior in the classroom with logical, easily understood rules for appropriate interaction.
5. Stay on task at all times. Enforce rules matter-of-factly unless behavior becomes so disruptive that it is necessary to interrupt the lesson plan.

Limit Setting

Level of Motivation	Behavior Style			
	Self-Assertive	Socially Interactive	Analytic	Accommodating
1. Self-Absorbed				
2. Approval Oriented			■	■
3. Interpersonal Loyalty	■	■	■	■
4. Others Oriented	■	■	■	■

▶ Announcing/Rehearsing the Rules

Establish rules regarding behavior in the classroom in order to define boundaries, expectations, and the consequences for misbehavior. Review them regularly.

1. At the onset of the school year, establish a rule that prohibits making fun of people. Make sure the students understand the need for such a rule.
2. Make the consequences for breaking the rule logical and clear.
3. Post the rule in a conspicuous place at the front of the classroom.
4. Repeat the rule daily until the students are able to recite and follow it without much thought. Occasionally, repeat the consequences for breaking the rule.
5. Enforce the rule consistently as infractions occur. Be careful not to allow even an occasional one-liner that violates the spirit of the rule.

▶ Describing Misbehavior as It Occurs

Describe to the student what he or she has just done, is doing, or is about to do.

1. Describe to the student exactly what just happened, without being judgmental (e.g., say, "I heard you say something to Bruce, and then he walked away looking angry").
2. Wait for a sign that the student understands how the behavior was wrong.
3. Allow the student to offer a potential solution to the problem.
4. Describe the effects of teasing and the possible consequences for continued misbehavior.

▶ Modeling Expected Behavior

Demonstrate by example the behavior you want the student to exhibit.

1. Discuss with the student the hurt or irritation caused by teasing.
2. Demonstrate the appropriate way to relate (i.e., be encouraging and respectful).
3. Ask the student how he or she would prefer to be treated. Once the student has identified the appropriate behavior, ask what sort of feelings his or her teasing has probably caused.
4. Monitor the student's behavior to be sure that teasing does not continue.

Reinforcement of Limits

Level of Motivation	Behavior Style			
	Self-Assertive	Socially Interactive	Analytic	Accommodating
1. Self-Absorbed		■	■	■
2. Approval Oriented	■	■		
3. Interpersonal Loyalty				
4. Others Oriented				

▶ Stopping and Redirecting

Stop the student's inappropriate behavior, and redirect his or her attention to the task at hand.

1. When teasing begins, tell the student to stop, then redirect him or her to the appropriate activity.
2. Check shortly thereafter to be sure that the student is on task.

▶ Charting Progress

Use charts to monitor misbehavior and check the student's progress.

1. Determine what circumstances tend to precede the student's teasing.
2. Talk with the student about his or her teasing, its effect on others, and why it is inappropriate. Be sure that the student understands what the problem is.
3. Work with the student to set goals to end the teasing.
4. Write the goals on a chart, and make enough photocopies of the chart for the next 3 to 4 weeks.
5. Every time the student teases someone, mark the chart. Plot the results on a graph, and share them with the student.

▶ Suggesting Parental Intervention Strategies

Enlist the parents' help in correcting the student's behavior.

Note. Before using this strategy, you may want to try the less intrusive Alerting Parents to Concerns and/or Exchanging Information With Parents strategies (see under *Prevention* and *Limit Setting,* respectively, in chapter 3).

1. Think of ways that the student's parents can help stop his or her teasing. If the student also teases at home, it may be appropriate to suggest consequences that correspond to those used at school.
2. Call the parents, remind them of the problem, and ask for their assistance in solving it. Offer your suggestions regarding what they can do to stop the inappropriate behavior.
3. Come to an agreement with the parents on what they will do to help remedy the situation, and arrange to be in contact with them on a regular basis to monitor progress and compare notes.
4. Within the next 24 hours, either mail the parents a written restatement of the plan or send it home with the student.

Control

Level of Motivation	Behavior Style			
	Self-Assertive	Socially Interactive	Analytic	Accommodating
1. Self-Absorbed	■			
2. Approval Oriented				
3. Interpersonal Loyalty				
4. Others Oriented				

▶ Isolation Within the Classroom

Temporarily move the student to an isolated area of the classroom where he or she can continue to work.

1. Designate an isolated area of the classroom as a hot seat from which the student can neither bother, nor be bothered by, others.
2. Explain that the hot seat will be used to isolate students who cannot or will not treat others with respect.
3. Establish consequences beyond the use of the hot seat for continued teasing.
4. Invoke penalties as promised. Whenever a student teases someone, send him or her to the hot seat, and do not allow further participation in the current class activity.

Level of Motivation	Behavior Style			
	Self-Assertive	Socially Interactive	Analytic	Accommodating
1. Self-Absorbed		■	■	■
2. Approval Oriented	■	■	■	■
3. Interpersonal Loyalty				
4. Others Oriented				

▶ Exclusion From Fun Activities

Exclude the student from an activity he or she enjoys.

1. Determine which activity the student enjoys most.
   Warn the student that any teasing will be punished by his or her exclusion from that activity.
2. When teasing occurs, promptly remove the student, thereby demonstrating that such inappropriate behavior will not be tolerated in the classroom.
3. Allow the student to observe the activity from a distance as long as he or she does not become disruptive.
4. Speak to the student in private after the behavior is under control.
   Allow the student to rejoin the group only if he or she can refrain from teasing.

Control *(continued)*

	Behavior Style			
Level of Motivation	Self-Assertive	Socially Interactive	Analytic	Accommodating
1. Self-Absorbed	■			
2. Approval Oriented				
3. Interpersonal Loyalty				
4. Others Oriented				

▶ **Time Out**

Move the student to a nonstimulating environment so that he or she can cool down and regain the ability to think rationally.

1. Establish an area within the classroom to be used to isolate misbehaving students.
   Establish the amount of time to be spent in that area, and increase the time with each occurrence.

2. Discuss the purpose of time out with the class. Establish the consequences for continued misbehavior.

3. Whenever a student teases someone, remove the offender to the isolation area immediately.
   Be consistent.

▶ **Requiring a Plan for Improvement**

Separate the student from the rest of the class, and have him or her prepare a plan for improved behavior. Do not allow the student to return to the classroom until he or she presents an acceptable plan.

1. Designate a relocation area, away from peers, where the student can complete a plan.
   This area should be free of any and all stimulation.

2. Have the student complete a written plan that addresses the following questions: What did I do? What rule did I break? Why is teasing a problem? How do I plan to avoid this problem?

3. Go over the plan with the student and work through any problem areas.

4. Tightly adhere to the plan. Have the student rewrite it if teasing continues.

THREATS OF VIOLENCE

Overtly stating intent to physically harm another; physical stance, body language, or other form of intimidation that leads others to believe that physical harm is intended

Prevention

Level of Motivation	Behavior Style			
	Self-Assertive	Socially Interactive	Analytic	Accommodating
1. Self-Absorbed				
2. Approval Oriented			■	■
3. Interpersonal Loyalty	■	■	■	■
4. Others Oriented				

▶ **Alerting Parents to Concerns**
Contact parents to express your concern about the student's attitude or behavior.
1. Determine the severity of the problem.
2. Organize the information to be communicated so that there is no misunderstanding.
3. If the problem is serious, be frank. If the problem is not serious, avoid alarming the parents.
4. Do not lead the parents to a solution.
5. Write down any information the parents provide that might be helpful in solving the student's problem.
6. In closing the conversation, reaffirm your support for their child's education and your willingness to work with them.
7. Thank them for their time and cooperation.

Limit Setting

Level of Motivation	Behavior Style			
	Self-Assertive	Socially Interactive	Analytic	Accommodating
1. Self-Absorbed	■	■	■	■
2. Approval Oriented	■			
3. Interpersonal Loyalty				
4. Others Oriented				

▶ **Probing for Motives**

Ask yourself questions to determine the goal behind the student's misbehavior.

1. Ask yourself the following questions immediately after the student threatens violence:
    *   Do I feel annoyed? Attention-getting may be or is likely the goal.
    *   Do I feel beaten or intimidated? Power may be or is likely the goal.
    *   Do I feel wronged or hurt? Revenge may be or is likely the goal.
    *   Do I feel incapable of reaching this student? Helplessness may be or is likely the goal.

2. Respond to the appropriate motive as follows:
    *   *Attention-getting.* Deprive the student of attention.
    *   *Power.* Do not allow open conflict. State the rules and consequences, and then move on.
    *   *Revenge.* Determine the reason for the student's hurt feelings.
    *   *Helplessness.* Provide opportunities for the student to succeed.

Reinforcement of Limits

Level of Motivation	Behavior Style			
	Self-Assertive	Socially Interactive	Analytic	Accommodating
1. Self-Absorbed		■	■	■
2. Approval Oriented	■	■	■	■
3. Interpersonal Loyalty	■	■	■	■
4. Others Oriented				

▶ Establishing Logical Consequences

Establish logical consequences for certain behaviors.

1. Post a list of classroom rules, and make sure that the students understand them.
2. Rehearse the rules with the threatening student, and review the natural consequences of his or her behavior.
3. Establish consequences that correspond to the seriousness of the misbehavior—for example:
   - Missing a break, recess, lunch, or other free time to make up missed work
   - Forfeiting participation in special activities such as field trips, films, and so on
   - Apologizing to the student who was threatened, and doing something positive for the wronged student
   - Referral to another person or agency (e.g., a parent, the principal, the police, etc.) for help in controlling this behavior

▶ Asking "What" Questions

Ask "what" questions until the student acknowledges his or her misbehavior; do not accept excuses.

1. Ask a "what" question that directly addresses the student's misbehavior.
2. Continue asking "what" questions until the student acknowledges his or her misbehavior without making excuses.
3. Ask a "how" question (e.g., "How did this help you solve the problem?").
4. Come to an agreement on appropriate behavior in similar situations in the future.

Control

Level of Motivation	Behavior Style			
	Self-Assertive	Socially Interactive	Analytic	Accommodating
1. Self-Absorbed	■			
2. Approval Oriented				
3. Interpersonal Loyalty				
4. Others Oriented				

▶ Relocation Within the Classroom

Move the misbehaving student to a less problematic location within the classroom.

1. Identify the object or person that is contributing to the student's misbehavior.
2. Move the student to a place in the classroom that is closer to you and farther from the source of disruptive behavior.
3. Leave the student in the new location until his or her behavior is acceptable.

Level of Motivation	Behavior Style			
	Self-Assertive	Socially Interactive	Analytic	Accommodating
1. Self-Absorbed	■	■	■	■
2. Approval Oriented	■	■	■	■
3. Interpersonal Loyalty	■	■	■	■
4. Others Oriented				

▶ Coordinating Outside Intervention

Coordinate help or support from an outside source
(e.g., a mental health or family service agency, the legal system, etc.).

1. Describe to the student appropriate methods of interaction, and give him or her specific directives regarding physical threats.
2. If you observe a pattern of violence or threats of violence, keep an accurate record of such behavior.
3. If you feel the behavior requires outside intervention, contact the parents, inform them of the situation, and ask for their help in resolving the problem. If the behavior may be caused by parental neglect, contact the principal or an outside agency directly.
4. Work with the parents, administrator, or agency personnel to resolve the problem.

Control *(continued)*

Level of Motivation	Behavior Style			
	Self-Assertive	Socially Interactive	Analytic	Accommodating
1. Self-Absorbed	■			
2. Approval Oriented				
3. Interpersonal Loyalty				
4. Others Oriented				

▶ **Time Out**

Move the student to a nonstimulating environment so that he or she can cool down and regain the ability to think rationally.

1. Determine whether the student has lost his or her ability to act rationally.
2. Designate a relocation area, away from any stimulating objects or people, preferably outside the classroom.
3. Bring the student back once he or she has cooled down, as evidenced by the completion of a simple assignment or task.
4. Have the student complete all assignments missed while away.

▶ **Requiring a Plan for Improvement**

Separate the student from the rest of the class, and have him or her prepare a plan for improved behavior. Do not allow the student to return to the classroom until he or she presents an acceptable plan.

1. Designate an isolated relocation area that is readily available.
2. Have the student prepare a written plan that addresses the following questions: What did I do? Why is it a problem? What rule did I break? How do I plan to avoid threatening behavior in the future?
3. Discuss the plan, and encourage the student to adhere to it as closely as possible.
4. Have the student sign the plan. Rewrite it if threatening behavior continues.

▶ **Having a Parent in the Classroom**

Bring one of the student's parents into the classroom to observe the student's behavior there.

Note. Before using this strategy, you may want to try one or more of the following three less intrusive strategies: Alerting Parents to Concerns, Exchanging Information With Parents, and Suggesting Parental Intervention Strategies (see under *Prevention, Limit Setting,* and *Reinforcement of Limits,* respectively, in chapter 3).

1. Call one or both of the student's parents, and ask them to attend class for one hour during a time when their child's inappropriate behavior is most likely to occur.
2. Let the student know that his or her parent(s) will be coming to class to observe; it should not be a surprise.
3. Have the parent(s) sit at the rear of the classroom and observe classroom activities without participating.
4. Schedule time afterward to discuss the student's behavior during the visit and how it compared with his or her normal behavior during that time period.
5. Come to an agreement with the parent(s) on a cooperative plan to help solve the problem.

TILTING BACKWARD IN CHAIR

Rocking backward in chair so that only two legs of the chair remain on the floor

Prevention

Level of Motivation	Behavior Style			
	Self-Assertive	Socially Interactive	Analytic	Accommodating
1. Self-Absorbed				
2. Approval Oriented				
3. Interpersonal Loyalty			■	■
4. Others Oriented	■	■	■	■

▶ Increasing Physical Proximity
Spend more time near the student throughout the class period.

1. Circulate throughout the classroom, especially while lecturing.

2. Walk up and down the aisles near the misbehaving student without interrupting the lecture.

3. Continue teaching or monitoring while standing near the student for short periods of time. (You may want to put your hand on his or her chair to emphasize your presence.)

4. Sit near the student for a short period of time.

Limit Setting

Level of Motivation	Behavior Style			
	Self-Assertive	Socially Interactive	Analytic	Accommodating
1. Self-Absorbed				
2. Approval Oriented			■	■
3. Interpersonal Loyalty	■	■	■	■
4. Others Oriented	■	■	■	■

▶ Announcing/Rehearsing the Rules

Establish rules regarding behavior in the classroom in order to define boundaries, expectations, and the consequences for misbehavior. Review them regularly.

1. Decide on five to seven classroom rules, and announce them.
   Be sure to include a rule regarding tilting backward in chairs.
2. Make the consequences for breaking the rules logical and clear.
3. Post the rules in a conspicuous place at the front of the classroom.
4. Repeat the rules at the beginning of the day until the students can recite and follow them automatically.
5. Add or change rules if necessary.
6. Carry out the consequences for infractions consistently.

▶ Disguising Directives

Disguise verbal directives to get the student to behave and to avoid confrontation.

1. Give the whole class a hint about tilting backward in chairs.
2. Give a disguised verbal directive to the target student
   (e.g., say, "Show us how to sit at your desk properly now").
3. Watch the student's facial expression to insure that you have not unintentionally invited a confrontation.

▶ Direct Commands

Make specific demands, spoken with authority, concerning the student's behavior.

1. Try some of the other strategies first, if possible.
2. Think of a positive way to state your command
   (e.g., "Please keep all four chair legs on the floor. I want to see your good writing posture.").
3. Anticipate situations where a command must be given, and practice your tone and posture.
4. Analyze the student's response.

Reinforcement of Limits

Level of Motivation	Behavior Style			
	Self-Assertive	Socially Interactive	Analytic	Accommodating
1. Self-Absorbed		■	■	■
2. Approval Oriented	■	■		
3. Interpersonal Loyalty				
4. Others Oriented				

▶ **Stopping and Redirecting**

Stop the student's inappropriate behavior, and redirect his or her attention to the task at hand.

1. Ask the student to stop tilting backward in his or her chair and to keep all four chair legs on the floor.
2. Tell the student to resume the appropriate task or activity.
3. Check back shortly thereafter to see if the student has obeyed.

▶ **Asking "What" Questions**

Ask "what" questions until the student acknowledges his or her misbehavior; do not accept excuses.

1. When the student tilts backward in his or her chair, ask, "What are you doing?"
2. Continue to ask "what" questions until the student verbalizes the behavior without making excuses.
3. Ask a "how" question (e.g., "How did tilting backward in your chair help you get your work done?").
4. Ask another "what" question (e.g., "What would be a better way to do your work?").
5. Give suggestions if necessary.
6. Get the student to agree on a plan that includes consequences for continued misbehavior.

▶ **Charting Progress**

Use charts to monitor misbehavior and check the student's progress.

1. Talk to the student, and be sure he or she understands why tilting backward in a chair is a problem.
2. Set a goal, or a series of steps toward a goal, to correct the behavior
   (e.g., no tilting backward in the chair for 2 hours in a row).
3. Write the goals on a chart so that progress can be measured.
4. Mark the chart each time the chair is not tilted during a specific period of time.
5. Establish a reward for attaining the goal.

Control

Level of Motivation	Behavior Style			
	Self-Assertive	Socially Interactive	Analytic	Accommodating
1. Self-Absorbed	■			
2. Approval Oriented				
3. Interpersonal Loyalty				
4. Others Oriented				

▶ Relocation Within the Classroom

Move the misbehaving student to a less problematic location within the classroom.

1. Move the student closer to the teacher or to a chair that cannot be tilted backward.

2. If necessary, have the student stand or sit on the floor for the same period of time that the chair was tilted backward.

3. If possible, leave the student in the new location. If it is necessary to move the student back to the original location, make it clear that other steps will be taken if the misbehavior continues.

TRIPPING OTHERS

Deliberately causing another student to fall

Reinforcement of Limits

Level of Motivation	Behavior Style			
	Self-Assertive	Socially Interactive	Analytic	Accommodating
1. Self-Absorbed		■	■	■
2. Approval Oriented	■	■	■	■
3. Interpersonal Loyalty	■	■	■	■
4. Others Oriented	■	■	■	■

▶ Asking "What" Questions
Ask "what" questions until the student acknowledges his or her misbehavior; do not accept excuses.

1. Ask a "what" question that directly addresses the misbehavior (e.g., "What did you do?").
2. Continue to ask "what" questions until the student verbalizes his or her mistake without making excuses.
3. Ask a "how" question that focuses on the negative result of the action (e.g., "How did tripping your classmate help you finish your assignment?").
4. Establish a plan for improvement that includes consequences for continued misbehavior.

▶ Positive Peer-Group Reinforcement
Provide incentives for peers to motivate students to behave appropriately.

1. Determine the overall maturity level of the class and their ability to respond positively.
2. Set an obtainable goal for the class (e.g., "If no one is deliberately tripped today, there will be an extra 5 minutes of recess").
3. Explain how the class can reach the goal (e.g., "Keep your feet under your own desk").
4. Closely monitor progress toward the goal.
5. Reward accomplishment of the goal.

Control

Level of Motivation	Behavior Style			
	Self-Assertive	Socially Interactive	Analytic	Accommodating
1. Self-Absorbed		■	■	■
2. Approval Oriented	■	■	■	■
3. Interpersonal Loyalty	■	■	■	■
4. Others Oriented				

▶ Removing Stimuli

Remove any object that acts as a stimulus for misbehavior.

1. Determine which activities or persons are most apt to incite the student to trip someone.
2. Separate the student from that activity or person.
3. Discuss with the student more appropriate ways to behave.

Level of Motivation	Behavior Style			
	Self-Assertive	Socially Interactive	Analytic	Accommodating
1. Self-Absorbed	■			
2. Approval Oriented				
3. Interpersonal Loyalty				
4. Others Oriented				

▶ Time Out for a Specified Period or Activity

Establish rules in advance for the use of specified periods of time out in response to angry outbursts.

1. Establish an area within the classroom that will be used for isolation.
2. Discuss the purpose of this area with the class.
   Establish consequences for continued misbehavior in the isolation area.
3. Whenever a student trips someone, move the student to the isolation area for a specified period of time.

▶ Detention

Keep the student after school for a specified period of time.

1. Establish that the consequence for tripping people will be detention for a specified amount of time.
2. The next time the student trips someone, assign detention immediately, as promised.
3. Utilize the detention time to establish communication.
4. Discuss the possible results of tripping people—from simple embarrassment to concussion or worse.
5. Formulate a plan with the student to find other, more appropriate, ways to indicate the need for attention.
6. End the detention on a positive note whenever possible.

WHINING

Complaining, begging, or making requests in an irritating, childish manner

Prevention

Level of Motivation	Behavior Style			
	Self-Assertive	Socially Interactive	Analytic	Accommodating
1. Self-Absorbed				
2. Approval Oriented				
3. Interpersonal Loyalty			■	■
4. Others Oriented	■	■	■	■

▶ Ignoring Misbehavior

Eliminate the student's payoff for inappropriate attention-getting behavior by refusing to acknowledge it.

1. Determine whether the whining is normal behavior for the student.
2. Decide whether the whining is simply a demand for attention or a genuine, but poorly presented, request for help.
3. If the whining can be endured without serious disruption to others, ignore it.
4. If the whining is disruptive to others and cannot be ignored, move to a more intrusive strategy, such as Direct Commands.

▶ Nonverbal Communication

Use eye contact, body movements, or hand signals to gain the student's attention.

1. When you see the student behaving appropriately, acknowledge that behavior with a smile, a nod, a thumbs-up, or some other recognized sign of approval.
2. Discourage negative behavior with a gesture such as raising your eyebrows, scowling, rolling your eyes, or shaking your head.
3. Monitor your physical responses, and try to use more positive nonverbal communication than negative.

▶ Using Humor to Relieve Stress

Use humor to lighten a stressful situation.

1. When the student begins to whine, respond with adult-level humor that he or she will understand.
2. Do not use humor that is childish, sarcastic, or cutting.
3. Focus on what is truly funny to try to get students to relax and evaluate their behavior.

Limit Setting

Level of Motivation	Behavior Style			
	Self-Assertive	Socially Interactive	Analytic	Accommodating
1. Self-Absorbed				
2. Approval Oriented			■	■
3. Interpersonal Loyalty	■	■		
4. Others Oriented				

▶ Reflecting Verbal Responses

Verbally reflect the essence of a student's argument in order to clarify his or her true feelings.

1. Listen carefully to the student to determine his or her hidden message.
2. Repeat that message to the student
   (e.g., say, "You complain because it is the only way to get someone to listen to you").
3. Continue to repeat such messages until no further clarification is forthcoming.
4. Ask the student to offer suggestions for resolving the situation.
5. Praise the student when he or she suggests an appropriate solution (e.g., say, "I like your suggestion that we spend a few minutes together a couple of times a week to see how you are doing").

▶ Probing for Motives

Ask yourself questions to determine the goal behind the student's misbehavior.

1. Ask yourself the following questions immediately after whining occurs:
   - Do I feel annoyed? Attention-getting may be or is likely the goal.
   - Do I feel beaten or intimidated? Power may be or is likely the goal.
   - Do I feel wronged or hurt? Revenge may be or is likely the goal.
   - Do I feel incapable of reaching this student? Helplessness may be or is likely the goal.
2. Respond to the appropriate motive as follows:
   - *Attention-getting.* Deprive the student of attention.
   - *Power.* Do not allow open conflict. State the rules and consequences, and then move on.
   - *Revenge.* Determine the reason for the student's hurt feelings.
   - *Helplessness.* Provide opportunities for the student to succeed.

▶ Student Self-Monitoring

Have the student monitor his or her own behavior using charts or other means to record progress.

1. Analyze the reasons for the student's whining to determine the root of the problem.
2. Chart occurrences of whining.
3. Use the charts as a nonthreatening way to make the student aware of the frequency of his or her whining.
4. Establish realistic, measurable goals with the student to decrease and eventually stop the whining.
5. Have the student maintain a neat, handwritten chart to monitor his or her progress.
6. Establish a reward for the successful completion of a goal.

Reinforcement of Limits

Level of Motivation	Behavior Style			
	Self-Assertive	Socially Interactive	Analytic	Accommodating
1. Self-Absorbed		■	■	■
2. Approval Oriented	■	■		
3. Interpersonal Loyalty				
4. Others Oriented				

▶ Stopping and Redirecting

Stop the student's inappropriate behavior, and redirect his or her attention to the task at hand.

1. Ask the student to stop whining as soon as he or she begins.
2. Redirect the student to another activity
   (e.g., say, "Please stop whining and finish your math worksheet").
3. Monitor the student to see if whining continues.

▶ Positive Peer-Group Reinforcement

Provide incentives for peers to motivate students to behave appropriately.

1. Appraise the overall maturity of the class to determine whether they can understand the problem.
2. Discuss the appropriate way to ask questions and register opinions.
3. Set a realistic goal to decrease whining, and reward good behavior (e.g., put a mark on the board each time the class goes 10 minutes without complaining, and when the class has earned 10 marks, give them 10 extra minutes of recess).

▶ Charting Progress

Use charts to monitor misbehavior and check the student's progress.

1. Identify the circumstances that precede whining.
2. Discuss the behavior. Be sure the student understands why the behavior is inappropriate.
3. Work with the student to set a goal, or a series of steps toward a goal, to end the inappropriate behavior.
4. Set a goal to reduce the number of occurrences of whining per day for a 2- or 3-day period, and write that goal on a chart so that the student's progress can be monitored.
5. Gradually decrease the number of allowable occurrences per day over a 3- to 4-week period.
6. Consistently reward the student for appropriate behavior.

Control

Level of Motivation	Behavior Style			
	Self-Assertive	Socially Interactive	Analytic	Accommodating
1. Self-Absorbed	■			
2. Approval Oriented				
3. Interpersonal Loyalty				
4. Others Oriented				

▶ Time Out for a Specified Period or Activity

Establish rules in advance for the use of specified periods of time out in response to angry outbursts.

1. Establish an area within the classroom to be used for isolation for specific periods of time.
2. Clearly explain the purpose of the time-out area—that it is a place to gain control of behavior before returning to the class.
3. Move the student to the isolation area whenever he or she whines. Be consistent.
4. Discuss alternate ways of dealing with whining in the future.
5. If whining continues, increase the amount of time spent in the isolation area.

▶ Deducting Points for Misbehavior

Deduct points (or tokens) or withhold privileges the student has earned.
(Deduction of points should occur in conjunction with a token reinforcement system.)

1. Choose the number of points that will be deducted for whining.
2. Inform the student that although he or she will earn points for appropriate behavior, the number of points you have chosen will be deducted when he or she whines.
3. Initially, a nonverbal signal could be given as a warning if the student begins to whine.
4. Deduct points exactly as you have stipulated if the whining continues.
5. If this strategy is not effective, consider increasing the frequency with which points are awarded and/or increasing the desirability of the rewards for which points can be redeemed (e.g., rather than 10 minutes of free reading time, substitute an opportunity to play a game with a friend).
6. If the problem persists, increase the number of points deducted for each subsequent occurrence of whining (e.g., 10 points for the first time, 25 points for the second time, etc.).

BIBLIOGRAPHY

References Cited in Text

Brophy, J. E. (1986). Research linking teacher behavior to student achievement: Potential implications for instruction of Chapter 1 students. In B. I. Williams, P. A. Richmond, & B. J. Mason (Eds.), *Designs for compensatory education: Conference proceedings and papers* (Vol. 4, pp. 121–179). Washington, DC: Research and Evaluation Associates.

Charles, C. M. (1981). *Building classroom discipline: From models to practice.* New York: Longman.

Curwin, R., & Mendler, A. (1988). *Discipline with dignity.* Alexandria, VA: Association for Supervision and Curriculum Development.

Gallup, G. (1984). The 16th annual Gallup poll on the public's attitudes toward the public schools. *Phi Delta Kappan, 66*(1), 23–28.

Gregorc, A. F. (1979). Learning and teaching styles: Potent forces behind them. *Educational Leadership, 36,* 234–236.

Harris, L., and Associates. (1993). *The Metropolitan Life survey of the American teacher.* New York: Metropolitan Life Insurance Co.

Hersey, P., & Blanchard, M. (1982). *Management of organizational behavior: Utilizing human resources* (4th ed.). Englewood Cliffs, NJ: Prentice-Hall.

Jones, V., & Jones, L. (1986). *Comprehensive classroom management.* Boston: Allyn & Bacon.

Keefe, J. W. (1987). *Learning style theory and practice.* Reston, VA: National Association of Secondary School Principals.

Marston, W. (1979). *Emotions of normal people.* Minneapolis, MN: Persona Press.

National Education Association. (1982). *Status of the American public school teacher 1980–81.* Washington, DC: Author.

Problems of discipline and violence in American education. (1978, January) [Special issue]. *Phi Delta Kappan, 59*(5).

U.S. Department of Health, Education, and Welfare. (1978). *Violent schools—safe schools: The safe schools report to the Congress.* Washington, DC: Author. (ERIC Document Reproduction Service No. ED 149 464)

Wang, M. C. (1992). *Adaptive education strategies: Building on diversity.* Baltimore: Paul H. Brookes.

Wang, M. C., & Walberg, H. J. (1986). Classroom climate as mediation of educational inputs and outputs. In B. J. Fraser (Ed.), *The study of learning environments 1986* (pp. 47–58). Salem, OR: Assessment Research.

Wilson Learning Corporation. (1990). *Social styles series.* Eden Prairie, MN: Author.

Wolfgang, C., & Glickman, C. (1986). *Solving discipline problems.* Boston: Allyn & Bacon.

Suggested Reading

Armstrong, T. (1987). *In their own way.* Los Angeles, CA: Jeremy P. Tarcher.

Bereiter, C., & Engelmann, S. (1966). *Teaching disadvantaged children in the preschool.* Englewood Cliffs, NJ: Prentice-Hall.

Canter, L., & Canter, M. (1976). *Assertive discipline: A take-charge approach for today's educator.* Seal Beach, CA: Canter and Associates.

Dreikurs, R. (1968). *Psychology in the classroom: A manual for teachers* (2nd ed.). New York: Harper & Row.

Elam, S., Rose, L., & Gallup, A. (1992). The 24th annual Gallup/Phi Delta Kappan education poll. *Phi Delta Kappan, 74*(1), 42–53.

Gettinger, M. (1988). Methods of proactive classroom management. *School Psychology Review, 17,* 227–242.

Glasser, W. (1969). *Schools without failure.* New York: Harper & Row.

Goldstein, A. P., & Glick, B. (1987). *Aggression replacement training: A comprehensive intervention for aggressive youth.* Champaign, IL: Research Press.

Gordon, T. (1976). *Teacher effectiveness training.* New York: Peter H. Wyden.

Jones, R. N., Sheridan, S. M., & Binns, W. R. (1993). Schoolwide social skills training: Providing preventative services to students at risk. *School Psychology Quarterly, 8,* 58–80.

Keirsey, D., & Bates, M. (1984). *Please understand me: Character and temperament types.* Del Mar, CA: Prometheus Nemesis.

Kohlberg, L. (1975). The cognitive-developmental approach to moral education. *Phi Delta Kappan, 56*(10), 670–677.

Kroeger, O., & Thuesen, J. M. (1988). *Type talk: The 16 personality types that determine how we live, love, and work.* New York: Dell.

LaHaye, B. (1977). *How to develop your child's temperament.* Irvine, CA: Harvest House.

LaHaye, T. (1987). *Transformed temperaments.* Wheaton, IL: Tyndale House.

Larson, J. D., & McBride, J. A. (1993). *Parent to parent: A video-augmented training program for the prevention of aggressive behavior in young children.* Milwaukee, WI: Milwaukee Board of School Directors.

Males, M. (1992). Top school problems are myths. *Phi Delta Kappan, 74*(1), 54–55.

Maslow, A. (1968). *Toward a psychology of being.* New York: D. Van Nostrand.

McCarthy, B. (1980). *The 4-MHT system.* Barrington, IL: Excel.

Neff, L. (1988). *One of a kind.* Portland, OR: Multnomah Press.

Rogers, C. (1969). *Freedom to learn.* Columbus, OH: Charles E. Merrill.

Wampler, F. W., & Hess, S. A. (1992). *Conflict mediation for a new generation: Training manual for educators.* Harrisonburg, VA: Community Mediation Center.